MONSTER SQUAD

MONSTER SQUAD

Celebrating the Artists Behind Cinema's Most Memorable Creatures

by Heather A. Wixson

Edited by Derek Anderson
Additional Editing by Patrick Bromley

BearManor Media

2017

*Monster Squad: Celebrating the Artists Behind Cinema's
Most Memorable Creatures*

© 2017 Heather A.Wixson

BearManor Media
P. O. Box 71426
Albany, GA 31708

bearmanormedia.com

Edited by Derek Anderson
Additional editing by Patrick Bromley

Cover artwork designed by Jared Moraitis, creator of BeastWreck

Typesetting and layout by John Teehan

Published in the USA by BearManor Media

ISBN—978-1-62933-221-5

Dedicated to my niece, Molly Mareci.
Never stop being creative and always dream big,
kiddo. I love you.

Table of Contents

Special Thanks

I DON'T EVEN KNOW where to begin. There are so many people that made this whole endeavor possible, and I am eternally grateful to so many people, because I never would have been able to tackle and complete this book without them.

In no particular order...

To all the artists who took a chance on me and agreed to be a part of this book: Jennifer Aspinall, Gabe Bartalos, Michèle Burke, John Dykstra, Mike Elizalde, Tony Gardner, Alec Gillis, John Goodwin, Kevin Haney, Steve Johnson, Bob Keen, Rick Lazzarini, David Martí, Todd Masters, Bart Mixon, John Rosengrant, Phil Tippett, Brian Wade, Steve Wang, and Tom Woodruff, Jr. I owe you all so much and will never be able to thank you enough for your participation, as well as the kindness and generosity all of you showed this humble writer.

To everyone who helped me gather materials for this project, including all the participants and their amazing staff members, the legendary Doug Drexler, as well as Matt Winston and Balázs Földesi from the Stan Winston School of Character Arts, and Cynthia Barron and Shannon Robles from The Jim Henson Company.

To my editor Derek Anderson, who toiled endlessly to shape my words into something worthy of those I had the honor of interviewing. Thank you for making me sound a lot smarter than I really am, and for being a driving force behind this project.

To those who helped me out with the gargantuan task of transcribing some of the interviews, including Nolan McBride and Brandon "Skinslip" Henriksen, I could not have done this without all your help.

To my entire Daily Dead team for being continually awesome. Thank you for pitching in to help make it easier on me to take on this book, including my editor Jonathan Smith, who is truly the best boss I've ever worked with throughout my 10-year career as a horror journalist.

To my brother-in-arms Patrick Bromley, who continues to be wrong about *Scream 4*, but was still a huge help to me in getting *Monster Squad* completed, with both editing and transcribing. Thank you for being such a great friend (with a sometimes unusual taste in movies).

To my amazing friends and family who gave me the courage and strength to follow my dreams back in 2009, and remain a huge part of who I have become over the last eight years: Jenna Mareci, Brian Barbier, Sharon Grosshauser, Margie and Nik Markevicius, The Tietz Family, Cully Johnston, John Rose, Christian Dawson, Fabien Ricard, and without a doubt, my mom, who is the reason I fell in love with horror movies in the first place.

And to every single person who has ever taken a moment to read something I have written over the last decade—THANK YOU. There's no way I would have continued to have any kind of success as a writer had it not been for your support. The same goes for Ms. Vicky Edwards, my high school journalism teacher, who saw something in me even before I did, as well as Mike and Mia Kerz, who were kind enough to bring me into the Flashback Weekend family, and continue to be hugely positive supporters of the world of horror and classic genre films.

Most of all though, I have to thank my partner in crime, Brian, for being the most incredible and encouraging force in my life, who has made so many amazing things in my life possible, but especially this book. Every day with you is truly a gift. I love you and I could not have done this without you.

Oh, and of course—thank you Johnny Utah for being a very good boy as I worked my way through nearly 75 hours of interviews, and many, many months of writing.

The best puppy ever, Johnny Utah.

Photo courtesy of Alec Gillis.

1   Alec Gillis

WHILE HE MAY NOT have foreseen just where his artistic tendencies would eventually take him in life, Alec Gillis realized early on that there was a creative streak inside him that was just waiting to be unleashed.

"Even back in kindergarten, I knew I was a creative kid," explained Gillis. "We would sculpt things out of clay and the teacher had a kiln. So even back then I was sculpting crazy things, like little *Flintstones* houses and these weird creations. At that stage, when you get a lot of positive parental and sibling feedback, it just encourages you, and you start thinking to yourself, *Well, this is who I am.* It becomes part of your identity, and I realize now how fortunate I was, because not everyone gets that kind of parental support."

"My father was in the Marine Corps, but he was also an insurance salesman and an artist, too. He was always drawing and he was very interested in special effects. My first recollection of him having a conversation with me about special effects was when I was about eight or nine and he was explaining to me how stop-motion worked, and how King Kong was actually a miniature. That fascinated me."

"He also told stories of people he had met in his days in New York City when he was selling insurance to people at NBC. These would be special effects artists for TV shows, as well as Dick Smith. He sold Dick Smith a life insurance policy. So he got to see life masks and clay and he had these tales about the fantastic world that these guys inhabited. That always was very, very attractive to me."

1

"When I was around thirteen years old, I saw a magazine interview with Ray Harryhausen, and that's when I saw that one person made all these great monsters I loved. That's when it clicked with me: *This is a job? Adults do this? That's what I want to do. Why would I want to do anything else?* There was no other choice for me, really."

Before he could get busy making monsters, Gillis set out to learn as much as he could about the art of bringing creatures and memorable characters to life in front of the camera.

"I started off doing animated films with G.I. Joe dolls or whatever I could find, and I even tried to sculpt in clay on their faces so I could manipulate them and what have you. There wasn't a lot of information out there when I was growing up."

"There were some little glimpses behind the scenes, like a *LIFE* magazine article that showed Roddy McDowall getting his makeup applied, so I was always hungry for more information. Then I discovered *Famous Monsters of Filmland* and I spent a lot of time reading those. Any time there was any kind of a behind-the-scenes look into how a makeup or a stop-motion puppet was created, that was like gold to me."

"When I was just getting into high school, there were two magazines I found: one was called *FXRH* and the other was *Cinemagic*. There were only four issues of *FXRH*, but it really went in depth about what Ray Harryhausen's techniques were, how stop-motion puppets were made, and how to create and work with molds, too. *Cinemagic* was cool because it was more fan-oriented. It was more about what amateurs were doing to attack problems, and it wasn't just about how to make a rubber mask or how to make a puppet creature—it also had camera information and thoughts about double exposure and trick photography, foreground, miniatures, things like that. *Cinemagic* gave you a total filmmaking perspective on effects and that always appealed to me. As much as I love the specifics of the technique—whether it's makeup effects or animatronics or miniatures—it's always, to me, about, 'How do you incorporate that into the bigger picture of telling a story on the big screen?'"

As Gillis continued to sharpen his skill set throughout high school, his hobby evolved into a career before he even knew it.

"As I got better, I took over my mom's garage and turned that into my workshop. As my work improved and became more sophisticated, people began to realize I was serious about special effects. I was nineteen and a

Alec poses with a special friend. Photo courtesy of Alec Gillis.

friend of my sister was working for Roger Corman. He saw what I was doing and said, 'Hey, I should get you an interview with Roger because we're working on this movie called *Battle Beyond the Stars*.' I agreed, but I was really nervous because these guys were professionals and not all of my stuff was all that professional."

"I asked him if I could bring a friend, just because I had met this guy recently who was five or six years older than me who was into similar stuff, and he had a great portfolio. I was hoping that might help bolster my chances. That guy, of course, was James Cameron, who back then was delivering books for a school district and had only done a short film, *Xenogenesis*, at that point."

"Jim and I interviewed with Chuck Comisky, Robert Skotak, and Dennis Skotak, who were in a model shop in Tarzana at the time, getting ready to start the miniature photography for *Battle Beyond the Stars*. The movie hadn't shot yet and it took them about six months to get back to us. I thought, *Well, that obviously didn't pan out*, but then we finally got the call that they were hiring us as a team."

"We commuted from Orange County to Venice every day to go work at Hammond Lumber, which was this old lumberyard Corman had purchased. *Battle* was a great opportunity for me, as I was able to do a ton of different things ranging from working with motion-control systems to building miniature spaceships, and the work was really formative for me. I loved that feeling of making a movie in a big, giant room in a warehouse. Over in one corner are the miniatures and creatures, and then you have the sculptures over there in the other corner. It's a very efficient and contained way to make a movie, and I loved it."

"*Battle Beyond the Stars* became a springboard for my career," Alec continued. "I got to work on a few more films, and right when Cameron was getting ready to start *The Terminator*, I got hired to work on *Friday the 13th: The Final Chapter*. Before that, I was going to UCLA [University of California, Los Angeles] film school, but I was already a working professional, and I would take the quarter off of school to work with Corman on another movie so that I could save the money up to go back to school. Eventually, it got to a point where I was saying, 'Why am I doing this? How many more film theory classes am I going to sit through?' I became very aware of the gap between the real world and the world of college, and it wore thin on me. That's when I left."

"But it did not hurt me in any way to not work on *The Terminator*. While I had just met Stan Winston through Jim and would probably have preferred to work on *The Terminator* at the time, I think Stan appreciated that I did not jump ship. He knew I was a man of my word and he knew he could rely on me in the future," Gillis added.

"To work on *Friday the 13th* [*The Final Chapter*], and to do those kinds of makeup effects with that particular group, was a great experience. Originally, I started working on it for Greg Cannom, but then he left the show and Tom Savini came on. To work with Tom, who came from a completely different background and was a self-taught makeup artist, was very illuminating because I had really thought of him as a cowboy up until that point. I didn't have a real appreciation for Tom's background and what he did when he came into this industry."

"Tom always had this knack for being able to problem-solve and come up with ingenious solutions. That speaks volumes about Tom's abilities as an artist. It also showed me that there's more than one way to do something, and if you get entrenched in any narrow sort of 'right way' to do something when it comes to the world of filmmaking, you run the risk of limiting yourself."

"Back in the '80s when Dick Smith's course came out, I had this conversation with Tom on how it was a valuable learning tool, but the downside to the course was that people considered it as the bible. It was the immutable word of the great Dick Smith, and they were afraid to do things differently than how they saw it done in the course, and Tom agreed."

"The thing that drives special effects, especially at that time, is that artists have to always be willing to experiment and come up with their own way to improve, to keep the craft moving forward and make it evolve. Nothing evolves if you just have a single way of doing things, and Tom was the epitome of evolving in his work. He was always coming up with something new, and I've always admired people who have that kind of rogue spirit to them."

After completing his work on *Friday the 13th: The Final Chapter* (1984), Alec got the opportunity to join a makeup team led by Greg Cannom for Ron Howard's sci-fi fantasy film, *Cocoon* (1985). It was another project that gave Gillis the chance to learn from one of the industry's most innovative makeup artists.

"In my early career, it was really awesome how with every different work situation, I was able to learn something wholly unique from that person. It was the same with Greg. He was a phenomenal artist and showed me a lot about the almost impressionistic approach to effects. He didn't over-fixate on detail, and was more interested in the overall impact of the design and how that could help those details come out."

"With *Cocoon*, Greg was very bold with his colors, and he was a very gutsy guy when it came to those kinds of decisions. We did a lot of last-minute work on *Cocoon*, fixing and changing things that I honestly didn't think were going to work. Of course, because Greg is a genius, it all worked beautifully because of his ability to understand how the camera would perceive the colors. I always likened Greg to an old-school matte painter, because those guys had an amazing understanding of what would show up on film and what wouldn't, and that was a very valuable experience to me."

Alec continued to explore the realms of cinematic science fiction when he came aboard Stan Winston's crew for Tobe Hooper's *Invaders from Mars* (1986), which would lead to several years' worth of work for Gillis.

Alec at work on *Invaders from Mars* (1986). Photo courtesy of Alec Gillis.

The drone crew poses on the set of *Invaders from Mars* (1986). (Alec is standing on the far right.) Photo courtesy of the Stan Winston School of Character Arts.

"By the time I got to Stan, I already had quite a well-rounded experience, from the Corman film school to working with Greg Cannom and Tom Savini. Plus, I was never pigeonholed into one job, so I had done a bit of everything. I had a very broad base, a very disparate set of experiences, and I think Stan liked that."

"At some point prior to *The Terminator*, Stan basically cleaned out his crew and started over. He was never specific about it, but I think he was trying to build his legacy and he was finding it difficult to do that with guys who would always be second-guessing him. So he brought in a crop of fresh faces: Tom Woodruff, Jr., John Rosengrant, Shane Mahan, and Richard Landon. I came in a little bit after that, and so did Rick Lazzarini, and we were all there to support the boss' vision."

"Because of my varied background, I was able to segue over nicely to be a valuable guy for Stan, and that's when all of us younger guys got a taste of the A-level movies. It was a great, exciting time to be working for Stan. *Invaders from Mars* was a valuable experience for me, too, because it peaked in terms of creating the drones and doing those effects while *Aliens* was coming in. That was my first taste of having to handle two shows at

Alec between scenes on *Invaders from Mars* (1986). Photo courtesy of Alec Gillis.

once, and two big shows at that. While we're painting a drone over on one side, Matt Rose is off in another corner sculpting an Alien tail. Everyone just divided up into teams and tackled everything we needed to get done."

"*Invaders* started shooting when Stan and the other guys had just packed up to go to London, and he left me behind to manage the on-set duties on *Invaders from Mars* while he took the other guys to really start getting into the build of *Aliens*. He trusted me, and that was amazing. That's one thing I took from working with Stan. The other was that nothing was off limits. If he wanted to make something, he would. It was never too big. He would always say, 'We're going to figure out a way,' and he'd plow into it with enthusiasm and energy. I always remember his can-do attitude to any project."

Shortly after wrapping their back-to-back sci-fi projects, Winston and his crew were given the opportunity to collaborate on a film that would celebrate the very creatures responsible for most of them falling in love with genre movies and special effects in the first place: Fred Dekker's *The Monster Squad* (1987). While they weren't initially happy with Universal's decision to not grant the likeness rights to the five classic monsters—Dracula, The Wolf Man, The Mummy, The Creature (a.k.a.

Gill-man), and Frankenstein's monster—they would base their characters on, their excitement far outweighed any disappointments, as Universal's decision ended up being a huge positive for them as artists.

"We were all excited when Stan told us about *Monster Squad*," said Gillis. "We were just thrilled to get that job, because who wouldn't be? At first, it was a bit shocking that Universal wasn't going to grant the rights to these characters, but at the same time, that gave us the opportunity to pay homage and still do something fresh, too. And because that was pre-Internet, we didn't have to contend with the early negativity. If we had tried to do that now, people would respond with something like, 'Oh, Stan Winston thinks he's better than Jack Pierce, eh?' It was nice to have nothing hanging over us going into those designs beyond just the basics."

"We flew into it by the seat of our pants. And because we were taking a chance anyway, we figured we might as well have fun with it. If you get too timid, that's probably when you're going to fall down, so we knew we had to be bold with our designs. Plus, this was also in the day when the makeup effects designer was the main creative force and you didn't have to run it through a studio where everyone has to sign off on everything.

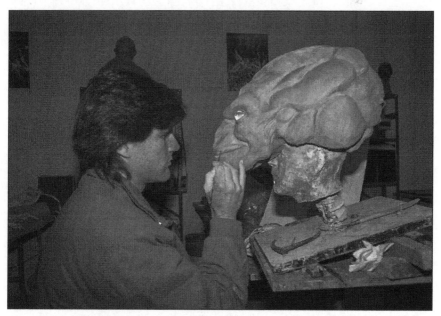

Alec sculpting the titular monster's face for Stan Winston's *Pumpkinhead* (1988).
Photo courtesy of the Stan Winston School of Character Arts.

These creatures were purely the vision of Stan Winston, along with the Director, Fred Dekker. And that's how it should be."

Once production on *The Monster Squad* (1987) wrapped, Gillis was at a crossroads, with his mentor continuing to explore his career as a director following the release of his first feature film, *Pumpkinhead* (1988).

"We got to a point where we had done *Pumpkinhead*," Alec said. "That had turned out great and Stan was on to making *A Gnome Named Gnorm*. Stan had made an industry announcement that he was no longer doing effects for other people, and that he was only going to do them for his own movies that he was directing. It was the perfect display of the bravado and confidence of Stan Winston, because if anyone could have done it, it would have been Stan."

"But Tom [Woodruff, Jr.] and I were looking around going, '*Hmm… we won't be able to work with the Steven Spielbergs or Robert Zemeckises or James Camerons anymore*,' which was kind of a bummer. It would be great to see Stan get his directing career off the ground, but they were probably going to be smaller-budgeted movies where we wouldn't really have a chance to strut our stuff as much."

"At that same time, Tom and I had co-written a script that was getting interest, and we thought that maybe this was the perfect opportunity to get that project going. We could bring all the creature effects back to Stan and then we could give back to him. When we pitched that to Stan, he said, 'Where I need you guys most is out there making monsters.' And we were like, 'Well, that doesn't really fit with our overall plans.' Stan saw us as the guys that did the creature stuff, and honestly, it didn't really make sense to me at the time. But I realized over the years that it was him giving us his blessing to go out there and make our own way."

"We left Stan on good terms, but then a writers' strike happened and the industry geared down for a while, which put everything we had been planning on hold. That was a good lesson, actually, because we realized it's not quite that easy to just go out there and make a movie. We had to figure out how to keep ourselves going. We did a couple of episodes of *Monsters*, the Laurel Entertainment show, and we did a couple of other projects, too. We ended up having to sublet a space from Rick [Lazzarini], and it was just Tom and I working over there because there was no ADI [Amalgamated Dynamics, Inc.] back then."

Tom Woodruff, Jr. and Alec with a Graboid on the set of *Tremors* (1990).
Photo courtesy of Alec Gillis.

"Out of the blue, Gale Anne Hurd called us up and said, 'I have this script called *Tremors* and I want you to look at it.' We still hadn't formed a formal company yet, so we did that while we were breaking down the script and having meetings with Ron Underwood, Steve Wilson, and Brent Maddock. As things were moving forward, we were like, 'Oh, this movie is really going to happen. Where on Earth are we going to build this stuff?' In the meantime, they kept asking to come and see our shop, but Tom and I would always just offer to meet them halfway because we were keeping the fact that we had no home a secret. So Marie Callender's in Toluca Lake was our go-to 'office' for a while."

"Once we got our first check, we put a deposit down on a building that was being built. But, of course, it never got finished in time. So we had to pull out of that. Luckily, we were able to sublet some space from Howard Berger, Greg Nicotero, and Bob Kurtzman at KNB [EFX Group]. We offered them some work, too, so we had those guys sculpting on *Tremors*, and when we found another building, that's when we were able to move. We basically had no equipment at the time, and even though *Tremors* was not a big-budget movie, we used every dime of it to get us established as

Alec prepares a Graboid puppet during production on Tremors (1990).
Photo courtesy of Alec Gillis.

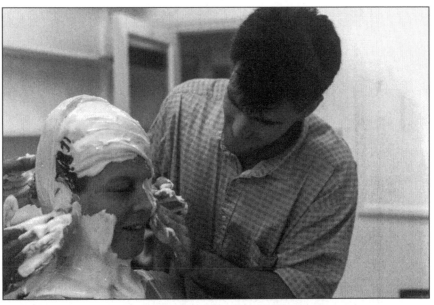

Alec preparing actress Sigourney Weaver for her lifecast on *Alien 3* (1992).
Photo courtesy of Alec Gillis.

a shop and buy what we needed. And that was the start of Amalgamated Dynamics. It was our first big job as ADI, and there couldn't have been a better one to start the company."

With ADI off and running, Alec and Tom found themselves returning to some familiar territory for their next project, David Fincher's *Alien 3* (1992), a sequel much smaller and more intimate in scope and scale compared to its immediate predecessor, *Aliens* (1986).

"*Alien 3* was a huge moment for us, and it came just in the nick of time, because we were out of work for seven months after *Tremors*," admitted Gillis. "The fact that we inherited the *Alien* series was pretty amazing. I think the reason we got it was that they went to Stan, but he said he wouldn't do the movie unless he could direct it. So it became a fantastic opportunity for us."

"In the first read of the script, I was a little disappointed that there wasn't something on the scale of the Alien Queen from *Aliens*, because we really wanted to do something big and bold. Tom and I both thought it was an odd choice that they were retracting back to the model of the first *Alien*, but that was kind of the vibe that they had going into part three. People had enjoyed *Aliens*, but they missed the spirit of Ridley [Scott]'s movie, where it was a single creature in a contained environment. It seemed odd to us to just kill off those remaining characters from *Aliens* and take it all in a new direction, and the film was certainly met with that kind of reaction when it was released, but it's cool to see that *Alien 3* has gained popularity over the years."

While in pre-production on *Alien 3* (1992), the sequel's original director, Vincent Ward, departed the project, ultimately scrapping some of the initial design ideas for the film.

"Vincent Ward actually left before we started building anything, so thankfully it wasn't like we had to switch horses mid-race. The ideas that were in the Vincent Ward versions of the script were much more risky than what you see now. He was taking more chances with it. He saw the Alien as a metaphor for the devil, and a lot of his influences were medieval influences. At one point, he had a woodcut of the devil with a human face on its ass, and he told us that he wanted to do that. He wanted Sigourney Weaver's face on the Alien's ass. That was a really, really risky concept."

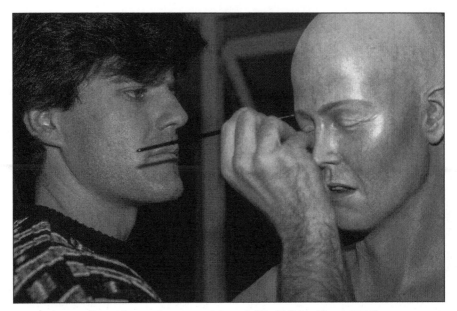

Gillis working on Sigourney Weaver's "double" for *Alien 3* (1992).
Photo courtesy of Alec Gillis.

"After he left the show, a lot of those medieval influences were minimized; there are still some in there with the monks, but that was only a small part of what Vincent wanted to do. From what I heard, there was a prison movie that [20th Century] Fox liked and they thought they could try and turn it into an *Alien* movie, and now what you see is a blending of those concepts. So when Fincher came on, it cleared the way for *Alien 3* to become a bit more of a straight sci-fi movie that fit more cleanly into the *Alien* legacy."

"The one thing that I always appreciated about Fox is that they did make interesting choices in directors when it came to the *Alien* sequels. They brought in James Cameron, who had two movies under his belt. Fincher became David Fincher with the release of *Alien 3*, and then you have Jean-Pierre Jeunet, who did *The City of Lost Children* and *Delicatessen*, directing [*Alien*] *Resurrection*. We got a chance to work with some unique talents with very strong voices on those films, and that doesn't always happen."

While Gillis may not have fully understood Jeunet's wildly evocative stylistic choices for the fourth installment in the *Alien* (1979) series, he had to embrace them nonetheless.

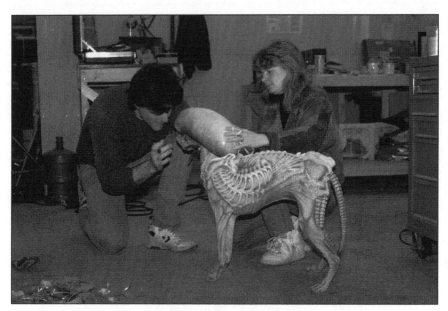

Alec prepares an unconventional Xenomorph on the set of *Alien 3* (1992).
Photo courtesy of Alec Gillis.

"We weren't in a position to question anyone's decisions, because our job is to make the director happy and give him quality creature work that will help support his film. That's on any film, not just *Resurrection*. But I do think there were some decisions made on that one that were just a little too outside of H.R. Giger's realm, like the Newborn Alien. Of all the things on that movie, he [Jeunet] was most passionate about and had the most to say about the design of the Newborn."

"Jean-Pierre had his reasons and his own logic behind why it should look like that, but it was such an out-of-left-field approach that it became this freakish sideline character and was a huge departure from the visual language that [H.R.] Giger established at the beginning. But at the end of the day, my job is to make the director happy. Sometimes you're doing corrective design and making the best of a situation."

At the same time they were working on *Alien Resurrection* (1997), ADI was also handling another ambitious sci-fi project, Paul Verhoeven's *Starship Troopers* (1997). To Gillis, while both directors were visionaries behind the camera, their approaches couldn't be more different from each other.

"Jean-Pierre is very soft-spoken, very considerate, and has this quiet sense of humor, so he was a little more predictable to manage in terms of where his passions were and his methodology. Paul is a genius of a completely different mold. He's very passionate, and when his blood boils, he lets his passion loose, and then he calms down just like that. Coming into

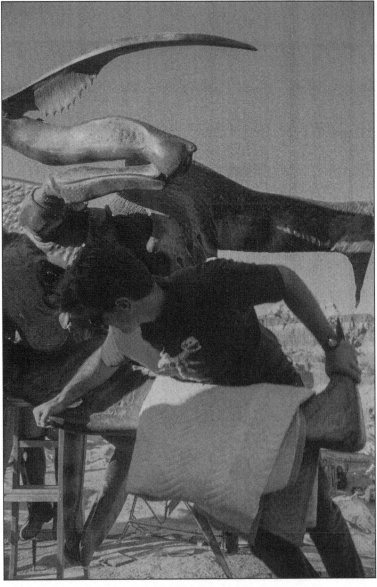

Alec in action on the set of *Starship Troopers* (1997).
Photo courtesy of Alec Gillis.

the project, Phil Tippett warned us in advance and told us, 'Paul will put you through some agony, but he appreciates that you hang with it and that you stay on the job.' I just tried to remain as unflappable as possible. Paul's energy level was amazing for however old he was [late fifties] while we did *Troopers*, because we were all twenty-five years younger than him and he was outworking us all every single day."

"For *Starship Troopers*, Phil's team designed those creatures, and our job was to execute and bring them into the real world. It was a much more manageable project than *Alien Resurrection*, where we had eggs, Chestbursters, death effects, Aliens, clones, and other makeup effects, too. For *Troopers*, we were dealing with essentially three different [types of] bugs—the Brain Bug, the Warrior Bugs, and the Arkellian Sand Beetles— and then we had to create variations of those designs. Where it got grueling was on set, because of the size and weight of everything and the fact that we were out in the middle of the desert."

Alec, Tom, and the rest of the ADI crew reteamed with Verhoeven a few years later for his horror film *Hollow Man* (2000), the director's modernized and deeply terrifying take on H.G. Wells' classic story *The Invisible Man*. Verhoeven's iteration featured Kevin Bacon in the titular role, and the project did a brilliant job blending ADI's ambitious practical effects with cutting-edge visuals spearheaded by Scott E. Anderson.

"When we first read the script for *Hollow Man*, we were like, 'Holy crap!'" Alec recalled. "We knew immediately that this was going to take a tableful of people to pull off. The logistics of determining where the overlap between practical and digital effects was going to be were monumental. There seemed to be something on every single page. It came down to both teams having to sit down and figure out the best ways we could complement each other. While a lot of those effects were done via a motion-capture suit, we still created a lot of skin elements and other effects to keep us busy."

"One thing Paul was very specific about on *Hollow Man* was that he really wanted a lot of those gore elements to be practical. There's the scene where Kevin Bacon goes into the cage and he grabs that dog and kills it because it was barking. We were able to use a stunt dog from the movie *Michael* for that, and he just bashed around as we had a tube running out of him, squirting hot slime everywhere. And for Kevin's burns, we had makeup pieces glued to his black leotard to help out Scott and his guys."

Alec between takes on *Hollow Man* (2000), with Tom Woodruff, Jr. performing in the gorilla suit. Photo courtesy of Alec Gillis.

"Then you have other fully practical elements like Tom [Woodruff, Jr.] in the gorilla suit. When they did the infrared scene with the heat-vision goggles, we just parked Tom under a bunch of 2K lights, where we would heat him up for about forty seconds, and then he'd run over and be hot enough to do the scene that way. Nowadays, people would probably leap to a digital solution for that, but it was so direct and straightforward to us, so we did it as a practical effect."

"Something else that I thought was really cool about *Hollow Man* was how different it was from *Starship Troopers*. *Troopers* was this larger-than-life movie about bug aliens, and this was much more about horror on a human level with this creepy, crazy guy who happens to be invisible and does terrible things to other people. That intimacy creates a very different kind of movie experience, and I enjoyed that both films were so uniquely different."

While Gillis is a believer in the idea that digital effects do have their time and place, he found out on Universal's 2011 prequel to *The Thing* (1982) that too much digital work can not only negatively impact a film's success, but can also visually destroy one's hard work at the same time.

Alec working with the animatronic effects on the set of *Hollow Man* (2000).
Photo courtesy of Alec Gillis.

"When we heard the movie was first out there, the producers reached out to us, sent us the script, and we read it and were like, 'This is pretty good.' Of course, our first question was, 'Well, just how much of this version of *The Thing* is going to end up digital?' Because these days, that's just the way things go."

"So, we had the conversation with the producing team, and we asked them how they saw us fitting in, and they told us that they wanted the movie to be 80% practical. My heart literally skipped a beat when I heard that. It was amazing news. The producers told us that they wanted to honor the legacy of the effects that Rob Bottin created on the original, so all the digital people would really be doing was just helping our work. We thought that these people were exactly talking our language, and that excited us."

"Tom and I started designing. Everything we were doing was carefully plotted out with the input of Matthijs van Heijningen, the Director. He wanted an aesthetic that felt contemporary but still in line with what Bottin did on the original *Thing*. What struck me as how different this process was on *The Thing* was that the feeling of pure joy when it came

Alec on the set of *Harbinger Down* (2015). Photo courtesy of Alec Gillis.

Gillis preps a tentacle burst effect for *Harbinger Down* (2015).
Photo courtesy of Alec Gillis.

able. The biggest challenge on *Harbinger Down* was to do this on a low-budget schedule. Even though we were in a contained location, we still had ten sets or so that we had to build, and we had to shoot this stuff in a timely fashion that didn't blow the budget, either."

"There were days where, like with any low-budget movie, you're running from setup to setup and you don't necessarily get the coverage you want or even get to do multiple takes. You just have to go with what you get and keep moving forward. It's exhilarating, but it doesn't give you 100% control over the process."

"It was an incredible learning experience and it really was the opportunity to do what Roger Corman did, which was to make a movie in a big, single warehouse. Also, what Roger did was make derivative movies, like how *Battle Beyond the Stars* was *Star Wars*, and so forth. And I love low-budget filmmaking, so what I hoped for this movie was that people who like low-budget filmmaking would say, 'Wow, that was really an impressive story to pull off,' even if they didn't like certain elements of it. A big part of what I wanted to accomplish with *Harbinger Down* was a different way that practical effects fans can share in the revitalization of the craft without it being backward-thinking, and show them that practi-

Gillis with Director Harold Ramis on the set of *Bedazzled* (2000).
Photo courtesy of Alec Gillis.

Tom Woodruff, Jr. and Alec Gillis with the Oscar for Best Visual Effects for *Death Becomes Her* (1992) (which Woodruff got to keep after a coin toss). Photo courtesy of Alec Gillis.

cal arts are not just nostalgia. They can also be applied to contemporary moviemaking styles as well."

As Gillis looks toward the future for Amalgamated Dynamics, he recognizes that the key to the company's continued success for over twenty-five years is having an indispensable partner to ride alongside through the ups and downs of the business.

"Having a business partner like Tom Woodruff is a big part of how my career and ADI have lasted so long. I've seen the toll this business can take on some of my friends who ran shops where they're in it by themselves, and a lot of aspects to this job can be very stressful and taxing to take on alone. The more of those experiences you have, the sooner you get to a point where you say, 'Screw this. I don't want to do this anymore.' The work becomes drudgery."

"Having a partner to bounce things off of and split the load with is great because we can carry the same load twice as far when we work together. I feel fortunate in that respect. There are not a lot of people that I could have done this with. Hopefully, Tom would say the same thing."

2 John Dykstra

FOR OVER FORTY-FIVE YEARS NOW, award-winning artist John Dykstra has left his indelible mark on modern cinema with a forward-thinking approach that utilizes technology hand in hand with special effects. He not only has changed the way movies are made, but has also inspired a generation of filmmakers looking to push the boundaries of what is possible to achieve on the big screen. Although his father's profession as a mechanical engineer influenced a few early hobbies in his formative years, Dykstra's passion began to expand into other avenues that shaped his eventual career path in special effects.

"While there might be an implication that somehow I was able to figure out my possibilities at a very young age," Dykstra said, "the truth is that I was just subjected to all the same things that kids are always subjected to, and certain things just stuck with me. When I was little, I really liked mechanical things, probably because my father was a mechanical engineer and he would build models to be representative of

Photo courtesy of John Dykstra.

company because he knew we were all young and hungry for the work. My experiences with Doug were seminal and he was a great mentor. Doug was and will always be ahead of his time," John added.

While he eventually moved on from working for Doug Trumbull after a few years, Dykstra continued to utilize his mentor's teachings as he embarked on his most ambitious project yet: George Lucas' *Star Wars: Episode IV – A New Hope* (1977).

"I was approached by Gary Kurtz and George Lucas about working on *Star Wars*. I think they approached me because they wanted somebody who wasn't an established visual effects person, like Doug [Trumbull]. What they were looking to achieve on the film was ambitious and unusual. George was blurring the line between an independent film and a studio film, so he was looking for kindred spirits who were willing to work in an unconventional fashion. And here I was, a college kid with a ponytail, so I was the epitome of unconventional."

"The truth is, I think they wanted somebody who was sort of a neophyte in the movie industry who they could have some control over," explained Dykstra. "I don't mean that in a bad way, I just think they didn't want somebody to come and say, 'Here is what your visual effects will be, and that's that.' They wanted someone who would be willing to continuously work with George and talk with him about what it was that he wanted to achieve in the movie."

"There were a broad range of new approaches that we used on *Star Wars*. The list goes on and on in terms of the mechanics of what we did differently or uniquely on *Star Wars* that made it what it is. The essence of it was that we linked the motion of the subject in the environment to the camera, and the camera became the controlling clock, if you will. If the camera ran fast, the system had to run fast, and if the camera ran slow, the system would slow down, too."

"I think George was surprised I ended up inventing a system [the Dykstraflex motion-controlled camera] in order to do what we needed to do on *Star Wars*. He probably figured that we'd do something cool with existing technology, but because we were here in Los Angeles and he was in London shooting, we were left to our own devices. I think that made George nervous, but we had a great team of people who had worked together before, so that made everything easier. We were all having a blast."

"Plus, the seminal movies that you see are usually because somebody has stepped outside the box. They didn't want to go to an established visual effects house because an established visual effects house would be afraid to step outside of the tried-and-true techniques, and we weren't afraid to push the envelope."

Due to the work that Dykstra and his *Star Wars* (1977) peers were doing at the time, a new division of Lucasfilm, Industrial Light & Magic (ILM) was born from their innovative spirit, becoming the benchmark for visual effects in the late 1970s and remaining the standard-bearer to this day. Dykstra, who was still establishing himself in the filmmaking world at the time, was chosen to supervise ILM, leading the charge with a team that included several other soon-to-be pioneers: Richard Edlund, Phil Tippett, Joe Johnston, Ken Ralston, and Dennis Muren.

"I brought in all of the people who I had worked with at various facilities, including Doug [Trumbull]'s place and Bob Abel's place, too. We all had a common language. Everybody who came there wanted to be there, enjoyed the work that they did, and trusted the people with whom they worked in almost a fraternal way."-

"We'd sit around, we'd talk about how we thought something new could be done, and the individuals would go off and build those components of that particular idea and would check back with the other people. They knew enough about each other's areas of expertise to know when they were getting into a situation where they'd better check with the guy from electrics or the guy from optics or the guy from wherever. It was like being part of a dream team."

While there are many landmark moments in *Star Wars* (1977) that became a reality because of the exemplary efforts of Dykstra and his entire team at ILM, one scene in particular still stands out to him even after forty years.

"The opening sequence in *Star Wars* is still my favorite moment," John said. "It's also what we used as our proof of concept to prove that we could do this kind of work. I just think it's really fun. It's really simple, too, but the way we put the viewers into space, where you were seeing a planet but then, suddenly, you were actually up close to a spaceship, still feels fun to me even now."

"Putting all of those things together in one continuous shot, and then finding the balance of all that imagery, was really stunning. Before we started that shot, we didn't know if any of this was ever really going to work, so to see it work as well as it does was a very proud moment for me."

Even though he was aware that the work they were doing at ILM on *Star Wars: Episode IV – A New Hope* (1977) was pushing the boundaries of filmmaking possibilities, Dykstra was surprised when they picked up the Academy Award for Best Visual Effects during the Oscars ceremony in 1978.

"I was beyond shocked," admitted John. "I was amazed that we were nominated to begin with, and that we would go on to win was astonishing. I didn't even have an acceptance speech prepared. I just went up and winged it, and I was even drunk, too. I figured we were just going to go to the Academy Awards and have a great evening. I didn't think it was really a possibility that we were going to be awarded an Oscar, but it was a great feeling to share an award with my friends, and it ended up becoming a huge boost to my career, too."

"The thing about *Star Wars* was the chemistry—it's an intangible part of making movies, but it's so important. No matter what you do, each movie that you work on has a chemistry, and sometimes the chemistry is constructive and the whole is greater than the sum of the parts, and other times the chemistry is destructive and despite incredibly good ingredients, the film itself does not become a particularly good product."

"It's a bit of a crapshoot, really. The producers and director obviously make every effort to assemble a team with whom they can communicate and have a rapport. That can be hard to do, because there are so many creative minds that have to coalesce and collaborate. It can be tough to get that chemistry right. And on *Star Wars*, the chemistry was exceptional."

After *Star Wars* (1977), Dykstra returned to the world of science fiction in Universal's TV series *Battlestar Galactica* (1978), a project on which he founded his own company, Apogee Inc., with many of the artists that contributed to *Star Wars* (1977). After leaving ILM, Dykstra continued his career as a special effects supervisor on his own terms. Just a year after *Battlestar Galactica* (1978), John found himself once again immersed in the realm of sci-fi for *Star Trek: The Motion Picture* (1979), a project that came with its own set of challenges.

"Honestly, it was terrible," Dykstra admitted. "Gene Roddenberry was around, so it was interesting to have him there, but the director [Robert Wise] didn't get along with the writer [Harold Livingston], Harold didn't get along with the studio, and the studio didn't get along with anybody. There was continuously one crisis after another. Then, on top of it, because they sold the film before they had a script even finished, they ended up with a class action lawsuit, and the studio was reportedly going to have to pay upwards of $100 million if they didn't have it finished in time for its release date."

"The one good thing about *Star Trek* was that I got to work with Doug [Trumbull] again. Originally, he was supposed to do the film all on his own. Because the producers had to step up the pace on everything and deliver a movie by a certain date, it meant we had to go crazy to try and get everything done on time. We were building one end of a model and photographing the other end of that same model on the same stage, and we were constantly working three eight-hour shifts to get the work done. I've never had to work like that in my career, and it felt much more like an emergency response than a collaborative effort. It was just, 'Let's just get this done.' It's amazing that it turned out as well as it did, honestly."

After surviving production on *Star Trek: The Motion Picture* (1979) and earning his second Oscar nomination, Dykstra helped bring the mischievous gopher to life on *Caddyshack* (1980) before teaming up with Clint Eastwood for his ambitious action film *Firefox* (1982), on which he once again used his expertise in shooting miniatures to great effect. However, there was another landmark project that he was almost hired for instead.

"I was approached by Ridley Scott to do *Blade Runner*, originally," Dykstra recalled, "and I had gone and interviewed with him. We got along just fine, but then, I don't know exactly how it worked, but Doug Trumbull ended up working on the movie. I guess the studio made a deal where they said they wanted me to take the Clint Eastwood movie *Firefox* because it was about all this flying stuff, and they wanted Doug to handle the artistic-type work for *Blade Runner*. I was really disappointed by that decision. But *Firefox* was great for different reasons, because we got to do a lot of flying, and we also got to invent a new matte photography process."

Dykstra did return to the world of sci-fi just a few years later for a pair of films from Master of Horror Tobe Hooper: his 1986 adaptation of the classic *Invaders from Mars* (1953) and *Lifeforce* (1985), which was originally shot under a completely different production name.

"*Spider-Man 2* came with its own set of challenges, particularly when it came to the character of Doc Ock [played by Alfred Molina]. We had to create tentacles that would work mechanically, but also had personality to them because they could act on their own. There were a few of us who worked together to create the tentacles as puppets. Edge FX designed how the puppets would work practically, and Imageworks handled the animation of the puppets on the visual effects side of everything. Alfred, who was going to be the one who had to wear these things, was giving us his input, too. He was a truly great villain."

Over the last fifteen years since *Spider-Man 2* (2004), John Dykstra has continued contributing to many blockbuster films, including *Hancock* (2008), *X-Men: First Class* (2011), *Godzilla* (2014), and *X-Men: Apocalypse* (2016), and he also lent his expertise to Quentin Tarantino's *Inglourious Basterds* (2009) and *The Hateful Eight* (2015). With a career that has lasted over four decades and earned numerous well-deserved accolades, Dykstra reflected on the secret to his success.

"Honestly, the key to this industry is to remain a student at heart. Always explore and embrace new approaches to your work. It's still hard for me to pinpoint. I was very fortunate to have made the transition from film to digital, which a lot of people didn't do, and I'd like to think it's because my input is more creative than it is technical. I believe that approach supports longevity in this business. You have to be ready to come up with imagery that is unique and provocative all the time, and if you can do that, then you work as long as you can get up every morning. You have to be ready to roll with the punches, and you have to realize that there are a lot of people out there who want to be doing the work that you're doing, so you have to always stay abreast of where the work and the industry is heading."

3 Kevin Haney

FOR AWARD-WINNING ARTIST Kevin Haney, it was his love of the Universal Monsters and live theater that forever cemented his career path in the world of special effects, even if possibilities in that field seemed like a world away during his younger days growing up in the Midwest. Monsters consumed Haney's childhood, though, and in high school, he would finally get the opportunity to further develop his talents as a budding artist.

"For as long as I can remember, I was always interested in monsters," Haney said. "I was raised in Cincinnati, Ohio, and we had the 'four o'clock movie' and late-night movies, so I saw everything from the Universal classics to really horrible Italian movies, too, stuff like *Caltiki: The Immortal Monster*. So I started doing all the Aurora monster models that were popular back then, and even though I hated them in regards to the designs, I was still very taken with them."

A caricature of Kevin Haney, drawn by artist Doug Drexler. Courtesy of Doug Drexler.

"Then, in high school, a friend of mine talked me into trying out for the school play and I managed to get a role in it. When it came time for me to be aged, I remember that the makeup guy, who was named Vic Johansson, had the Dick Smith handbook. I remember thinking, as I looked through the pages, that this was cool as hell. I told Vic that I wanted him to teach me how to do all of this stuff, and he told me I had to talk to Suzy Ritter, the makeup department head."

"So the next day at math class, I was still thinking about that book and thought it was going to be great because I'd be able to do The Wolf Man now and Quasimodo, too. And then a friend of mine comes up to me in class and says, 'Hey, Kevin, can I be on your makeup crew next year?' And I said, 'My makeup crew? What are you talking about?' He told me how Suzy had said to him that I was going to be the makeup chairman next year, so I went to her and said, 'What the hell? I don't know anything about makeup.' But I guess Vic had told her how I was interested in Dick's book, and because I showed interest, they were going to spend the summer teaching me how to do makeup, and that's how it all began for me. I learned rather quickly, and I found that I loved it all instantaneously."

Haney would get more opportunities to flex his creative muscles post-high school, but not through college.

"When I graduated, I went to Ohio State University, and I soon realized that the theatrical department couldn't really teach me anything beyond the basics in makeup. Then, I found this group of guys there who did this summer theater down in Chillicothe, Ohio, and they needed someone to come and do makeups on them."

"I would spend my summers going around to where all these productions were going on. I was hired to do rubber makeups of old Native Ameican chiefs and frontiersmen, and they even gave me my own shed to work out of. It was great, and I was doing work that I was really proud of there."

"It was also work that I was able to send off to Dick Smith to get his attention, so he would bring me out to New York. And it eventually worked; I realize how lucky I am in that regard, because I'd be a very different person if Dick hadn't taken me in. If I'd come out to Los Angeles at that point, I would have been in a very different environment, which may not have been as supportive, because Dick was a very forgiving mentor. Because there was heavier competition on the West Coast, I was this big

Kevin Haney and Doug Drexler look on as Dick Smith does a makeup application.
Photo courtesy of Doug Drexler.

fish in a small pond in New York, and there were a few of us who helped jump-start the makeup scene there in the late '70s and early '80s."

"When I began studying under Dick, I was able to meet so many other people, too," added Haney, "and that became a real defining point in my young career. I didn't work on that many things with him, but I spent a lot of time sitting up in his little room. I remember once, while he was sculpting David Bowie for *The Hunger*, he stopped what he was doing just for me, and began explaining where the clay went and why it went there. It was like a master class on aged sculpture, and why he chose me, I'll never know, but I'm just grateful he did."

Another fixture in Haney's early career was John Caglione, Jr., a multi-award-winning artist who would go on to work on memorable films such as *Dick Tracy* (1990) and *The Dark Knight* (2008). One of Haney's first professional gigs as a special effects technician was on Frank Henenlotter's low-budget cult classic *Basket Case* (1982), and that's where he first forged his friendship with Caglione, Jr. However, Haney was initially slated to work on another project with Henenlotter before the now-iconic character of Belial from *Basket Case* (1982) was even a twinkle in the filmmaker's eye.

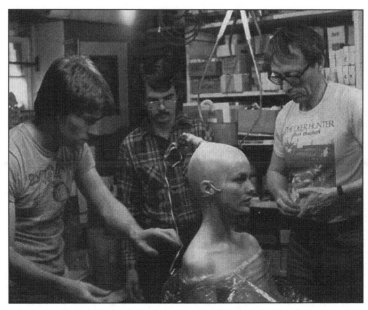

Doug Drexler, Kevin Haney, and Dick Smith in action on *Altered States* (1980).
Photo courtesy of Doug Drexler.

"Originally, Frank Henenlotter and [Producer] Edgar Ievins brought me on because we were going to do a show called *Ooze*, which was an exploitation of Legionnaires' disease. Frank's idea was that there was this respiratory/circulatory disease where you would get these boils and then it would cause your extremities to explode off your body. Frank even had me do a little maquette and ship it to him from Ohio so he could use it for fundraising."

"But when we finally met to discuss the project, he said, '*Ooze* is out and now I'm going to do something very different.' He gave me this book about genetic anomalies of nature, and Frank had found a picture of what we would eventually base Belial off of. It took him a while to get his financing, so by that time I had already started working with Dick on *Altered States*, just helping out here and there."

"But, Dick loaned me his lab and his oven to run the foam for *Basket Case*," Kevin said, "even though Frank had set me up in a little place down in the Village, which is where I first built the monster. There was a lot of running back and forth, and all I really had on that shoot was four hundred bucks, a bag of UltraCal, a gallon of foam latex, and a box of

Roma. Back then, you were not really paid for your time, so you did it for the thrill."

"The biggest mistake I made on *Basket Case* involved how I sculpted the hands," Haney added. "I thought an easy way to do the hands was to make them off the mold, but they weren't sculpted to go on a human being. Frank was a little irate with me because they were very, very small and very tight and very hard for him to manipulate, and Frank was the one doing the puppeteering of the monster for most of the shots."

"I needed help to finish everything up, and that's when John came in; I really owe him a lot, too. There was a baby monster that needed to be done and several other effects that I had engineered out, but they still needed to be executed. We were shooting in Upstate New York, which ironically was John's hometown, so I brought in John to do the baby monster and he was having trouble, too. Because he was working at NBC at the time, which had great facilities, he had me come in and we were able to fix the problems there. We ended up having such a great time working together that John said, 'You know what? This has been really fun. You should work here. I'll put in a good word for you.' And frankly, between John and Dick Smith, I couldn't do much better. Plus, I now had a special effects family, so that clinched everything for me."

Haney soon found himself on the fast track at NBC upon the recommendation of Caglione, Jr., who had been a fixture at the network for several years.

"What was great about working there was that I was able to do an accelerated apprenticeship, because they felt that my training under Dick had already put me beyond where most would be during the trainee period. Soon enough, I started doing commercials, and one of the staff requirements was to do *Saturday Night Live,* so John and I would muck around there, too. John left about halfway through 1980 to work on *Quest for Fire,* and then I inherited the show from him until Peter Montagna took over in 1985."

During his time at NBC, Haney continued to work in the world of film, contributing his talents to projects like *Amityville 3-D* (1983) and *C.H.U.D.* (1984), on which he assisted Caglione, Jr., who was heading up the movie's makeup effects. In addition to working on the film's special effects, Haney lent his vocal talents to the C.H.U.D., too, often roaring into paper towel tubes for the sound department.

Right around the time he was wrapping up with NBC, Haney was brought on to Brian De Palma's comedic crime caper *Wise Guys* (1986), co-starring Danny DeVito, Joe Piscopo, and Harvey Keitel. Although he was a bit nervous working with such top-notch talent, his director was nothing but kind to him throughout production.

"Brian De Palma was very patient with me on *Wise Guys*, because I was still so green and definitely not experienced when it came to running a show at that point. But he didn't fire me, which was nice, and he would listen to my ramblings, which were often. I remember after one instance, he just looked at me and said, 'You don't know what your job is, do you, young man?' And then he chuckled."

Shortly after *Wise Guys* (1986), Haney got the call that forever changed his career when he was requested to join the effects team for Ron Howard's *Cocoon* (1985), a science fiction fantasy film that utilized brilliant practical and cutting-edge visual effects to bring its otherworldly creatures to life.

"*Cocoon* came about because of a union thing," explained Haney. "They had an L.A. guy for my position, and the unions came down and said, 'No, you've got to have an East Coast guy on your team.' So I came in and worked with Bob Norin, which meant I was walking onto a set with people who already knew a hell of a lot about how to work on a show of that magnitude and how West Coast people were doing things."

"I came in with my little cantilever makeup kit that was very popular in New York, but Bob told me that it would not be sufficient for me to keep using. So, on my next payday, he had me order the proper upright wooden kit everyone else was using, and then he helped me get all the proper materials together. He walked me through that, which was really important and helpful, as I was taking my next steps in my career."

"*Cocoon* was also interesting for me because I was able to see Greg Cannom and Kevin Yagher come in and do their thing. Rick Baker was acting as a consultant, but Greg designed the aliens. I basically had two things to do for Greg—one involved Don Ameche's double during the dance scene, and then I worked on the effect where Brian Dennehy pulls his eye socket down. I also had to age up Wilford Brimley. He bleached his moustache and hair, and we added liver spots and lines with makeup and colored pencils."

Even though he had found success on a West Coast project, Haney still remained loyal to New York for several more years, including through his work on Orion Pictures' satanic thriller *The Believers* (1987), starring Martin Sheen, Helen Shaver, and Robert Loggia.

"I am really proud of the work I did for *The Believers* because that was still very early in my career and I had to do a lot of gelatin work in that film. It was a lot of fun for me because we had to make spiders come out of Helen Shaver's face. I learned a lot on that movie, especially how lighting can affect your makeups."

"The film's Director of Photography, Robby Müller, was so all over the map as far as how he would light his scenes, so it was hard to anticipate what I needed to do to make sure my work still looked good. It was always different with each scene, so I'd always go to him and say, 'Okay Robby, give me the gels du jour.' At one point, I remember him coming up and saying, 'Kevin, don't yell at me, but I have her walking through six different gels, and going from neon and into daylight.' I couldn't believe that and I tried to protest, but all Robby said to me was, 'Your makeup is so good, dude, that I know it'll hold up.' While I appreciated his vote of confidence, I wasn't so sure. It did all come out looking pretty good, though," Haney added, "for that time and that budget."

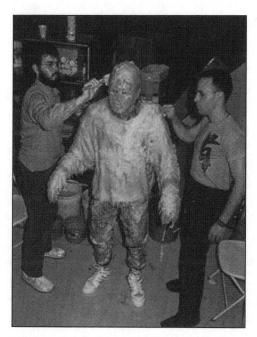

Kevin Haney and Doug Drexler working behind the scenes on *Poltergeist III* (1988). Photo courtesy of Doug Drexler.

In the late 1980s and early 1990s, Haney found himself working on much bigger productions, including *Poltergeist III* (1988), *Driving Miss Daisy* (1989), and *Dick Tracy* (1990). The new opportunities came about from his reputation as a dedicated artist and the strong collaborative relationships he had forged with the producing team of Richard D. Zanuck and Lili Fini Zanuck, as well as his longtime friend Caglione, Jr., who brought Haney onto the hugely ambitious production of *Dick Tracy*.

"Everything in my career during that era really converged at the point when I worked on both *Driving Miss Daisy* and *Dick Tracy*," recalled Haney. "Thanks to *Cocoon*, the Zanucks chose to call me for *Driving Miss Daisy*. I was unavailable because I had started working on *Dick Tracy* and I had a pact then where I said, 'If I'm working on something, I don't ever jump ship, even if it means turning down a whole feature.' So I stayed on *Dick Tracy*, which ended up being a great project in many ways, but it also made it so I could join the West Coast artists' union, along with my friends John [Caglione, Jr.] and Doug [Drexler]."

"What was nice was that they ended up having to redo some stuff with Dan Aykroyd's makeup in *Driving Miss Daisy*, and the Zanucks were able to bring me back because I had already wrapped on *Dick Tracy*. But then, John and Doug got to take home an Oscar [for *Dick Tracy*] a year after I won an Oscar myself on *Daisy*, which was pretty incredible."

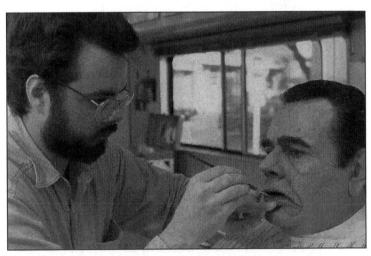

Haney works to transform Paul Sorvino for *Dick Tracy* (1990).
Photo courtesy of Doug Drexler.

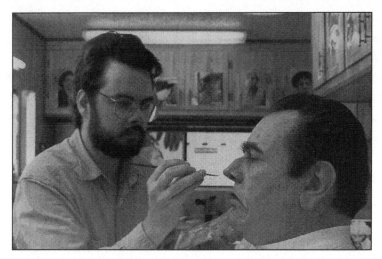

Kevin puts the finishing touches on Paul Sorvino for *Dick Tracy* (1990).
Photo courtesy of Doug Drexler.

"I didn't get a statue for *Dick Tracy* or anything, but that's okay because it was not in John's or Doug's hands. My work stands for itself, so I wasn't concerned about that. I might have been more devastated, though, if I hadn't won the Oscar the year before for *Driving Miss Daisy*, so this could have been an entirely different conversation had it not been for the Zanucks," Haney added.

"All of this happened right around the time I started working on the television series *Monsters*. That was a show where I had to try and cut corners everywhere because of the budgetary limitations, so it was a very different experience than some of the films I had been working on. I usually take it upon myself to put my own money up on the table to just make the work look cool—especially with monsters—but that one was tough."

"I didn't do a lot on *Monsters*, but I was able to create a vampire and a mandrake root character. That production was really difficult, especially with the budget they gave me. I basically had $1,800 to do a monster a week, and at one point, I ended up in the hospital because I couldn't afford an assistant—or rather, I felt that I couldn't afford an assistant because I wanted every cent to be on the screen. Dick [Smith] had to come down and save my ass on that one when I got sick."

Shortly after coming to this crossroads in his career, the now award-winning Haney had to make a tough decision: stay in New York and continue to help sustain the special effects scene there, or head west and make a name for himself among fellow artists in Hollywood.

"In 1990, I was called to do *The Addams Family* [1991 movie], and I just stayed out there, because at that point, Los Angeles was where all the work was being done. There was so much going on with television and with film, so I never really had a reason to go back to New York. I ended up working on both *Addams Family* movies, and I really appreciated the approach that both [Director] Barry Sonnenfeld and [Producer] Scott Rudin took to those films."

"They were very smart. They knew exactly what they were doing and they were respectful to the original characters. We all got a book of the original *Addams Family* cartoons and that was our bible. That was the feeling we were going for, and there were actually some cartoons in the film that were recreated. It was also very well-written and had a brilliant cast."

Soon after he helped bring the Addams family to the big screen, Haney enjoyed another turning point in his career when he was tasked with turning legendary actor Jason Robards into Mark Twain for the TV movie *Mark Twain and Me* (1991), a project that would go on to win Haney and Donald Mowat an Emmy Award for their makeup effects.

"*Mark Twain and Me* was another big moment for me in different ways. Usually, I'm good about separating the artist in me from the emotional side of myself, but that wasn't the case here, and that was due to Jason Robards. He was a delight and he helped me get through a really hard time of my life, which was my first divorce. He was fantastic and he made the work a total joy."

"We also did another TV movie together, *Lincoln*, and because Jason's face was very distinctive, a lot of people said early on that he didn't have the right face to play Abraham Lincoln. Well, I worked hard to make it the right face for Lincoln, and I'm really proud of how that makeup came out. But Jason was a great person, and I loved being able to work with him a few times."

Right around the same time he was transforming Robards into one of the United State's greatest presidents, Haney also worked on *Death Becomes Her* (1992), the savagely dark comedy featuring Meryl Streep, Bruce Willis, and Goldie Hawn. Looking back at the project, Haney discussed how differently things could have been had director Robert Zemeckis kept in one key cast member who was cut from the final version of the film.

"Originally, Tracey Ullman was in it, and I worked with her. She was going to be Bruce's girlfriend, and for some reason they cut her out. They thought that the ending was too soft and predictable with her in it, and so Robert completely cut her out, which was very strange because she was in the whole thing. I'd still like to see a cut with her in it, because she was very good, but I guess they just decided to go a different way with the film. I know from a conversation we had that Mr. Zemeckis doesn't want me to ever print those pictures of the aged makeups on her and Bruce, which is a shame because they turned out fantastic."

Over the next few years, Haney lent his talents to several more genre-centric projects such as *Hocus Pocus* (1993), *Addams Family Values* (1993), and *Stigmata* (1999), while still finding success in mainstream movies like *The Shawshank Redemption* (1994), *The Chamber* (1996), and *Air Force One* (1997), as well as the comedic sequel *Austin Powers: The Spy Who Shagged Me* (1999).

"Michèle Burke and Kenny Myers brought me in for [*Austin Powers: The Spy Who Shagged* Me] to help out, and I mainly worked with Will Huff. That was great to be a part of because we were always having a good time on set. [Director] Jay [Roach] had learned his lesson from the first *Austin Powers*, and so he would just keep the camera running to get all this hilarious stuff. What was even better is that we wouldn't start until late, because there was a theory that comedy and early mornings didn't mesh, so the hours were very good and I had a lot of fun doing all the makeups on Verne [Troyer] for that shoot. For the third *Austin Powers*, it seemed like they just eliminated as much as they could with the makeup, so I didn't work on that one at all. Two was very ambitious though, and a lot of fun to be a part of."

In the early 2000s, Haney was called to work alongside special effects legend Rick Baker on several ambitious projects—*How the Grinch Stole Christmas* (2000), *Planet of the Apes* (2001), and *Men in Black II* (2002)—that featured some of the best makeup work he had been around his entire career.

"Rick prepares a show like nobody else," Haney said. "He gives every single aspect of that show his full attention and he also makes sure the crew has everything they could possibly need to do their job. For *Grinch*, I was given a couple of background characters, but my main person to work on was Jeffrey Tambor's Mayor of Whoville. Jeffrey's just a joy to be around, but the appliance that I was given to work with was one of the best I'd ever been given. It was beautiful and so easy to use, and looked seamless when we would finish Jeffrey up."

"With *Planet of the Apes*, the shoot was cool and the makeups were amazing, but the film itself wasn't very successful. Rick, Kazuhiro [Tsuji], and Bart [Mixon] did a fantastic job of putting together everything and brilliantly designing those ape appliances in a way that felt like it was befitting of the original. I think we all knew the movie itself wasn't going to be great, but we were all happy to be working on it, since the original *Apes* was a film that so many of us were fans of. Rick even said once while we were working on it, 'Go get Rod Serling's script. Let's make that. That's a great script, so why can't we just make that?' Tim [Burton] tried really hard on *Planet*, but all he really did was just pull together certain elements that made the first film iconic, and not much else."

"And for *Men in Black II*," Haney continued, "I worked again with Kevin Grevioux, who I had done makeups for on *Planet of the Apes*. He was playing this third-eye guy and it was a lot of fun, and again, all of those appliances were top-notch. Every creature mattered to Rick, so you never had to worry about 'making do' or anything like that. I was so happy to work with Rick on those three jobs—everything was very well-thought-out, well-planned, and absolutely beautiful."

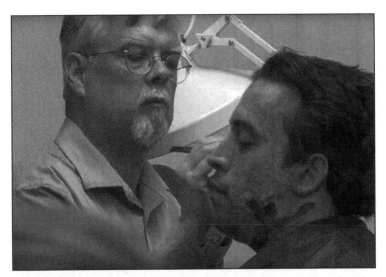

Kevin works on a zombie for *Scouts Guide to the Zombie Apocalypse* (2015).
Photo courtesy of Tony Gardner.

(Left to right) Doug Drexler, Dick Smith, and Kevin Haney.
Photo courtesy of Doug Drexler.

After beginning his special effects career in the early 1980s, Haney is still working steadily after thirty-five years in what can be a cutthroat business. He's been the Creative Director at Makeup & Effects Laboratories since 2010, and over the last few years has lent his talents to a wide array of films, including *Alice in Wonderland* (2010), *John Carter* (2012), *Iron Man 3* (2013), *Captain America: The Winter Soldier* (2014), *Guardians of the Galaxy* (2014), and *Star Trek Beyond* (2016), on which he was part of a vast team tasked with bringing over fifty alien species to life via practical effects in honor of the franchise's fiftieth anniversary. While he can't pinpoint the exact reason for his career's longevity, Haney does admit that a bit of extra effort can go a long way.

"Asking me how I've managed to enjoy my career for as long as I have been able to is a tough question. I've just been lucky and I think that I could be anybody, really. I know I have some talent, but I see a lot of talented people's careers passing on, too, so I guess I've done something right. The longevity comes from basically showing up on time, doing your work, and don't ever create trouble. It's pretty straightforward."

"Something else that has always been important to me is that I've never been afraid to do the small stuff. There are a lot of people who get all hoity-toity and say, 'I'm not going to go out and paint bodies. I'm above that. Don't you know who I am?' For me, I've always been like, 'What time? Three thirty in the morning? I'll be there.' What we do is still a service industry, so you have to try and give each production your very best service. A lot of people in this industry don't even bother to try to ask names, and while I'm not very good at remembering names, I will always make the attempt. Because when a person sits in that chair for me, I like to know who they are and I want them to know that I care about them and the process."

"So, maybe in the end, it's really about not being so full of one's self. In saying that, I'm reminded of the story about Arturo Toscanini, who was a conductor of the NBC Symphony Orchestra. There was an opera singer who was getting ready to do this big performance. She turned to Toscanini and said, 'Mr. Toscanini, you know that I'm a star,' and he said to her, 'Yes, but music, she's the sun, and when the sun comes up, you don't see the stars.'"

4 Jennifer Aspinall

FROM AN EARLY AGE, Jennifer Aspinall knew she was obsessed with the art of illusion, but she wasn't exactly sure just what path her career would end up taking over the thirty-plus years she has enjoyed in the makeup business. A highly driven and multi-dimensional artist who wasted no time honing her skills, there's a reason Aspinall has continued to find success, both within the world of special effects and outside of its realm as well.

Photo courtesy of Jennifer Aspinall.

"I didn't grow up wanting to be a special effects makeup artist," explained Aspinall. "It all happened much more organically. For me, it was more about illusion. I wasn't really sure whether that meant I was going to end up being a makeup artist, or if I would end up acting or directing or producing. I just liked creating illusions."

"When I was a kid, I liked to disguise myself and make myself up into different people, primarily because I was painfully shy. When I was nine, I found Richard Corson's *Stage Makeup* book. That book rocked my world; it gave me all the tools that I needed to create different illusions on myself. I received my first professional makeup from my next-door neighbor who produced dinner theater. By the time I was twelve, I was working for her, doing everything from makeup to performing."

"I worked doing theater from the age of eleven until I graduated from high school. My daily routine would be: go to school, come home,

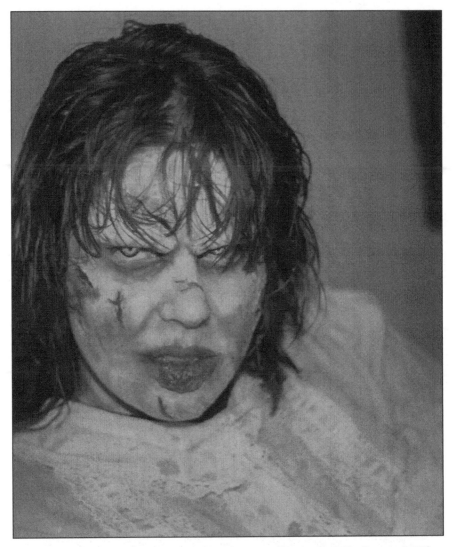

Jennifer transforms herself into the possessed version of Regan from *The Exorcist* (1973).
Photo courtesy of Jennifer Aspinall.

do my paper route (which was a five-mile bike ride), go to theater, and do the show. Then, come home, do my homework, go to bed. And then do it all again the next day. I was very blessed to have such supportive parents."

Not one to rest on her laurels, while still in high school Aspinall branched out from her work on those dinner theater shows and helped bring a stage production of a beloved cult classic to the Philadelphia theater scene.

"At seventeen, I produced and performed in a live stage version of *The Rocky Horror Picture Show* in Philadelphia for a local theater. Producing a theater piece was the next level of me breaking out of my shell. I learned a lot."

Jennifer wearing a dramatic glam makeup that she designed and created during her younger years. Photo courtesy of Jennifer Aspinall.

"Producing and performing in *Rocky Horror* proved to be helpful in a couple of ways when I decided to move to New York City to pursue makeup opportunities," Aspinall added. "While performing the role of Frank-N-Furter, I ended up having a fan club. The woman who was the president of the fan club introduced me to a friend of her mother's, who happened to be a very successful hairdresser in New York. Peggy, the hairdresser, was very kind and introduced me to several commercial directors and production companies. That started my working career in New York."

"And through *Rocky Horror*, I also met a makeup artist named Arnold Gargiulo. Arnold was the first person I had met creating prosthetics. He shared a lot with me. After watching him, I was very inspired and thought, *I could do this*. What really spoke to me about using appliances was that it was another way to create an even better illusion. What Arnold taught me really changed my career yet again."

It wasn't long before Aspinall put her new skills to good use on the low-budget cult classic *The Toxic Avenger* (1984), which not only introduced horror fans everywhere to Toxie, the film's soon-to-be iconic hero, but also launched Troma Entertainment and the careers of Lloyd Kaufman and Michael Herz to new levels in the indie filmmaking world. While she

A young Jennifer at work. Photo courtesy of Jennifer Aspinall.

Toxie and a friend pose between takes on the set of *The Toxic Avenger* (1984).
Photo courtesy of Jennifer Aspinall.

was grateful for her big break, Aspinall still cannot recall exactly how the stars aligned for her on that project.

"You know, I'm not really sure how I got the job; that would be a question for Lloyd, because I don't know why he chose me for *Toxic Avenger*," admitted Aspinall. "I'd never done a movie before, and even though I had watched Arnold do mold-making, that was something I had never really done before on my own. The character of Toxie was my first sculpture for a mask. He was my first real mold, and the first time I created something to that extent from scratch. That was a big deal to me. I had to figure it all out on the spot, and I had to do it all with just $200."

"Luckily, I'm blessed with a brain that likes to figure out puzzles. I was also blessed to have met a guy named Tom Lauten. He was my right hand on that show. He was very helpful, and he had done some special effects makeup before *Toxic Avenger*. It was a little like learning how to

A close-up look at the Toxie makeup, as designed by Jennifer for *The Toxic Avenger* (1984). Photo courtesy of Jennifer Aspinall.

break down magic tricks. I don't know if I can verbalize it precisely, but because I can storyboard things in my head, it made it easier for me to figure out what angles we would be seeing the effect from, and then I knew how to build it from there."

"Even though we had literally no budget, I remember being very committed to doing the best I could do under the circumstances. At the end of the day, I just wanted to create interesting, realistic effects and a version of Toxie that felt alive. I believe even if you're working on a low-budget movie, or if you've got only a certain amount of time, the work you do has to look alive—it has to look organic, or it just doesn't work."

"Working on *Toxic Avenger* was great, though. On a technical level, I learned a hell of a lot on that show, and on a personal level, it taught me so much about what actually goes on when you're making a movie, and that gave me even more insight into our industry."

A few years later, Aspinall found herself challenged once again on one of the horror genre's most storied independent productions, *Spook-*

ies (1986), a low-budget haunted house chiller that after three decades has still not made its home entertainment bow (there's even some debate over whether or not the film received a proper theatrical release back in the day). Looking back on the project, Aspinall recalled how things continuously evolved throughout the production of *Spookies* (1986), which underwent several directorial and crew changes as the shoot wore on.

"Originally, I didn't have anything to do with the effects. I was hired just to do the straight makeup, but there were two or three different groups from beginning to end. At one point, Arnold [Gargiulo] was hired to do some effects, and his assistant, a kid named Gabe Bartalos, was there, too. John Dods was hired to do some of the big mechanical creature-y stuff, but then, at some point, things began to shift on *Spookies*."

"Some people left, other people came in. I ended up doing the straight makeup, as well as some of the effects. I helped apply the prosthetics on the little girl, on the Grim Reaper character, and the Spider-Woman, and I sculpted and applied one of the Muck Men creatures. It all happened by default, though. All I remember was a lot of weirdness. On top of everything, we were shooting in a real haunted house."

Both makeup stages of the Spider-Woman character from *Spookies* (1986).
Photos courtesy of Jennifer Aspinall.

One of the Muck Men creatures Jennifer worked on for *Spookies* (1986).
Photo courtesy of Jennifer Aspinall.

"There was an old woman who had owned it, and she had recently died," Aspinall continued. "I believe her family thought they would make some money by renting it out to this production before they sold it, so we had the run of this estate for the entire shoot. We all lived there during the shooting of the production. And I'm not sure if it was the old woman or not, but there was something that was haunting us. We'd hear doors slamming all the time by themselves, things would get moved when no one was around—there was a lot of really weird stuff."

"*Spookies* led to another low-budget film called *Street Trash*. After *Street Trash*, I began to realize that I needed to shift gears and determine which direction I wanted to take my career. I had to come to grips with what I enjoyed and what I didn't enjoy in our business, and what I wanted to do as an artist."

As she searched for answers, Aspinall happened upon another artistic figure who would leave a huge imprint on her blossoming career.

"I met an artist named Dean Howell. He was a resin artist in New York. Dick Smith was even a fan of his. He was one of the first people that I knew of who was doing gigantic, realistic heads completely out of resin."

"I still remember a conversation we had so vividly. He spoke to me for hours, just talking about art and life. One of the things Dean said to me was, 'Well, you're an artist and that's what you need to be. Just be an artist and just look at everything that you do as art.' That's when I realized, *I'm not a special effects artist, I'm not a makeup artist—I'm simply just an artist.*"

"I'm lucky enough to work in an industry that I can make a living in doing something I love to do. But the bottom line is that it's all about the art. I feel very blessed, and that discussion transitioned me into a different

Jennifer was in charge of the ambitious practical effects needed for the cult classic *Street Trash* (1987). Photos courtesy of Jennifer Aspinall.

place where I was like, *Okay, this is what I get to do as an artist to make money. I'm doing commercial art, and I'm just going to create the best and most organic work for the people who hire me.*"

"It's different once you get rid of the ego. When you detach the ego from the work, it's very freeing. The bottom line is that we are all doing commercial art. It's not our show. It's somebody else's show, somebody else's vision. It's my job to help the writer, the director, and the actor to realize their vision," Aspinall added.

It was right around that time that the live theater environment Aspinall grew up in came calling again, only on a much grander scale.

"I ended up working for the New York City Opera for about six years. Because I love doing theater and theater is one of my passions, the fact that theater came back into my life when it did was amazing. It was great to be in that live setting again, plus, all the things that I had been doing in the horror films were techniques I now was able to bring into the opera."

"And, much like the rest of my career, everything was building on itself. I wasn't doing horror films then, but I was still doing prosthetics, and because of my work there, I ended up getting a random call to leave the opera to be in charge of *Saturday Night Live*. Working in that environ-

Jennifer hard at work on the set of *Street Trash* (1987). Photo courtesy of Jennifer Aspinall.

ment was great, because it allowed me to incorporate my theater skill set of having to do quick changes with prosthetics, creature, and beauty makeups."

Aspinall spent three years backstage in charge of the makeup department at *Saturday Night Live* (1975) (for which she received her first Emmy Award nomination), and the experience served her well, preparing her to become a part of *MADtv*'s (1995) sketch comedy family for over fourteen seasons. She enjoyed much success on *MADtv* (1995), nabbing one Emmy Award, fourteen Emmy Award nominations, and five Make-Up Artists & Hair Stylist Guild Awards along the way.

Unfrozen Caveman Lawyer (portrayed by Phil Hartman) was one of the popular characters Jennifer created during her time on *Saturday Night Live* (1975). Photo courtesy of Jennifer Aspinall.

"Fox Television brought me to Los Angeles in 1995 to head up the makeup department for *MADtv*. To be present at the birth of a show like that was really amazing. It was a really great experience to watch a show grow and develop, and I'm honored to say I was there from the first day until the last."

One of the many transformative makeups Jennifer created for comedian/actor Jordan Peele over the years. Photo courtesy of Jennifer Aspinall.

Television has been particularly good to Aspinall's career, as she worked as the department head on several shows over the years, including *The Jamie Kennedy Experiment* (2002), *The Tonight Show with Jay Leno* (1992), *Key & Peele* (2012), and *Walk the Prank* (2016), and she also returned to *MADtv* (1995) as the head of the makeup department for the show's revival run in late 2016.

Films have also kept her busy throughout the years, with Aspinall lending her talents to a wide range of productions, in-

When not keeping busy on feature films, Jennifer also runs another business called Human Vase that brings together intricate makeups and floral designs. Photos courtesy of Jennifer Aspinall.

cluding *Basquiat* (1996), *The Mexican* (2001), *A Cinderella Story* (2004), *Indiana Jones and the Kingdom of the Crystal Skull* (2008), *Guardians of the Galaxy* (2014), *Star Trek Beyond* (2016), and *Kong: Skull Island* (2017).

Beyond her illustrious career as an artist in both film and television, Apsinall has also branched out by starting two different companies: Skin Saver Lotion, which features a revelatory skin barrier lotion, and Human Vase, which celebrates living art by combining exotic flowers and body paint. When she's not busy working professionally, Aspinall also enjoys teaching aspiring artists in Los Angeles the importance of versatility in their creativity.

"I believe the reason I'm still working is because I do all kinds of makeup, so I'm not locked into just doing special effects. Plus, there is the love of being creative, too, because I have to stay creatively busy. One of the things that I teach my students is that above all else, you need a varied skill set in order to find any kind of longevity in this business. That way, if there aren't any prosthetics jobs out there, you can work doing beauty makeups and so forth."

"That broadens your marketability, and that way, you're always working and continuing to grow as an artist. This industry can be rough, so the most important thing I've learned along the way is that you have to figure out how to take the ride without getting overly attached, and at the same time remain centered on your own integrity—artistically, personally, and professionally."

Jennifer poses with some of her Emmy awards. Photo courtesy of Jennifer Aspinall.

5 John Rosengrant

FOR OVER THIRTY YEARS, animatronics specialist and makeup artist John Rosengrant has left an indelible mark on the special effects industry. From the very first film project he contributed to back in 1983 to the groundbreaking work he's doing now as part of Legacy Effects—which he co-founded with Alan Scott, Shane Mahan, and Lindsay MacGowan in 2008—Rosengrant has remained a vital creator in the world of modern effects.

Photo courtesy of John Rosengrant.

Rosengrant grew up on the East Coast during the 1960s, quickly falling in love with classic movie monsters that would become a lifelong obsession, fueling his desire to be an artist and helping him during a huge transitional phase throughout his childhood.

"I lived in New Jersey, right across the George Washington Bridge from New York City, until I was seven years old," explained Rosengrant. "My dad worked for the phone company and they were building a plant that made telephones in Shreveport, Louisiana. So I moved from basically New York City to Shreveport back in 1966. It really was a huge shift for me, from being a kid going to the Natural History Museum, seeing Radio City Music Hall, and growing up around such an iconic city, to basically cotton fields and not much else going on. It was definitely different, and monster movies were a big help to me."

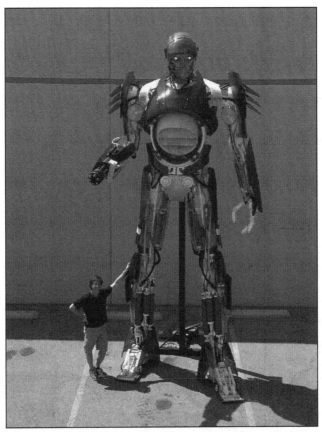

John poses with an oversized friend created by Legacy Effects.
Photo courtesy of John Rosengrant.

"I always knew, since I was about five years old, that I wanted to make monsters, but nobody in that time period had any clue how to go about making it into a career. Plus, when I moved to Shreveport, I was so far removed from everything that I had no idea that any of this could be a possibility. I was always building those monster model kits from Aurora or drawing, and I was just obsessed with these movies. I remember seeing *King Kong* for the first time on TV, or seeing the *Bride of Frankenstein* and *Frankenstein* and all of these classic horror movies, all of which had quite an impact on me. I was just obsessed with them, but didn't know what any of that meant at the time because I was just a kid."

"And even though I was in a place like Shreveport, which is so far removed from what's going on in Hollywood and the movie industry, I never let that stand in the way of my love of monsters and wanting to create them. I discovered *Famous Monsters of Filmland* and would spend days just poring over every scrap of information on those pages religiously. *Famous Monsters* became my connection to this whole thing. As I got older, I did more painting and learned how to sculpt, too. I was doing this stuff on my own, becoming more and more of an artist as I got older, but I still didn't know how to get into that world at all."

Once he graduated from high school, the next logical step for Rosengrant was to head off to college, so he enrolled at Louisiana State University (LSU) and headed to New Orleans to begin the next chapter in his life.

"I always tell people that at LSU, I majored in Fine Arts and Partying, which wasn't exactly doing much to get me on my path to making monsters in the movies. After about a year and a half of that, I came back home to Shreveport to try and figure out what I wanted to do. For a while, I even thought about going to film school because I thought that might help, so I spent some time working on my grades and putting this plan together, all while biding my time working at a supermarket."

As John struggled to determine what course of action he should take, two iconic movies, *Alien* (1979) and *An American Werewolf in London* (1981) lit a fire under him and pushed him to make the biggest move of his entire life.

"*Alien* was pretty much a game changer for me at that point in my life. It was like a whole different level of movie to me. I love all the B-movies and the Universal horror films, but *Alien* just resonated with me differently. It affected me more than *Star Wars* [*Episode IV - A New Hope*], even,

John would eventually get a chance to work on *Aliens* (1986), the sequel to Ridley Scott's *Alien* (1979). Photo courtesy of John Rosengrant.

and I just loved the gritty, scary realism of that world. I wanted to be part of that. Fortunately, later I was able to work on *Aliens* with Jim Cameron, but that wasn't something I ever could have foreseen happening. Ever."

"Then, *American Werewolf* came out in 1981, and it was a very exciting time for special effects that I really wanted to be a part of. My parents weren't artistic, but they were always very supportive, especially my mom, who told me, 'If you don't go and do this and find out whether you can be successful at this, you'll never forgive yourself.' And that's when I realized, *What was the worst thing that could happen? If I go off to Hollywood and I fail miserably, then I'm right back where I started. No harm, no foul, and at least I tried.* So I took the plunge and moved out to Los Angeles in 1982, and I've been out here ever since," John added.

When he transitioned to the West Coast, Rosengrant was thankful that he had a familial support system in place, with his grandmother living in Pasadena and an aunt and uncle residing in Beverly Hills. One fateful day, Rosengrant's uncle made a phone call on John's behalf that would not only lead to the start of his professional career in special effects, but would also alter his life in unimaginable ways.

"As it turns out, my uncle was an entertainment lawyer who also happened to be Stan Winston's entertainment lawyer. I remember thinking to myself, *This is an amazing coincidence. How lucky could I possibly be?* So, he called Stan up for me and asked if his nephew could come by and see him because he was an aspiring artist, and Stan agreed. I was so excited and still could not believe my luck."

"I went by the shop, and I remember meeting Stan and watching him as he looked at my book. I was so nervous. He flipped through it in about ten minutes and he handed it back to me and said, 'Yeah, reminds me of when I was starting out. Great. You want to have a look around?' He was completely open to me just poking around and told me to take my time, so I stayed for two and a half hours and looked at every square inch of his shop. That was the first time I had ever seen what Hollywood effects really looked like up close, and I was amazed. Seeing all the molds and the sculptures, I thought all of it was fascinating. But I knew that what Stan had said was his roundabout way of saying that I still had stuff to learn, so I was very determined to learn and get better."

While he was still regularly in contact with Stan and hoping to work with him, Rosengrant's first break in the industry came via Makeup &

While they didn't start working together immediately, Stan Winston, pictured here with John during pre-production on *The Monster Squad* (1987), would go on to become John's mentor. Photo courtesy of the Stan Winston School of Character Arts.

Effects Laboratories, Inc. (MEL, Inc.), when he was hired onto the crew for Charles Band's cult movie *Metalstorm: The Destruction of Jared-Syn* (1983).

"The guys at Makeup & Effects Lab gave me my first break, and I was in heaven the entire time. I was getting to do what I wanted to do for real, and I didn't really care if it was a bad movie. It was incredible. I also met Tom Woodruff [Jr.], Shane Mahan, and Kenny Myers—a lot of people who are still working in the industry—and that was a fun crew to be a part of. Plus, it would eventually help me land the biggest job of my career that kick-started everything."

"Right around that time, Tom Burman was, for whatever reason, giving free classes to learn makeup effects at night out of the goodness of his heart. I would go to those and learn all kinds of techniques from Tom. I don't really know why he did that, except for the fact that Tom is a nice man. I am thankful for it, though, because I learned quite a few things and I was meeting more people, too. That's how you get your foot in the door. It's not only the friendships aspect of the industry, but it's also about people seeing whether you can do the work or not."

In 1983, John finally got the call he had been hoping for from Stan Winston, who was putting a crew together for an independent sci-fi project helmed by an up-and-coming director named James Cameron.

"I was still regularly in touch with Stan, but for some reason he never really called me to do anything before *The Terminator*. That was a big job for him, and he had to put a pretty big crew together, and some of those people he crewed up with were guys I had known from Makeup & Effects Lab. Stan was looking for more help, and those guys recommended me, and that's all Stan needed to hear in order for him to finally hire me. When he called me up, I was absolutely over the moon."

"I didn't know what *Terminator* was at the time," John continued, "and I certainly didn't know what it would end up becoming. I couldn't care less, honestly. It was a job with Stan, and that's all I wanted from the experience. That being said, my experiences on *The Terminator* absolutely spoiled me, because you just think every project is going to be like that—from the great script to Jim's vision to everyone on the cast and crew, it was beyond my expectations."

"I know there are a lot of people who have said, 'Oh, my God. Jim is so hard to work for,' but I don't have another perspective because he's the first real director that I ever worked for. For me, [Cameron] became the definition of a director in my eyes—someone who is so hands-on involved with every aspect of filmmaking beyond just directing. I loved when he'd come

A behind-the-scenes look at John in action during pre-production on *The Terminator* (1984). Photo courtesy of John Rosengrant.

John supervises a key effects scene on the set of *The Terminator* (1984).
Photo courtesy of the Stan Winston School of Character Arts.

to the shop and I remember watching him sketching the Terminator with Stan. They'd go out together scavenging, picking up all these various housing and mechanized parts from the car junkyard. We had all this stuff scattered everywhere in the shop, and Stan and Jim would stand around talking for hours about how they could incorporate different parts to make this robot."

"Jim was coming from his science and mechanical backgrounds and blending that approach with the artistic process, and there was this magic happening between him and Stan. It seemed so organic to me that I just felt like this is how it always should be. *The Terminator* was all about innovating and learning what to do, and it was an interesting combination for everyone involved. There was just an energy to it, too, where you had the feeling it was going to be something special."

"Jim was so all-encompassing throughout production and involved from all levels—he just poured himself into it. We did, too, because we were all so in love with this whole process and what we were creating. It was thrilling to have been part of something like that."

The Terminator (1984) was the beginning of a longstanding collaboration between Rosengrant and his mentor, as he continued working for Stan Winston over the next twenty-five years.

"I would say that I became Stan's right-hand man over time," John said, "and he was a great mentor. I learned so much from him. He was

John doing some sculpting for *The Terminator* (1984). Photo courtesy of John Rosengrant.

a great artist, but he was also a great businessman and his approach to it all was very insightful. He was great about putting things in a perspective from the business point of view, because he realized it's called 'show business,' not 'show art.' And that's something that you really have to come to grips with as a young artist."

"When you work in this industry, you have to learn that in the end it always comes down to business. You can slave over your version of a design, your little sketch, and maybe it ends up getting passed over or they want to change something or they don't like your work. That kind of rejection can leave you crestfallen if you take it personally. But, if you think about all those brilliant painters—Renoir, Gauguin, Michelangelo, or Rembrandt—if you like one more than the other, it doesn't make that artist any less of a genius. Everyone has his or her own preferences, so if your work isn't picked, that doesn't necessarily make it bad. Stan taught me that, and Legacy Effects wouldn't be who they are today without that kind of understanding of how the business side of the art can be."

After *The Terminator* (1984), Rosengrant and his fellow team members at Winston's shop kept busy on a low-budget Canadian movie before reteaming with James Cameron on another landmark science fiction film, *Aliens* (1986).

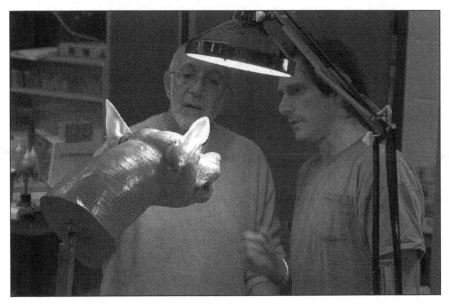

John consults with Stan Winston for Tim Burton's *Big Fish* (2003).
Photo courtesy of the Stan Winston School of Character Arts.

John sculpting the Alien Queen torso maquette for *Aliens* (1986).
Photo courtesy of John Rosengrant.

"I remember after *The Vindicator*, Jim called us all together for a screening of *Alien*, and after it was all said and done, he turned to all of us and said, 'You guys want to go to England and work on *Aliens*?' I couldn't believe it. It felt like this amazing dream come true."

"I was a single guy at that time in my life, in the middle of this crazy wave of special effects that was going on during the 1980s, and I was getting to go work on *Aliens* and live in London for seven and a half months? How cool is that? We were all excited, but what was interesting was that there were a lot of English guys on that crew who initially weren't thrilled that a bunch of Americans were working on a sequel to Sir Ridley Scott's masterpiece. We all got along by the end. In fact, we ended up working with a lot of those guys again on *Interview with the Vampire*, and that was a great experience."

"Shane [Mahan] and I spearheaded the Alien Queen sculpture; I sculpted the torso of it, he sculpted the head, and then various sculptors did the limbs and tail and all of that stuff. That was an incredible process, and I'm so proud of the fact that she still looks amazing even today. It was a tough shoot, though. There was a time when we had the scene in the APC [Armored Personnel Carrier]—where the Alien acid goes shooting everywhere—moved up on us, and we weren't anticipating it yet."

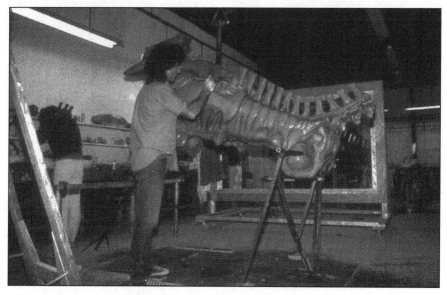

John working on the full-size version of the Alien Queen torso on *Aliens* (1986).
Photo courtesy of John Rosengrant.

"That was pretty stressful because we had to build this animatronic puppet version of an Alien with hardly any time. We knew it had to get done, so Steve Norrington and I dove in on it and both said that we would do whatever it took to get it done. Steve was doing the mechanical aspects of the design and I was handling the art side of it, and we worked for about thirty-five hours straight on that thing without going to bed. We got it ready to shoot, though, and made our deadline. It was exhausting, but we were so proud that we got it done. I do remember falling asleep on a soundstage that day when I was waiting for them to start shooting," Rosengrant added, "but it was worth it."

Right as *Aliens* (1986) was wrapping up, the next challenging project soon came knocking on Stan Winston's door: John McTiernan's *Predator* (1987), which had halted production due to issues with the initial design of its titular space warrior. Thankfully, Stan and his crew already had a fan on set in Arnold Schwarzenegger, who suggested they take on the re-design of the Predator, which needed to happen in an almost impossibly quick amount of time.

"We got the Predator creature done in something like six or seven weeks," Rosengrant reflected. "We had *The Monster Squad* going on at that time, so I remember there was some chaos in the shop. Not too much, because we all knew what we had to do, but we weren't used to juggling two productions like that, and one that had to move as quickly as *Predator* did. It was pretty crazy, but it was just thrilling to be involved. I didn't know much about what happened prior to us getting involved. All I know is that they had a failed Predator that didn't work, and everyone involved was scratching their heads going, 'Oh, shit. What are we going to do? Are we going to turn this movie into Arnold vs. the Sandinistas in the jungle, or are we going to try and fix this monster?' They were stuck."

"Because we had worked with him before on *The Terminator*, Arnold reached out to [Producer] Joel Silver and told him that he needed to meet with Stan," John explained. "Arnold told Joel that if anyone could get this done, it would be Stan and his crew. Producers kind of had an idea of what they wanted because they knew what hadn't worked already, but Stan still drew up a bunch of concepts that he could show everyone. He actually was on the plane from Japan with Jim Cameron after they had been promoting *Aliens*. Jim was the one who recommended that Stan should add some mandibles to his [the Predator's] mouth, and Stan loved the idea."

"Hats off to Steve Wang and Matt Rose, too," Rosengrant added. "They were living and breathing that show while a bunch of us were busy on *The Monster Squad*. I remember a lot of us were jumping in and sculpting the feet of the Predator and helping finish the suit, but Steve and Matt were the ones who really put everything they had into that suit. And between having *Predator* going on and *The Monster Squad*, there was a really cool energy in the shop at that time, but we were all so busy that we barely had any time to enjoy it."

"The best thing about *Monster Squad*, beyond the fact that the movie itself was a lot of fun, was that it gave us the opportunity to reinvent these iconic Universal Monsters that we had all grown up loving. I've always loved werewolves, so the Wolfman was the character that I got involved with, and that was a dream come true. You very rarely get opportunities like that as an artist, and I loved every minute of it."

Over the next few years, Rosengrant lent his talents to several other notable productions, including *Alien Nation* (1988), *Leviathan* (1989), and *Predator 2* (1990). Then, in 1989, a young filmmaker by the name of Tim Burton came to Stan Winston in search of an effects team to work on his modern Gothic fairy tale, *Edward Scissorhands* (1990).

John examines his work on the Wolfman character for *The Monster Squad* (1987). Photo courtesy of the Stan Winston School of Character Arts.

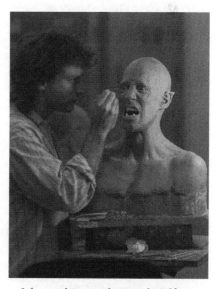

John working on the initial Wolfman sculpture during the design phase on *The Monster Squad* (1987). Photo courtesy of the Stan Winston School of Character Arts.

"I remember when we first heard about *Edward Scissorhands*, Stan wasn't even sure what to make of it," John said. "Up until that point, Tim [was only known for] *Beetlejuice* and *Pee-wee's Big Adventure*, so we didn't really know what to expect from him other than it was probably going to be quirky. But as we all dug deeper into the script, we were all convinced that this could be something really neat and definitely unusual."

"Shane and I designed the scissor hands after hearing what Tim's vision for the character was. I happened to find this weird book on Pennsylvania locks and keys from the eighteenth century, so that became a tool for us to use during the design process. We had a ton of fun coming up with that and being part of that process of this amazing character. You know when you're working on a film, and you can just feel like it's going to be something special? That was the feeling we all had on the set of *Edward Scissorhands*. It was magical."

"Something else amazing that happened on *Edward Scissorhands* was that Johnny Depp arranged to let us come down to the set and meet Vincent [Price] one day and get a picture taken with him. Shane and I were huge fans of his and had our copies of *Famous Monsters of Filmland* with Vincent on the cover that he signed for us. Vincent was so, so gracious—such an old-school Hollywood class act, and that was an amazing mo-

John Rosengrant and Shane Mahan apply makeup to actor Danny DeVito during a makeup test for Tim Burton's *Batman Returns* (1992). Photo courtesy of the Stan Winston School of Character Arts.

ment for me that I will never forget. Something else I loved about working on *Edward Scissorhands* was that it was a nice change of pace from all the things that we had been doing up until that point, so it was a chance for all of us to spread our wings and get involved with a completely different style of filmmaking."

Just a few years later, Stan and his amazing crew of artists and technicians reteamed with Burton on his ambitious sequel, *Batman Returns* (1992), providing Rosengrant with the opportunity to reimagine yet another iconic character for the silver screen: the Penguin. Due to Burton's wildly imaginative approach to *Batman Returns* (1992), John had carte blanche to give the memorable villain an audacious overhaul.

"Honestly, I don't think it really dawned on any of us at the time just what we were doing," Rosengrant said. "We were really young and stupid, so it never crossed our minds to think that fans wouldn't approve of what we were doing, or that they would get mad at us for messing with something that everybody already loved."

"We all believed in Tim's vision, though, and our job was to honor what he was trying to do with this world as the director. I hate it when somebody records a classic song, but it sounds almost exactly the same as the original version. What's the point of that? So our mindset was, *'If we're*

John watches as Stan Winston does some makeup touch-ups on Danny DeVito for *Batman Returns* (1992). Photo courtesy of the Stan Winston School of Character Arts.

going to do this, we need to really do it.' We couldn't go too far away from some of those iconic touches that make the Penguin so memorable—the nose, for example—but we did take those touches in a hyper-real yet fantastical direction."

"Also, Danny DeVito was such a great actor, and that can really help take a makeup to another level. I still think that one of the most fun makeup tests I've ever done in my life was when we put Danny DeVito in the makeup for the Penguin when he came over to Stan's shop. That day we only did his nose and a little bit of a brow, but Danny just loved the fact that he could get lost in this character and it wasn't exactly him looking back at himself in the mirror. The minute he looked in that mirror and he saw this new character, he just lit up. It was a really fun day."

Right around this time, John began to see the cinematic tides shift towards visual effects, first on the set of *Terminator 2: Judgment Day* (1991) and later while working on *Jurassic Park* (1993), Steven Spielberg's landmark adventure film that would forever change how movies are made.

"I definitely saw things changing on *Terminator 2*, but we still must have had over two hundred different practical things that we had to prepare for the shoot. That was probably the hardest movie I have ever worked on in my life because the dates got moved up, and when you're building practical stuff and your time gets taken away from you, it can

John reviews a reference photo while working on a sculpture of Arnold Schwarzenegger for *Terminator 2: Judgment Day* (1991). Photo courtesy of the Stan Winston School of Character Arts.

John on the set of *Terminator 2: Judgment Day* (1991) with Director James Cameron and co-stars Robert Patrick and Linda Hamilton. Photo courtesy of the Stan Winston School of Character Arts.

make things nearly impossible. Honestly, I didn't even know how much CG [computer graphics] work was going to go into *Terminator 2,* because we had been so busy on the practical side of things. It wasn't until I saw everything come together in the final version of the movie when I realized how much of a landmark movie it would become in that regard."

"One thing about *Terminator 2* that I don't think a lot of people realize is just how much practical work went into that film. The shot where the T-1000 is frozen and he gets shot and blown into a million pieces? That was all done for real. I'm very proud of that work, because it really is one of those great moments of suspended disbelief. It still looks great, too."

"I don't know the exact timeline of when technology began to take over, just because there had been some advancements on films like *The Abyss,* and even *Young Sherlock Holmes* had a CG sequence, too, but *Jurassic Park* was definitely that first 'holy shit' moment I can distinctly remember. When we saw the test footage of what they could do with the dinosaurs, I knew halfway through *Jurassic Park* that this was going to be a game-changer for our industry. Stan knew it, too, and understood it was something he needed in

John working on the mechanics of the practical Velociraptor used in *Jurassic Park* (1993). Photo courtesy of the Stan Winston School of Character Arts.

John tests out the Velociraptor leg mechanics created for *Jurassic Park III* (2001). Photo courtesy of John Rosengrant.

his toolbox as well, because first and foremost, he always said to us, 'We're creating characters,' and if this could be another way to create a character, then we all needed to adapt."

"Stan started buying some machines and we set up a computer room at the studio," John continued. "He gathered us together and asked, 'Well, who wants to keep doing traditional stuff and who wants to move into this digital world?' I embraced it because I knew it was important, but I didn't want to do it myself. I didn't like the idea of sitting in front of a computer screen all day, but I still realized it was this new frontier that we all needed to embrace, whether we liked it or not."

"But, like we learn in the story of *Jurassic Park*, just because you can do something doesn't mean you should. So, of course, ever since 1993, we've seen a lot of bad CG work in movies, especially in the late 1990s and early 2000s. It just felt for a while like people were forgetting the simple laws of gravity, which is so important when you're creating these things using visual effects. Above everything else, you always have to make sure it looks real and that it works within the laws of physics, or you end up with something like Ang Lee's *Hulk*."

John continued to stay busy at Stan Winston's studio over the next fifteen years, working on a variety

Stan Winston and John Rosengrant share a laugh with Jon Voight on the set of Michael Bay's *Pearl Harbor* (2001). Photo courtesy of the Stan Winston School of Character Arts.

of films, including *Interview with the Vampire* (1994), *Congo* (1995), *The Lost World: Jurassic Park* (1997), *Small Soldiers* (1998), *The Sixth Sense* (1999), *Galaxy Quest* (1999), *Jurassic Park III* (2001), *Terminator 3: Rise of the Machines* (2003), and *Constantine* (2005). Then, on June 15, 2008, the unthinkable happened when Stan Winston lost his battle with cancer. The loss of John's friend and mentor was immeasurable, but he and his fellow artists at Stan Winston Studio still had to keep their leader's legacy alive on various productions that were already underway.

"I remember we lost Stan right around Father's Day," Rosengrant said, "and it was tough on all of us because he was much more than just a boss. He always felt like he would beat it. He did beat the odds for years. I think he was diagnosed with multiple myeloma in 2000 and he lasted eight years. He was fighting it the entire time. But, during that time, he started turning the reins over more and more with us, and by 'us,' I mean Shane Mahan, Lindsay MacGowan, Alan Scott, and myself. We were responsible for these shows, so we started having to make these budgets and oversee all these different aspects, and we became the face of these movies while on set, interacting with the directors and producers. The world didn't really know that Stan was sick and fighting cancer at the time, and he didn't want that, either. He didn't want the sympathy."

"I was off in Albuquerque, New Mexico, in the middle of *Terminator Salvation*, and I just had a bad feeling after the second or third trip back, because I had been in L.A. visiting Stan at the hospital. About two weeks before it happened, I called Jim Cameron to tell him that he needed to go see Stan. I called Steven Spielberg, too, and said the same thing. I don't know if Steven ended up seeing him, but I know he ended up talking to him. Somehow, I could just feel like this was coming and knew that it was important that some of Stan's closest friends knew what was happening before it was too late."

"I was really sad to lose Stan because I spent twenty-five years with him as my mentor and as a close friend, too. Plus, we had to move forward and finish up all these movies that Stan was still committed to, so we wrapped up *Terminator Salvation* and we had to finish our work on *Avatar*. Once we were finished with those, the biggest question we all had was just, *'How do we move on, exactly?'*"

That's when Legacy Effects was born, bringing together John, Shane, Alan, and Lindsay as co-founders of a company that would honor Winston's impact on them both professionally and personally, as well as the makeup industry as a whole.

"We all felt an obligation to all of these people, this family of artists and craftsmen, and even accountants and business people, who had

John consults with Stan Winston for *Big Fish* (2003). Photo courtesy of the Stan Winston School of Character Arts.

been a part of this huge family that had been growing for years," Rosengrant explained. "It just felt like a very natural thing to keep it all rocking and rolling and doing what we were doing. We've been very lucky so far—knock on wood. We've been growing and keeping it together and we're constantly trying to innovate how to create the same high level of art that's expected, but to do it with less money and less time than we had in the past, because that's the nature of the business today."

John Cherevka and John Rosengrant put the finishing touches on one of the T-1 robots from *Terminator 3: Rise of the Machines* (2003). Photo courtesy of John Rosengrant.

"We've learned a lot. We've adapted and we've never been afraid of technology, and I have to thank Stan for that. We're always beta testing new types of machines at Legacy that aren't even out on the market yet, because we are always trying to push the bar and figure out cool, new ways to get things done and make something cool for our clients, too."

"The one aspect that's been sort of painful for me is that I have found myself working less and less hands-on, because it's really hard to go into the zone of sculpting and painting and then get disrupted every five minutes by business-related calls. It's two very different mindsets, so learning to hover between those two worlds is a big part of being successful in this industry. The other part of the success is embracing technology and not ever being afraid of it. You have to try and be intuitive enough to make your own luck, too."

6 Bob Keen

BORN IN THE U.K. IN 1960, artist and director Bob Keen's fascination with the world of special effects began to percolate at a very early age when he was just discovering movies and magic.

"When I was six years old, I was really into performing magic," Keen said. "All I wanted for my birthday and for Christmas were magic tricks and illusions, because I just could not get enough. One day, my father took me to a mu-

Photo courtesy of University of North Carolina School of the Arts.

seum where they were showing episodes of *Thunderbirds Are Go*, which was all done with puppets and models, and I fell in love with those things very quickly."

"Whenever we would go to the cinema, they would give you this special magazine printed just for those audiences that would give you these behind-the-scenes looks at different movies. That really fascinated me and I remember turning to my dad one day and saying, 'These people are the modern-day magicians. I want to be that.' So, from a very early age, it was focused in my head that special effects and makeup effects, and this wonderful world that we now live in, was what I wanted to do."

"My dad was a very creative person, but he kind of rolled it off at first. I started going to bookstores to try and find books about special effects, but back in the '60s there was very little to find out there. I started playing around with everything myself, and eventually my dad bought me an 8mm camera, so I started shooting my own movies and doing makeups on my friends. One time, I made up my friend's terrier as a werewolf. I was just trying to learn how to do these things I'd see in the movies when there were no real resources available."

"I started going to all of these film fairs, where I would buy up all these secondhand magazines and cut out different articles so I could make my own books on the subject matter. I did that throughout my entire early childhood. When I was about fourteen, Shepparton Studios had an open house where they were selling off all of their props and special effects items. My mum, God bless her, took me on a bus and a train and another bus, which was absolutely horrendous, and then we had to walk about two and a half miles to actually get to the studio finally."

"We got to tour the studio and see different sets on the backlots and all of these fantastic warehouses full of these amazing pieces of film history. My favorite was the special effects storage house, because it had all the props and the creatures from films like *Day of Crickets* and a great deal of the Hammer films, too. It was an incredible day. As I was learning more and more about everything, I felt like my interests were being split in two, where half of me was interested in makeup effects and the other half was interested in special effects and miniatures."

While Keen had a clear understanding of just what he wanted to do with the rest of his life, he had no idea how he was going to achieve his dreams. Then, one fateful day, he got some advice that would further fuel his desire to pursue special effects.

"I had a really amazing metalwork teacher at my school who, by sheer coincidence, had a brother who worked for the BBC [British Broadcasting Corporation]. He took me to the special effects department there and I got to see everything they were doing. The biggest piece of advice he gave me was that if I really wanted to get into all of this, I needed to go and be an apprentice somewhere."

"Since the only place I really knew my way to was Shepparton Studios, I decided that was the place I needed to be. So, one Sunday I took the train and two buses and walked myself two and a half miles to get to

Shepparton. Of course, you are not allowed into the studios, but I found a hole in the fence around the back of the lot, and I climbed through it. A security guard caught me immediately and kicked me right out the front door. So, after that, I went straight back to the fence so I could go and try again. I was obviously a terrible criminal, because he caught me again right away."

"I was on the way out and he said to me, 'You know, I have never seen anybody try to break in here twice like that. Why did you want to get in here so much?' I explained to him that I wanted to be a special effects artist, and he said, 'I am probably going to regret this, but [special effects artist] Derek Meddings is doing a film here right now called *The Land That Time Forgot*.' He took me to see Derek, and he was kind of amused that I had climbed through the fence twice, and he said to me, 'Do you want to stick around and make the team coffee today?' I couldn't say 'yes' fast enough."

"I ended up staying there that day until nine o'clock at night, and my mum went nuts. But Derek asked me to come back for a week or two, and I think I did ten full days that time. After a few days, Derek asked me to lend a hand on this sequence of this big submarine coming through the ice, and then we were going to make a volcano blow up, too. I loved it all."

Enamored with the brand new world he had found a place in at Shepperton Studios, Keen continued working for Meddings throughout his next summer break.

"I rang Derek up once my holiday began and I spent five weeks doing some other films with him. The first thing we started work on was a film called *Micronauts*, which was going to be this big science fiction film about shrinking people down to the size of ants so that they could save the population. It was a very bizarre film."

"We were working away on the film, but then one day the producer came in and said, 'Sorry lads, some idiot over at Elstree Studios is making another science fiction film, and in all honesty, there isn't room for two science fiction films. We are just going to cancel this film now.' So, we all realized the only thing we could do was to get in a car and go over to Elstree and see if we could get work on it."

"And here I am, only sixteen years old, going over to Elstree with all these other artists who were regular people working in the film industry. No one realized I wasn't a true professional at this point, so I ended up getting hired, and it turned out to be *Star Wars: [Episode IV] – A New Hope*. I didn't know what it was going to end up being, of course. When I got hired, they just shoved me into a hut around the back of the shop, where I was in charge of creating six helmets. All I knew about *Star Wars* was that there were men running through corridors wearing my helmets, so you can imagine that I was completely shocked when I went to see it in the cinema for the first time."

"The other thing you don't realize when you're a sixteen-year-old kid is that the glue we were using to stick the helmets together at the time would make you high as a kite, so you would be constantly bumping off the ceiling with these glue fumes in your hut."

After working on *Star Wars* (1977), Keen realized it was time to make some decisions about his future, considering he was now finished with high school and had a better understanding of the world of professional special effects.

"I had an offer to go to a university, but I kept delaying it because it wasn't what I wanted to do. Because of that, my father went out and found an apprenticeship for me with a company called Aeronautical General Model Makers. What I liked about this apprenticeship was the fact that they would lend people out for films, and you would also be working in the shop, too, so you actually earned a proper apprenticeship experience on it because it ran for four years."

"I started working for them, and because they already knew Derek and he had recommended me, I would get hired out at a very young age to these other films. I did films like *The Medusa Touch*, *Alien*, *Superman*, and *Superman II*. It was such a great experience, and to work on all of those films was absolutely brilliant."

"I was working my way through this four-year apprenticeship. I was three years into the apprenticeship, and that's the first time you get a chance to take the actual exam, so I sat [down for] the exam, and by some sort of miracle, I passed. The guild said that even though I passed my exams, I still had to complete my last year to be an apprentice. I didn't think that was very fair, so I moved from there to another model-making place which was much closer to Pinewood Studios."

"It was Brian Johnson who hired me on a couple of things, which was really good. Brian called me up one day and told me that he was about to start on [*Star Wars: Episode V –*] *The Empire Strikes Back*, and he wanted me to come down and talk to his team about being an apprentice in the special effects department. I was so chuffed. I was so pleased. I went over to Elstree Studios, and his secretary told me that Brian was out at the moment visiting the set, but that I should go over and talk to Stuart Freeborn, because he was employing people right now and they were trying to build a bridge between makeup and special effects."

"I went over and saw Stuart, and Stuart was amazing. I remember him saying to me, 'Well, I could offer you maybe a week or two's worth of work,' and I thought that all sounded brilliant. He told me that we were going to build a creature, and after everything, I ended up working with Stuart and then back with Brian for eleven months on [*The*] *Empire Strikes Back*. While working on it, I got on really well with Stuart's son, Graham Freeborn, and another makeup effects artist, Nick Maley. They took me under their wing and got me into the union, too."

"Working with Nick, I would get to do all of this great stuff on some wonderful films over the years, and it was a great opportunity for me to learn. I just kept working my way up, and Nick decided one day that I was in charge of the workshop. I think it may have upset a few people because I was still incredibly young, but it seemed to work. I got the job done, and Nick liked that."

"We had a very good working relationship all the way through to *Highlander*. When Nick started *Highlander*, he got very sick. I think it was just sheer exhaustion, because Russell Mulcahy, who was a fantastic director, was much more used to a music video type of environment where everything would happen very quickly. Nick was much more used to a longer time for development during these longer production films, so he ended up leaving the picture on the recommendation of his doctor. I was asked if I would take over the picture, and so *Highlander* became my first film as a supervisor, which was fantastic."

After *The Empire Strikes Back* (1980), Keen found himself on board another ambitious project filled with a variety of creatures: Jim Henson's *The Dark Crystal* (1982).

"*The Dark Crystal* came about because Frank Oz had been the puppeteer for Yoda, and he and I got on really well. He asked me if I would come over to the Henson's and do some stuff with them. I got an interview over there, which was a really strange setup because it was in Hansford Heath, and it was an old post office building."

"They had been based there for about a year, and when I came on, I got a little corner where I was going to be working. The first character they introduced me to was Fizzgig, and they told me that was going to be my creature. I was very excited, and within about a week and a half, I had finished off all the things I needed to do on Fizzgig. Then I was asked to work on all the Garthim, and I started doing all the mechanics and working everything out. Once I finished with them, they gave me the Landstriders to work on. That's basically how it went, and I ended up doing a lot of the background creatures."

Keen reunited with many of his peers on another fantasy project, *The NeverEnding Story* (1984), which was directed by Wolfgang Petersen.

"Brian Johnson gave me a call and asked me if I wanted to come out to Munich and work on *The NeverEnding Story*. Because I had just done *The Dark Crystal*, and I enjoyed working with that crew and many of them were going to be on this, I flew out and stayed in Munich for almost nine months."

"I mainly got to work on the Rock Biter, and then I worked with Colin Arthur on a lot of the other creatures, too. The only creature I didn't work on was Falkor the Luckdragon. But there were a lot of people who had come over from working on *The Dark Crystal*, so that was great, and we just had the best of times over in Munich. Wolfgang Petersen was a fantastic director who would really give us the time to let us explore things, and I even got the chance to direct the puppet unit. It was all really exciting, and being in the middle of this whole world that was pulsating around animatronics was a once-in-a-lifetime experience."

"Somewhere between *The Dark Crystal* and *The NeverEnding Story*, I had the opportunity to work with Stuart [Freeborn] again, and he gave me Jabba the Hutt to supervise on *Star Wars: Episode VI – Return of the Jedi*. Being able to supervise the building of an eighteen-foot gangster slug was awesome. How many times in your life do you get to work on something like that? We had a very quick prep time to get him done, and it was pretty intense shooting him right at the beginning of *Jedi*'s shoot, but it still was just great fun to do."

Bob found himself consistently busy throughout the mid-1980s, and after finishing up on back-to-back-to-back projects, he was hired to work on both Tobe Hooper's *Lifeforce* (1985) and the aforementioned *Highlander* (1986), with the latter film providing Bob with the opportunity to take the reins a bit more as the film's Special Effects Makeup Co-Designer. All of these opportunities helped prepare Keen for the most ambitious project he'd spearhead throughout the 1980s, Clive Barker's *Hellraiser* (1987), which had an immense amount of gore and blood-related effects, and also gave birth to several now-iconic characters in horror: the Cenobites.

"I got a call from *Hellraiser*'s Producer, Christopher Figg, and he said, 'I just heard you've done a great job on *Highlander*, and we would like to talk about a film that we're doing.' I went into London and I met with Christopher and Clive Barker. Clive and I just hit it off immediately. I still think he's one of the most imaginative and fast-thinking directors I've ever worked with—he's amazing. He and I would bat ideas back and forth over a table, and it was really, really hard work to keep up with him because he had so many ideas. At the end of that initial meeting, they said to me, 'Okay, we'll be in touch.' I thought to myself right at that moment, *Oh, well. Usually you get a 'yes' or a 'no,' so that's the end of that.*"

"But about a week later, Clive actually phoned me up and said, 'I really, really want you to do the film. We don't have any money yet, but would you want to come and talk to us and work it through in the meantime?' So we spent the next six to eight weeks working up ideas. He was still writing the script and trying to push it out to find people to finance it. We would kick around what we could do for no money, and all of that ended up being some of my favorite times and memories around *Hellraiser*."

"The process started off with Clive sketching out ideas that we would work through together, and then we would kick other ideas around based on those sketches. Originally, Pinhead wasn't like he is now at all. He was much more like the character Shuna Sassi in *Nightbreed*, where it was all quills coming out of the top of his head. I was looking at this and going, 'Clive, we can't do this on this budget.' I knew that this makeup would go on for six days and that we couldn't do that on this micro budget. He said, 'Okay, well, let's have a think about it.' That's when we came up with this drawing of a grid on a lifecast, just to work out where we were going to put in what was originally going to be six-inch nails. Clive looked at the grid and decided he really liked the symmetry of it, so we left it in."

"We were having real problems contending with the aesthetics of a six-inch nail, though. It was very crude and made the design look almost comical when the nails got too deep. I suggested that maybe they should be thin pins, and because of this series of conversations, through trial and error we ended up with that design of Pinhead, which has become so iconic over time."

"To this day, I still credit the success of Pinhead to Doug Bradley," Keen added. "Only 10 percent of what Pinhead has become is due to our work, and 90 percent of Pinhead is what Doug brought to it and what Clive insisted that he was. He became this bishop of pain and it just elevated him above all the other monsters that were around at that time. It put him onto a different plane to a much more laid-back type of a character. Doug worked on that, and it just became this magical thing."

"Butterball came out of the fact that we were just talking about an idea of this really fat character and how he'd play with his wounds all the time. Chatterer came out of what we were calling at the time 'the poor bastard,' because we decided to design a mask where poor Nick [Vince] couldn't see anything at all. Nick had this ability to make his teeth chatter. It was almost weird, like it was freezing cold and he could chatter his teeth, so that became part of that character. The female Cenobite came out of a direct drawing from Clive."

"The look of these Cenobites would go on to be copied and rehashed and remade on so many other films, but what made the work we did on *Hellraiser* so great was that it really was a group of people working through a group of problems, with a genius like Clive right at the top of it."

Beyond the Cenobites, Keen and his crew were given the Herculean task of trying to create Barker's audaciously bold and visceral gore effects without many resources to work with—something previous films helped prepare him for.

"We had to create all the other effects, which I thought was all the real fun stuff to do in the film. I could draw on all my experiences from the other films I'd done effects-wise. To design the [Lemarchand puzzle] box and the mechanics of the box, I worked with Simon Sayce. We had about four people who would then work out the problems of the box. We came up with the little beating heart thing that's under the floor almost on the day we ended up shooting it. It was made up out of a condom, a piece of tubing, some glue, and some bits and pieces to pull the whole thing together and make it look like a real human organ."

"There was The Engineer, which was the big creature, and we built that, but I still say that they overshot it. It's really something that should

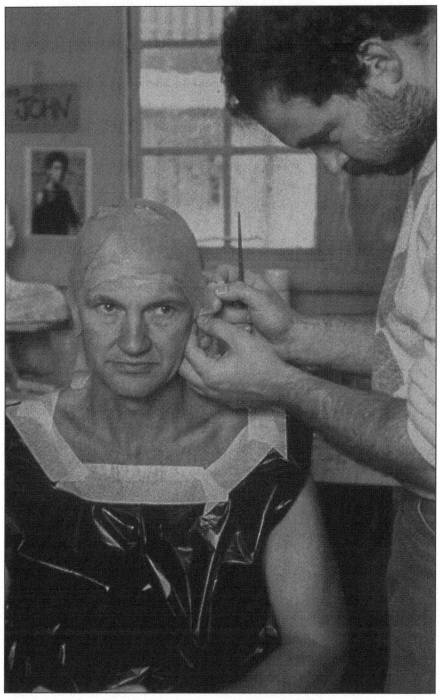

Bob works on Andrew Robinson's prosthetics for *Hellraiser* (1987).
Photo courtesy of The Clive Barker Archive.

have been seen in very, very small glimpses. Then there was this skeletal puppet, too. There were just so many great effects that were created on *Hellraiser*, and it was on a budgetary level that was nearly impossible, but we made it work."

"I remember that when we officially went into production on *Hellraiser*, it was all very sudden," Bob recalled. "One day we're talking and then suddenly we were making the movie. The one thing I can say about *Hellraiser* is that we were putting our fingers into places where no one had really gone before in horror. The whole pain and pleasure thing—we knew we were going to push some buttons, but we knew they were risks that needed to be taken."

"The shoot was incredibly quick and incredibly intense. We had to create the Cenobites at an extremely fast pace, but my entire team was unbelievable. They were really put through their paces on that shoot. We got all the way through to the end, and when the executive producers saw the footage, they said, 'We really like this. We really think it's great. We want to put more money in and we want to invest to make it even better.' So we did the scene where Frank [played by Sean Chapman] bursts at the end, and a couple of other pieces were redone, too, about seven or eight weeks after principal photography had finished."

"It was great that we had the opportunity to go back and correct a couple of things which we didn't think had worked in the film the first time, particularly in relation to the first time you see Frank after his rebirth. It became very clear that we had to reshoot that stuff because we'd gone in one direction, and now with this human kind of birth, we definitely had to go in another direction."

"But the whole process of making *Hellraiser* was this tumbling, creative tour de force. You either strive to keep up with Clive or you fall behind. You are pushed every second of the day, and with me being so early in my career at that time, to find myself pushed by my director so hard really did me a great deal of good. It changed my entire view. Having gone from these huge, great, epic movies where we'd be eight months to a year on the movies and we had a lot more time and freedom, and being put into this low-budget, extremely fast-moving, extremely creative environment, it really changed the way I thought about how to do things and what was achievable. It was really that film that focused me in."

"I decided at the time—which, financially was probably a terrible idea—but I decided that it was a really good idea to stay with the lower-budget films and be a bigger cog than to go with the big-budget films and be a very small cog in a huge machine. I don't regret that, looking back, because I had the best of times doing that. You also have to be more inventive. You have to think on your feet, you have to create quicker and cheaper. You can't just throw money and time at it. You have to work the problems out. That served me well, and I really enjoy that aspect."

Bob poses with the unused Frank effects from *Hellraiser* (1987).
Photo courtesy of The Clive Barker Archive.

"I'm very proud of what the team and I did, too," added Keen, "and I'm very proud of how we pulled off so much with so little. We were all very young, we were all very enthusiastic, and we all wanted this to be the film that would break us out and get us noticed."

"I remember that I was shooting *Waxwork* out in Los Angeles when *Hellraiser* came out, and every single bus stop had Pinhead on it as a poster. It was mind-blowing, because to all of us, *Hellraiser* was this little film that we thought would be a stepping-stone up. No one had an idea that this film was going to take off the way it did, and it was incredible to be a part of that."

Bob would reunite with Clive Barker just a few years later for his next directorial project, *Nightbreed* (1990), a modern fable that celebrated monsters instead of making them strictly instruments of fear, an approach that appealed to Keen when he joined the ever-innovative Barker on the adaptation of his novella *Cabal*.

"There were two main aspects of the project that ultimately convinced me to do *Nightbreed*," he explained. "One was the chance to do so many different creatures with Clive, and to have that creativity flowing around us. The other reason was that I am a great lover of [Mary Shelley's] *Frankenstein* book, so to have that opportunity to do sympathetic monsters, where there is a humanity to them and a vulnerability, too, just spoke to me as a fan."

"The creative process on *Nightbreed* was unlike anything I've ever been a part of," Keen added. "It was wonderful. We had a very small, very select team start the film months in advance, and both Clive and I spent the first four weeks just playing around with textures and colors and different techniques to really push us away from what other movie monsters had been. We both wanted to go down a road which hadn't yet been traveled by other people in movies."

"Making *Nightbreed* was entirely different, though, as it felt like everything was constantly snowballing on us. We started off at one climate and we shot that period of time out, and then there was more shooting, and then there was even more shooting, and there was just this constant feeling of Clive and us versus the people who were releasing the film. We were doing our monster stuff, and their reaction to everything was that this film should be more about [Dr.] Decker [played by David Cronenberg]. When you are working with other people's money, you try and accommodate them, you try and make things work, but it was clear they wanted a slasher movie instead of Clive doing monsters."

"Because of that constant push and pull, we were doing all the blood and guts stuff during the day, and whenever we could find the extra time, that's when we kept working on the breeds themselves. I burned an awful lot of favors I had with my crew throughout the filming of *Nightbreed*. We really ended up pushing ourselves beyond what we could possibly do, and we achieved what we wanted to do, but it all came with great sacrifice. We had worked harder on that movie than we had ever worked before. Even though *Nightbreed* was so tough, I still hang onto my fondness of the first six months on that film, when we were really creatively free and we were making Clive's vision."

In the late 1980s, Keen had the opportunity to collaborate with another rising filmmaking talent from the U.K., Anthony Hickox, who was putting together *Waxwork* (1988), a horror comedy about a group of unsuspecting high schoolers in a wax museum that paid homage to a variety of notable characters in horror and the tropes that modern fans had come to expect from the genre.

"Anthony Hickox is just one of the most fun people to work with," said Bob. "He's a bubbling, enthusiastic fanboy of a filmmaker whose energy always drives the production. I have done a lot of films with him—actually, I've done more films with him than any other director I've ever worked with—and we have a great working relationship. He let me do some directing on *Waxwork*, too, which is how I got my start in directing, so he helped me open up a lot of the things I wanted to try out and let me do them on his films. "

"When Tony asked me to do *Waxwork*, I was on my holiday from having just done *Hellraiser*. After just having gone down some very dark tunnels with Clive, I was excited to just build some monsters. It also meant I would get to work in L.A. on the Universal backlot. We did a lot of work on a micro budget, to be honest, but it was so much fun that none of us minded. We got to do something like eighteen types of monsters or entities for that movie in the end. We did all the prep in England, and then we flew out to Los Angeles with a really small team and just had a ball, so I definitely have some strong emotional attachment to *Waxwork* after all these years."

In his career, Keen also had the good fortune to collaborate with forward-thinking filmmaker Richard Stanley on his debut feature, *Hard-*

ware (1990), a post-apocalyptic cyberpunk horror/sci-fi mash-up that has gone on to become a cult classic.

"Richard is the strangest filmmaker I have ever worked with. If I had to guess when I worked with a director whose career was just going to take off like a rocket, I would have guessed Richard back then, because Richard has got it all. He is a good director, he's great with images and the story, and he's got an extremely interesting personality. I got on with him really well."

"*Hardware* was made with this grunge-pop video approach, where it has this hard-edged look at our future and what we have done to our world. And Richard's dark view of the world almost feels like a prediction now, especially in the last few months."

"Richard was a pleasure to work with, even though we had a ton of problems on the film. We had gone down one road, where we built a real robot that was operated by actual robotics, and it was a nightmare. We were radio-controlling it, and every time a taxi or someone who had a radio frequency would drive by, this thing would suddenly freak out and just tear itself apart or swing around dangerously. So, over the course of a weekend, we went in and ripped all the guts out and put it back together again. That film had no money at all, and what he managed to pull off on that picture is a miracle, really."

Keen returned to the realm of Clive Barker's imagination in the early 1990s when he came aboard Bernard Rose's *Candyman* (1992), an adaptation of Barker's short story "The Forbidden," which went on to become a revolutionary film.

"*Candyman* was just one of those rare experiences where you have the intelligence of this really clever idea, and you bring that together with the smartness of the director, so that the end product doesn't feel like any other horror films happening at the time."

"Our biggest nightmare on that film, that we kept putting off until we just couldn't put it off any longer, were the bees. Originally, I had this really expensive mechanical head in my budget and it was going to be able to open its mouth and have bees come flying out of it. I knew that if you try and do a human mechanical head, if there's even one hair wrong on it, somehow you can always spot it. I got it in my head that there must be another way to do this effect, so I went and spoke to the bee person and asked him, 'Is there a version of the bees that don't sting?' And he told me there was."

"So we figured out that, for the first two weeks of their lives, bees don't sting and they don't fly, either. That's when we came up with this idea for a mouth condom that we could clip inside Tony [Todd]'s mouth, fill it with bees to get those shots, and then it would be easy to pull it out. I showed it to Clive and Bernard, and they thought it was great, but they told me that I was the one who had to tell Tony that this was going to happen. But Tony was all for it, and so when we did those scenes, we were inside a bee net where it was just the beekeeper, the actors, and myself. You have never heard anything in your life like twenty or thirty thousand bees flying around you."

While it may seem like wrangling thousands of bees would be one of the more challenging things one would have to contend with on a film project, Keen found even bigger challenges awaiting him and his crew on Paul W.S. Anderson's horror/sci-fi movie *Event Horizon* (1997).

"*Event Horizon* was pretty intense to shoot," Bob recalled. "It was well-organized, though, and well-made, but it was not an easy film to do, and we had a lot of technical problems. We had some internal problems within my group, too, so it wasn't one of the more fun movies I've ever worked on. I remember the first time I walked onto those sets, though, I thought they were amazing. For all its issues, *Event Horizon* had some of the most brilliant production-designed sets I have ever walked on. It felt like we were making a real epic horror movie in space."

"It was a big-budget film, so we had plenty of time to prep it and we had time to do everything we were supposed to, but most of that work ended up being cut out. There were a couple of circumstances where we pulled things off in the rehearsal time better than we did on the camera time for certain effects. There was this scene where someone is frozen and they break into a million pieces. The first time we did it in rehearsal, it worked like a charm, but when we went to actually shoot it, it took us eight or nine times to get it to look the same again."

"We were trying to do things on *Event Horizon* that were very hard to achieve, and we eventually got there, and we got all of the effects done, but it was such a killer film to do. In hindsight, the film turned out really well considering what Paul was up against. It has a lot of stuff going for it, but when we were in the middle of it, it just wasn't a lot of fun to do."

In the early 2000s, Keen teamed up with another burgeoning filmmaker, Neil Marshall, who was about to embark on his feature film directorial debut, the werewolf-centric action thriller *Dog Soldiers* (2002).

While he was excited to get a crack at making lycanthropic creatures, it was the script's more humanistic qualities that first drew Keen into the project.

"I still say to this day that *Dog Soldiers* wasn't a pure werewolf movie. To me, it feels more like an 'enemy at the door' movie, where it just happened to be werewolves. It could have been the Viet Cong, it could have been the Germans, it could have been zombies, it could have been anything, and it still would have been just as effective. Neil was very smart about how he framed that threat in his story."

"I was excited to do the werewolves, but I knew *Dog Soldiers* was going to be different because most werewolf movies are about these characters who turn into monsters. *Dog Soldiers* was much more about the people in the house than it was about anything you would normally expect from a movie about werewolves. And that is part of the genius of the film. It was made a few years ahead of its time, because horror and the DVD market were really struggling at the time it was released, so it's been great to see that it's a movie fans have continued to embrace after they finally discovered it."

Wanting to challenge his own sense of creativity in new ways, over the years Keen began directing different projects, all while still continuing to create special effects for others.

According to Bob, "Anybody who works in the film industry long enough always gets to the point where they think they would like to start directing. I had an opportunity to do that throughout the '90s and a little bit into the 2000s, too. I really enjoyed my time that I had directing, but I found a new level of respect for directors afterwards because it's an entirely new level of dealing with people. Everybody wants to henpeck you about all these details you normally don't care about, and here you are trying to concentrate on performances and the story."

"I thoroughly enjoyed the time while I was directing, but it was something that I kind of wanted to do, I got to do it, and then I couldn't find the scripts that I liked, so I just stopped doing it. A lot of times people want to make a movie just so they can turn a movie around to make some money, and that rotating door syndrome is what has probably done more harm to the film industry than anything else."

"Now I teach at the University of North Carolina School of the Arts, and that has become a great opportunity for me to pass back the knowledge I've gained during my career, and to try and give people an idea of what they need to do in order to prepare themselves to make it. My big-

Bob (squatting, far left) helps oversee a miniature setup for *The Dark Crystal* (1982). Photo courtesy of The Jim Henson Company.

gest advice I always give to my students is that no matter what job you are doing in the world, whatever that job is, try and do the best you possibly can at it. Just be in the moment and stay focused. It's so important."

"As far as my career is concerned, I think I did very well because I got thrown into problem-solving very early on, and so I got the reputation as being the person who could fix things," Keen reflected. "Being able to solve problems is one of the most important skill sets you need to thrive. You need to be creative, but being able to work through issues in order to achieve those creative goals is so important."

"I also think a big part of it was that I really enjoy the business. My career is still going strong because I still enjoy what I am doing. The day that you stop enjoying what you are doing is the day you should quit, because it seems pointless otherwise. I have loved every minute of my career. I love the way that it has consistently morphed and changed, and I have been able to enjoy the chance to work with some amazing, and sometimes crazy, people on some really brilliant projects."

7 Rick Lazzarini

FROM A VERY EARLY AGE, Rick Lazzarini, President of The Character Shop and a thirty-five-year veteran in the world of special effects, was drawn to both the monsters and the illusions provided by the world of makeup. That fascination continued to grow throughout his childhood, and as Lazzarini honed his skills, he turned his artistic obsession into his own business enterprise, all while still in high school.

"I was always creative as a kid and even created my first prosthetics when I was six years old," Lazzarini said. "I played Jesus in the school play

Photo courtesy of Rick Lazzarini.

and I made stigmata wounds for myself with crayons and binder paper, taping them to my hands and feet, and one to my side. I didn't know that was a prosthetic, but that's basically what it was. It was my first illusion!"

"Then, I ran across an issue of *Famous Monsters of Filmland* one day after church. We went to the market, and my grandma saw that a copy on the shelf had caught me wide-eyed, so she got it for me. I just plowed through it at home. I loved how it talked about all these monsters that I liked and gave me more monsters to check out, too. That's when I started going through the *TV Guide* to try and find these monster movies and Hammer movies so I could watch them. When I was in seventh grade, I had a date to go out with one of the hottest girls in school. I hadn't dated much because I was a nerd, but when I found out that the original *King Kong* was going to be on Channel 5 that Friday at 8 p.m., I had to cancel. I was too much in love with monsters to miss that."

"I also had a Super 8 camera growing up, and all these Aurora and dinosaur models, too, so I would try to make my own movies with these models, animating them very crudely. In 1968, when *Planet of the Apes* came out, a friend of the family and her boyfriend took me to see it, and soon I began seeing the behind-the-scenes stuff. That really clicked with me. Eventually, I started going to the city library, where I would read up on stage makeup and those kinds of things just so I could learn everything possible."

"As I got into high school, I started doing makeup for our plays, and that's when I got into the three-dimensional stuff that I really liked," Lazzarini continued. "I got a reputation as the guy who would make cool stuff, and bands would call me up and say, 'Hey, can you airbrush a backdrop for me?' or, 'Can you make this cool prop?' I was around fifteen, making custom masks and *Planet of the Apes* masks and selling them to costume shops in San Jose. I turned myself into a little entrepreneur while I was still in high school."

Before he began making a name for himself in the worlds of film and television, Lazzarini was living a fantasy life filled with eccentric rock stars that most high schoolers at the time could only dream of meeting.

"My brother introduced me to a guy who was working for a rock band called The Tubes. The Tubes had this character, Quay Lewd, and he had these big-ass platform shoes and light-up glasses. This guy, Tim Zoch, made cool props for them. I hooked up with him and we started making effects for The Tubes for photo shoots. I started driving up to San Francisco, going to the Mabuhay club, watching the punk explosion happen all while I was underage. It was pretty awesome."

"We just kept the rock-and-roll thing going, making effects for bands coming into town, especially if they had a theatrical kind of show. We'd call up managers and see if we could watch the show so we could give them our ideas on what we could do for them. That would happen all the time. Once, I even got to see a David Bowie show, and yeah, I'll admit there were times where we'd call people up just so we could go see the show."

"One thing that was really cool was that we hooked up with Kiss. I was seventeen when I did a lifecast on Gene Simmons' and Paul Stanley's faces. That took big balls, of course. I offered to do masks for them, because they were putting makeup on their faces all the time. I just thought if we made some really thin masks out of foam latex, they could put them on quickly and take them off just as quickly. They liked that idea and here I was, just a seventeen-year-old kid."

Lazzarini almost set out for a career in rock FX (visual effects) after working with Kiss. Fate, however, had different plans for him at that pivotal time in his life.

"Originally, I was going to go on a tour with Kiss, but then they delayed the tour. Around the same time, I had been going to film school and I had already finished one semester at Loyola Marymount University. They delayed so long that I figured I had to either go back to school, or I had to go to work. So I chose school. I rented a garage just off campus from this woman named Mrs. Keeney, and I set up a workshop there. I worked on music videos, TV shows like *The Greatest American Hero*—which was a Steven Cannell show—and Roger Corman films, even though I was still going to film school. I went to film school and learned how to make films, but I didn't learn anything about how to do special effects there because I was already doing it."

Eventually, Lazzarini decided to make the transition from Northern California down to the Los Angeles area where the special effects industry was booming. There, he landed his first professional gigs at Makeup & Effects Laboratories, Inc. (MEL, Inc.) alongside other future heavyweights coming up in the business, including the masterminds behind Legacy Effects, as well as Alec Gillis and Tom Woodruff, Jr., who would later form their own highly successful company, Amalgamated Dynamics, Inc. At MEL, Lazzarini was quickly thrown into the feature film world as part of the crew for an early 1980s cult horror movie.

"My first job at MEL was *Evilspeak*, where I was working for Allan Apone and Doug White. The scene I worked on was where the woman had to be nude in the tub and then eaten by pigs. The idea was to make an edible gelatin body and fill her full of fruit scraps so that the pigs would just go nuts. I was mainly working at the shop, but they had me go to the set because they had some gelatin appliances that they needed."

"They gave them to me in this ice chest, but it was all the way down in Inglewood or City of Industry at this abandoned church where they were shooting, and it took me forever to get there. By the time I got there, these things were all melted. It was a mess. But the cool thing about working at MEL was that Frank Carriosa (who doesn't go by that name anymore) was working on the animatronics for this boar, and I got to take a look at what he was doing while I was there."

"The boar had this fiberglass core and Frank was mechanizing this thing so that the jaw opened up and I could see the insides. He was using some springs and bicycle cables. I thought it was the coolest thing ever because I hadn't done much in animatronics at that point. I fell in love immediately."

The next project that would come through MEL's doors was Amy Jones' slasher masterpiece, *The Slumber Party Massacre* (1982), and Lazzarini found himself heading up the special effects on the film alongside Larry Carr.

"I have a lot of memories from *Slumber Party Massacre*," Rick said. "Michael [Villella], who played the driller killer, was a method actor, so he spent a lot of his time on set just walking around, trying to perfect his walk. It was crazy. I also remember we questioned them about using a drill, because where would the power cord go? But producers just said, 'Don't worry about it,' so we learned not to question some of the specifics of it."

"We also got to kill Aaron Lipstadt, who was one of the producers. He played the pizza boy who got his eyes drilled out, and we made these appliances for his eyes so that they could be drilled out. There's a kid that got drilled through the shoulder, and we made a piece for that. The thing I remember most about *Slumber Party* was when they shipped us a gelatin hand that we had to use for a gag where the driller killer's hand was chopped off with the machete. They sent me down to the set that day as the rep."

"The thing about gelatin is that you can make it really light and fluffy, or you can make it really dense," Lazzarini explained. "In fact, we learned on this movie that you can make it so dense that a sharpened machete will bounce right off of it, which is what happened. They wanted the cut to happen with one fell swoop, and all we could do was whack away at the thing, which is the way it ended up in the movie. I know it wasn't what they planned, but it ended up being a really effective scene."

A short time later, Lazzarini was contacted to work on one of the more highly anticipated sequels of the 1980s, *A Nightmare on Elm Street 2: Freddy's Revenge* (1985), on which he was tasked with bringing several demonic pets to life for director Jack Sholder. The project was not without its difficulties, though, especially since right around the same time, Rick caught a break that would forever change his life.

"I got the call to work on *Nightmare 2*, and I was supposed to create a demonic parakeet, a demonic rat and cat, and then two demonic dogs. While I was moonlighting on *Nightmare 2*, I had just begun to work on *Invaders from Mars* [1986] over at Stan Winston's. Honestly, I wasn't keeping track of things, but then movies change schedules on you, too, so that was part of it. At some point they said, 'Oh, we need the parakeet next week,' and I hadn't even started on it. So I made this demonic parakeet with a Freddy-looking bird body with wings that flapped around and some head movements, too. It was just a disaster. It looked stupid. Everybody hated it and it was very embarrassing. It's one of the worst things I have ever done."

"The demonic rat and cat that we created were hand puppets," Lazzarini continued. "I worked on the cat and the rat was done by Alec Gillis, who I was friends with, and we would often work together on stuff. In fact, we both started at Stan's on the very same day. The rat definitely looked better than the cat, which was strike two for me on *Nightmare 2*."

"The one thing that we did hit a home run on were the demonic dog faces that were basically homages, which is a nice way of saying 'rip-offs,' of H.R. Giger's boil-faced babies. They looked pretty cool on the dogs, although trying to get measurements off a Rottweiler was an absolute nightmare. But we got a general idea of the size we needed to do and decided that the best way to sell the effect was to use a collar to hold the head pieces on."

"Alec and I went to The Pleasure Chest and got these spiked collars, because they had this punk look to them and we thought that would be very cool and very weird, too. [Producer] Bob Shaye was really into these dog masks, and when we brought the masks to set he turned into a big kid. He was styling the hair and helping with the slime on the face, and I think that's when I finally won him over," added Rick.

Rick sculpting the Supreme Being's legs for *Invaders from Mars* (1986).
Photo courtesy of Rick Lazzarini.

Prior to wrapping up on *Nightmare 2*, Lazzarini had to make a decision that would forever change the course of his journey in the special effects industry. Rick had been slated to take on a job at a Los Angeles prop house, but he got an offer that he found very hard to refuse, ultimately putting him on a path to work alongside a pioneer in the industry and setting him up to break out on his own as an artist.

"I was going to jump to another prop shop and supervise all the special stuff there," Lazzarini explained. "Right around the same time, Stan Winston had a small project, so he wanted to know if I wanted to come on board, too, because they needed help for a couple of days. So I called up the prop house and said, 'I know I'm supposed to start Monday, but Stan Winston called and asked if I could work a couple of days? Can I do those two days and then come in?' The guy said to me, 'You've got to make a choice, and I'll give you a day to think it over.' I said to him, 'I don't need a day. I'm going with Stan. See you later.'"

"I totally took the leap. I didn't have any guarantee of more than two days and I just thought, *I'm going to make this work.* So, we jumped right into this small project, then immediately afterwards came *Invaders from Mars*, and we made some crazy-ass creatures for that. By this time, I had worked in this prop shop called Ellis Mercantile and I had used mills and lathes and drill presses. I knew the tools that you needed to make this stuff. So, imagine my surprise when I got to Stan's shop and realized he didn't even have a machine shop set up, mostly because he had farmed out that stuff previously and had never had to set one up."

"I basically set up the machine shop there. Dave Nelson did the animatronics for one of the giant creatures for *Invaders from Mars* called the Supreme Being. They were these big, lumpy creatures with skinny legs that we worked on, and Richard Landon and I were in charge. There were two of them, and the job was to make these things support the little person inside a backpack on the main actor's back, but be really lightweight and hold the rest of the damn thing around it. *Invaders* was a really fun shoot— I remember seeing Karen Black from *Five Easy Pieces* and *Trilogy of Terror* while on set, and that was pretty cool, even though she was very intimidating. Tobe Hooper was a blast to work for, too."

Right as they were wrapping up the effects on *Invaders from Mars* (1986), Winston's shop was awarded with one of the biggest projects they had ever seen come through their doors: James Cameron's *Aliens* (1986), a project ambitious for many reasons, but primarily due to the large number of Xenomorphs that needed to be created, including the gravity-defying Alien Queen, who would go on to become one of the most iconic monsters of modern horror cinema.

Rick works on the Alien Queen head for *Aliens* (1986). Photo courtesy of Rick Lazzarini.

According to Lazzarini, "Originally, Jim had said, 'Well, we can have a crane lift the Queen from the top, or we can have a crane support her from the bottom and I'll just frame those shots depending on how we do that.' Stan was a big fan of strapping people onto people, so he asked Jim, 'What if we have two guys inside the Queen that are mirroring each other side by side, so they have a little T-Rex arm here and then the bigger arm over here? Let's get a right-handed guy so he can use his right arm for the strength of the big arm that he's holding, and we'll get a left-handed guy for over here, and they both could use their feet to move her hips.' That's what we ended up going with, which gave Jim a lot more freedom with shooting those scenes."

Stan Winston oversees the Alien Queen garbage bag test (Rick is pictured directly next to him on the right). Photo courtesy of the Stan Winston School of Character Arts.

"My job was to start designing the basics for the Queen. I had to figure out just how would two guys fit in there? We had to make this fiberglass lifecast, which was then integrated with a steel plate, and I was doing all this work utilizing real primitive CAD [computer-aided design] stuff, because the technology wasn't there yet to design the interior mechanisms for the Queen. I ended up working on a

Rick working on the Faceghugger mechanisms for *Aliens* (1986). Photo courtesy of Rick Lazzarini.

lot in *Aliens*. I was really pleased to have a hand in the Queen, the running Facehugger, the opening egg, and the close-up mechanisms for the Queen that allowed the front face to move around, open her jaw, and shoot out the inner jaw."

While Rick was hard at work back in the States, Alec Gillis and most of his team members were over in England overseeing special effects production on *Aliens* (1986) at Pinewood Studios. Initially, he wasn't going

Rick (pictured on the right) next to the Alien Queen on the set of *Aliens* (1986). Photo courtesy of Rick Lazzarini.

to be a part of Stan Winston's U.K. team, but the always forward-thinking Lazzarini made the case for why it was imperative that he should be sent over to join his colleagues.

"I remember talking with Stan and he told me, 'I'm sorry to tell you this, but I'm only budgeted for five people over there, so we can't send you, too.' I knew I had to push for this chance, so I said to him, 'Okay, here's the deal. Your five people over there are four art department guys and one mechanical guy, Richard [Landon], and he can't handle all the mechanical stuff by himself.'"

"Somehow, from that discussion, we wrangled some sort of a deal where I became Stan's subcontractor. I told him, 'If we do it this way, you can save money and you can just put me up on the same house as the other guys. The house is already paid for, so I'm just another roommate.' He finally agreed, and that's when I decided to incorporate myself and everything I did on *Aliens* under the Creature Shop, which is what my company was called at that time—that is, until the Hensons sued me since I had no idea they had trademarked that name. So we changed our company name to The Character Shop, and that's been our name ever since."

"We all lived together in this cottage in England and I remember Steve Norrington was on the crew," recalled Rick. "He was a wild man. Julian Caldow was there, too. We had a bunch of great guys, including all the guys who now comprise Legacy Effects. One cool thing I remember about that time in particular was that they were working on *Little Shop of Horrors* [1986] at Pinewood at the same time we were doing *Aliens*, so we could go and see the entire New York set, which was phenomenal. We shared the same foam room as that crew and we would help each other out all the time. It was great."

After *Aliens* (1986), Lazzarini ventured into the realm of science fiction once again, albeit on a film that could not be more different than Cameron's sequel, the Mel Brooks sci-fi parody, *Spaceballs* (1987), starring Bill Pullman, John Candy, Rick Moranis, and Daphne Zuniga. Rick was tasked with creating the animatronic ears for Candy's dog-like character, Barf, which he found to be a rewarding experience beyond just the work itself.

"*Spaceballs* was a job that I did out of my home shop in Westchester, California. They needed mechanical ears for John Candy and I thought that sounded like a fun job. I made two sets of ears, one set that was radio-controlled and could move forward, side to side, and could bend

Rick poses on the set of Spaceballs (1987) with John Candy.
Photo courtesy of Rick Lazzarini.

and wave and rotate as well, and another set that was Waldo®-controlled, which was like a form of robotic manipulation, but was very cumbersome because that meant you had to have cables running off the back of John. That set was quickly nixed because it didn't lend itself to shooting the way they wanted to, so it became the radio-controlled version all the time."

"I got to spend days on days with John and [makeup artists] Ben Nye Jr. and Ken Diaz in the makeup room on *Spaceballs*. Every day, Ben, John, Ken, and I would just sit there and joke around with each other. John was just the most wonderful actor and human being that I have ever worked with. He would call me up at home and go, 'Hey, you like lobsters?' 'Yeah, John, who doesn't like lobsters?' Then he'd say, 'Great, I'll send you a crate of lobsters because I can't eat them all myself.' He was that kind of guy, so thoughtful. Some people just have this 'thing' about them, where you instantly can feel that there's a unique presence, something special about them. That was John."

Rick's time on *Spaceballs* (1987) would end up being far more involved than just his effects work, as he performed two minor roles involving heavy prosthetics.

"Someone eventually realized that there was this scene near the end which ended up being a *Planet of the Apes* parody, but nobody had even talked about the prosthetics for that yet. Me being me, I went to Robert [Latham Brown], the Production Manager, and I said, 'Hey, you have this thing here where you've got people in makeup on horseback that you haven't even thought about yet, so I'll tell you what. Since I'm already puppeteering on this thing, can I get a role as one of the apes? And just to sweeten the deal, I'll even sculpt my own appliance.' He agreed to it after he saw the appliance I had sculpted, but then, for a moment he hesitated

Rick in his ape makeup next to his dressing room on the set of *Spaceballs* (1987). Photo courtesy of Rick Lazzarini.

and asked, 'Wait a minute, do you even know how to ride a horse?' And I told him that I was an 'excellent horseman.'"

"But, of course, that was a lie," Rick admitted. "I just wanted to do it so bad. I wasn't totally unfamiliar with horses because my sister had ridden when I was growing up, but beyond that, I didn't know much about riding. And it just so happened that they got this really ornery horse that wouldn't do what I wanted, so that became this whole situation in itself. Then the stuntman who was playing the other ape switched with me, but he was having trouble with the horse, too, so my secret was safe."

"The one thing I will always remember about that scene was that when we were filming, I started doing this Roddy McDowall impersonation, but Mel wanted me to sound mean and intimidating. I said, 'Mel, in the canon of *Planet of the Apes*, the chimps were the intellectuals, the orangutans were the law givers, and it was the gorillas who were the mean, militaristic ones.' He didn't want to hear any of that shit, but later on when *Spaceballs* came out, they had dubbed it with a Roddy McDowall impersonation."

"Another cool thing I got to do on *Spaceballs* was perform as Pizza the Hutt. They had already shot the Pizza the Hutt scenes with this actor named Richard Karen, and he hated it. They also didn't like the way the footage turned out, so Mel wanted to do it over again and Richard said, 'No fucking way.' So, because I had already been in a suit and makeup,

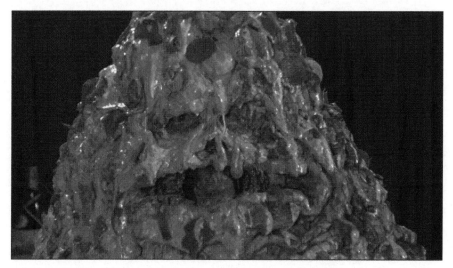

Rick performs as "Pizza the Hutt" in *Spaceballs* (1987). Photo courtesy of Rick Lazzarini.

they put me in the getup. They still used Richard's pre-recorded track, so that's not my voice at all, but you can see my mouth and my eyes."

After *Spaceballs* (1987), Lazzarini continued to stay busy throughout the mid-to-late 1980s, contributing to a variety of films, including *The Unholy* (1988), *Dead Heat* (1988), and *My Stepmother Is an Alien* (1988), before working on *Ghostbusters II* (1989) and *A Nightmare on Elm Street 5: The Dream Child* (1989) back to back, all while keeping busy on multiple commercial projects in the very same year. While Rick experienced a great deal of stress due to his workload during that era, he also relished the fact that the industry was at an all-time high.

"For *Nightmare 5*, we made this animatronic translucent fetus-type baby, and then we created this thing where Freddy was ensconced in the wall of the womb, with all these textures that melded into Freddy's face when he says, 'It's feeding time!'"

"Funny story: Adam Jones was working for me at that time. He eventually went on to become the guitarist for the band Tool, and now he's a freaking millionaire. He was the one who sculpted the Freddy appliance. How we did everything for the effect meant that whoever was going to do it was going to be glued into the wall of this womb for the entire day, and Englund was like, 'Screw that.' So I volunteered myself, and if you watch that scene, you can see me wearing the contacts and the Freddy appliance, and I even got to say the line."

"When I was working on *Ghostbusters II* and *Nightmare 5*, it truly felt like the golden age of animatronics and practical effects. At that time, nobody was crying about budgets, nobody was crying about the schedule. If you said, 'This is what I need,' that's what you got. It was just fun. There were a lot of good times, and there was a lot of innovation, too, because when there's more work, there are more opportunities for innovation. I even pioneered my own flocking technique of applying hair to creatures back then, because I was always trying out new methods and techniques."

"There was just an explosion of practical effects at that point, so we were all fat and happy. We weren't at that point where everyone thought, '*Oh, we could do that with CG* [computer graphics].' It was for the bragging rights, so you could say to the world, 'Look how smart I am.' That is, unless you failed. It was a big gamble every time. Beyond that, there is a part of the work to me where I just want someone to give me a problem to solve, and I won't stop until I figure it out. But then, not long after, that

A behind-the-scenes look at the impaled heads scene in *Ghostbusters II* (1989).
Photo courtesy of Rick Lazzarini.

amount of work started to dry up right around the time when CG technology began to take over in the late 1990s."

Despite the technological advancements of filmmaking in recent decades, both Lazzarini and The Character Shop have weathered the storms, keeping busy on a multitude of film and commercial projects, including *Hook* (1991), *Hocus Pocus* (1993), *Operation Dumbo Drop* (1995), *Outbreak* (1995), *Escape from L.A.* (1996), *Mimic* (1997), *Willard* (2003), and *Snakes on a Plane* (2006), and they were even tasked with bringing Slimer (and his girlfriend) to life with practical effects for Paul Feig's *Ghostbusters* (2016).

While his talent is a big reason why he's still working steadily, there's another key factor to his success: keeping it all in the family at The Character Shop by working with his wife, Debra, whom he has known since he was nineteen years old.

"There are guys that I could be jealous of because they have bigger shops or they are working on bigger pictures, but the way I see it is that they also probably have bigger problems than I do. When I did

Rick working on the theater ghost for *Ghostbusters II* (1989). Photo courtesy of Rick Lazzarini.

A crane was utilized to get the animatronic elephant to the set of *Operation Dumbo Drop* (1995). Photo courtesy of Rick Lazzarini.

Rick doing some sculpting for the main creature in *Mimic* (1997). Photo courtesy of Rick Lazzarini.

Mimic, there were seventy people that I had to be accountable for. The toughest thing wasn't wrangling budgets or dealing with changing delivery schedules, or even technical challenges. It was managing seventy different egos. I don't want to be a professional babysitter, though, which can happen when you get to be a shop of a certain size, so I've since deliberately focused on doing smaller-scaled projects. It doesn't stress me out as much, and because I have better control of it all, that means I take smaller risks."

"I used to have regulars here," Lazzarini explained, "folks who worked here full-time. But then technology came in, and CG started taking more work away. Everything in the business started to fragment, and so you had to be more flexible and more frugal. I stopped having full-time workers. I would only have people come in when I had a job. Meanwhile, Deb got work as a film editor, and she kept working until we had kids. After the kids got set, we found out that it was more cost-effective to have Deb in the front office. It made sense. She's incredibly intelligent, so I rely on her to be diplomatic. If I'm going to write something to somebody, it goes through her first."

Rick, Debra Lazzarini (pictured left and right in the front row), and their crew during a Cadbury chocolate commercial shoot. Photo courtesy of Rick Lazzarini.

"Over time, I realized that I could give Deb work beyond the office, too. Many of our puppeteering jobs require manipulation of radio-control transmitters, so why not get her proficient in doing that? Then it made even more sense to have Deb around. Plus, our company does not pay Deb and myself a salary. Whatever build comes in here, zero of that income goes to Deb and myself. Zero. The only way that we take income in is by performing as puppeteers, and so I choose jobs that maximize our opportunities to be puppeteers."

Rick credits his business approach to the time he spent working under Stan Winston, specifically something he overheard one day that continues to impact the way he handles things at The Character Shop.

"I remember Stan talking on the phone one day with somebody who was trying to shortchange him, and he said, 'Fine. If you're not going to do that, then you're not going to get this.' The person on the other end was clearly arguing with him. And then Stan said, 'Because what I gave you was a gift. I gave you a gift.' He was very clear about the situation and he wasn't shying away from it, either. Stan stood his ground and I took that lesson to heart. I'm all about over-delivering for my clients, but if Stan taught me anything, it was to always stand up for yourself and the work that you do."

Rick (far left) listens as Stan Winston and other team members (Alec Gillis, David Nelson) work on troubleshooting the Facehugger for *Aliens* (1986). Photo courtesy of the Stan Winston School of Character Arts.

Rick poses with his version of Slimer for *Ghostbusters* (2016).
Photo courtesy of Rick Lazzarini.

The other big lesson that Lazzarini has learned over the years? "That one 'aw, shit' moment can erase twenty 'attaboy!' moments every single time. You never want to be the guy holding everything up because things are going wrong, so always, **always** over-prepare."

8 Mike Elizalde

FOR ALMOST THREE DECADES NOW, Mike Elizalde has worked hard to establish himself as one of the premier creature effects artists in Hollywood, from his initial days working at various studios, to 1994, when he first opened the doors at Spectral Motion alongside his wife, Mary. While his creative talents have thrust his work into the spotlight on ambitious films like *Hellboy* (2004), *Hellboy II: The Golden Army* (2008), *Pacific Rim* (2013), and *Hansel & Gretel: Witch Hunters* (2013), Elizalde

Photo courtesy of Mike Elizalde.

experienced a modest upbringing, and he never could have imagined that being a part of such memorable movies would be in his future.

"I was born in Mexico, in Mazatlán, Sinaloa," Elizalde said. "My dad passed away when I was two, and my mom decided that it'd be better for me and for her if we immigrated to the United States when I was four. So I came to the States when I was very young and grew up in South Central Los Angeles in Compton. We were very poor, so there weren't a lot of resources available to me in any capacity. We basically lived in the middle of an industrial park, right by the railroad tracks. That was an interesting way to grow up, because there's so much stuff to look at. None of it is particularly beautiful, but it helped me begin to think creatively."

"But as a kid, you don't really know any better. You think, *Well, this is where we live, and this is our environment, and that's that.* It was always

A picture from Mike's (seated in front) early childhood. Photo courtesy of Mike Elizalde.

Mike and his team at Spectral Motion discussing the creature suit they created for *Attack the Block* (2011). Photo courtesy of Mike Elizalde.

a dream of mine to go beyond that life. Most people who live in those circumstances—whether they acknowledge that or not—somewhere in their heart, there's an ambition and a need to grow beyond that kind of poverty. We also lived in a trailer park for a little bit, and we were poor. We were living on food stamps and welfare and barely surviving. But I still had a fun childhood. I still had creative stuff going on that I did on my own, and that's what kept me going."

While the possibility of working in special effects wasn't necessarily something on Elizalde's radar as a child, he quickly fell in love with creatures and monsters as he grew older and began learning more about horror movies. Eventually, Elizalde watched one film in particular that would forever change his life, inspiring him to keep building upon his creative nature and utilize that passion for his eventual career path.

"For me, the earliest creative spark I felt came from watching monster movies," explained Elizalde. "I had a stepdad for a few years and he was terrific. He was the guy who'd make me stay home on Friday nights, saying to me, 'Hey, there's a horror movie on. Let's go watch it!' He helped my dream come true in a way that he probably never really even knew.

But I really enjoyed that time, and horror movies were something that gave me a very tangible look into a creative field."

"Even though I didn't fully understand it at the time, I was immediately drawn towards the world of effects. But I didn't find my true creative streak until after high school, as that's when I really started diving into this stuff in earnest. A big part of that was due to *An American Werewolf in London*. That movie changed my life, and it's also when I started figuring out that there's a guy behind all of this. There's a person who created these things and had to put a team together, too."

"I started reading a lot about Rick Baker, and once I realized that he was the protégé of one of my heroes, Dick Smith, I just thought that was the coolest. It drove me forward, and to end up working on any project that I did with Rick throughout my career was an incredible dream come true. I never could have dreamed up something like that. The other movie that inspired me was *The Thing* [1982], and I'm sure that one also influenced several generations of creative people to follow their dreams. They're both still incredibly powerful to this day."

"As I grew older, that's when I started learning names like Jack Pierce, who did the Frankenstein's monster makeup, and Karl Silvera, who had created the Herman Munster makeup on Fred Gwynne. Those characters stayed with me, so when I got old enough to start looking for my own research material, those were two I found immediately."

Not one to let life's limitations hold him back, Elizalde began teaching himself the art of practical effects and prosthetics through any books and other literature he could find. As he worked hard to fine-tune his techniques, he connected with a Hollywood innovator who encouraged him to follow his dreams of creating his own kind of monster magic on the big screen.

"If you're passionate enough about something," Elizalde said, "you're going to figure it out one way or another—whether it's a formal training situation, or you implement and figure out ways to do it on your own. You're always going to chase that dream until you find enough traction and enough momentum to dive right in and start making a living out of it. And that's how it worked out for me."

"Another thing that I had always been interested in was magic. I made a friend while I was in high school who also enjoyed magic, and I even used to hang out at the Magic Factory where they built illusions for

Mike performing a magic trick. Photo courtesy of Mike Elizalde.

Doug Henning and David Copperfield. That was a really cool place, and I learned a little bit of craftsmanship there—how to use tools and how to do things properly and not haphazardly. I also learned how to have a really good work ethic while I was there," Elizalde added.

"One of the people who would come in on Saturdays to hang out with us was a guy named Bill Taylor. Bill used to own a company called Illusion Arts, and they did visual effects for movies. All of a sudden I'm with this guy who works in the movie business, and he was someone I really looked up to, and still do to this day. I wanted to be like him, and he became my inspiration in many ways. So, when I was still in the Navy, I started getting better at makeup, and I would do them on myself and my friends there, so I could take pictures and show them to Bill for him to critique."

"He told me to keep practicing and that I just needed to keep working at it, which is what I did. And, eventually, I started sending all my pictures off to a few different studios in Los Angeles and just hoped for the best."

While Elizalde initially had to pursue an alternative career while dreaming of his break in the special effects industry, one day fate intervened and gave him his first chance to begin proving himself as an artist.

"After I left the Navy, I took a temporary job as an air conditioning repair and installation guy, so I was driving around in my air conditioning

Mike working on a sculpture project. Photo courtesy of Mike Elizalde.

van. I drove past this place, I looked down the alleyway, and I could see that there were molds and lifecasts of actors sitting out there in the alley. I thought to myself, *Oh my gosh, that's the stuff that I want to learn about and get into.* So, I quickly parked in the lot and grabbed my pictures, because I always had them with me."

"As it turned out, it was one of the places that I had sent my stuff to, called MMI: Magical Makeup Industries. So I knocked on the door, I went in, and I spoke with a guy named John Foster, who looked over my pictures and said, 'Your stuff looks pretty good! Why don't you come in here and talk to the owner?' We went into the main office, and the next thing I knew, I had a job. It was three months after I left the Navy, so I felt like, *Oh my gosh, my dream's coming true so fast. This is amazing!* I worked there for several months doing different things, including sculpting and painting. I was getting an all-around education while working with my idols."

"It was almost like a Dorothy moment for me, when she walks through the door and all of a sudden the world is no longer in black and white. Everything was now in Technicolor, and that's how my life felt every day going into work. Once that job concluded, based on the work that I'd done for them, MMI was very happy and pleased, so they recommended me to a lot of other people. I just kept on working, and I haven't stopped in thirty years."

Early on in his career, Elizalde found himself working for another modern visionary in the world of practical effects, David Miller, who was responsible for creating the iconic look of Freddy Krueger, and who also worked on countless genre projects as well, including *The Terminator* (1984).

"I spent a good amount of time working for David Miller's shop, which was a great experience. Back when I was trying to get into the business, I remember the first time I saw Freddy Krueger and thought to myself, *Wow, that's a really cool makeup. I wish that I could work on something like this some day.* So, as you can imagine, I was very excited to be a part of [*A Nightmare on Elm Street 3:*] *Dream Warriors*. We built a bunch of puppets and had this whole puppet crew on set, which was an amazing experience."

"I got to work with David and his crew for three more years," Elizalde continued, "and that really was a very special time in my career, when it was still the early years and all these doors were just beginning to open for me. To do something like Freddy Krueger was a very lofty goal for

Mike touches up Ron Perlman's makeup between takes on *Hellboy II: The Golden Army* (2008). Photo courtesy of Mike Elizalde.

me, to either try to emulate something like that or to work on a *Nightmare* movie. But as I grew in the business, my sensibilities became a little more focused on the final work, whether it was doing a realistic old-age makeup or creating a really lifelike puppet that looked so remarkably real that you wouldn't be able to tell the difference. That became much more of a passion for me, not so much it being about a specific character, but the objective of mimicking reality to a certain degree."

Elizalde's thirst for knowledge propelled his career, and the more varied experiences he garnered, the deeper his love for the artistry grew.

"The thing that drew me further into special effects, as I worked in different studios, was realizing how much detail went into the work and how important it was to have that hyper-realism to your work. That really kept me hooked, and it's still one of the things that fascinates me even today. The process of punching in one hair at a time, or creating skin textures on clay, or even creating the eyes and the teeth on a creature. I learned how effects can be a form of alchemy, where all these elements come together to simulate something in reality."

"I saw the process almost like a magic trick. You're creating an illusion, but it's just in a different mode of expression. I also always believed that it was important to vary interests and approaches, to change things up and keep it all interesting, which was something I applied to my career. All of those things combined gave me a good perspective on what I wanted my studio to be like and where the emphasis would be in our creative processes. The more you spread yourself out, the more you learn," Elizalde added, "and the more you pick up information from different sources."

"We call it cross-pollinating—where you learn a certain method of doing things in one studio, and then you go to another studio and you learn that method in cadence, but you also bring something different to the table and say, 'When I was working over here, we did this and that was cool.' It's a great breeding ground for creativity and to always come up with new ways of achieving things. Plus, I never felt comfortable staying in one studio for a very long time, so I worked at a lot of different shops before creating Spectral [Motion]. In fact, the longest I stayed anywhere was at Rick Baker's studio, where I was at for about five or six years collectively."

Before finding a temporary home with Rick Baker, Elizalde contributed to numerous films throughout the late 1980s, including *Watchers* (1988), *Food of the Gods Part 2* (1989), *Turner & Hooch* (1989), *A Nightmare on Elm Street 5: The Dream Child* (1989), *Look Who's Talking* (1989), and *Howling V: The Rebirth* (1989). One of his biggest professional challenges would come at the end of the decade, though, under the supervision of Mark Stetson during production on Paul Verhoeven's *Total Recall* (1990).

"*Total Recall* was a completely new challenge for me as an artist," explained Elizalde. "I was working at Mark Stetson's studio, and by trade, Mark is a model-maker, a miniature set designer, and a visual effects master. That was a completely different world for me. It was not prosthetic makeup, and it wasn't puppets, either. It was a whole different creative process that also served as a great education for me, and it became a huge component of my learning process."

"I worked on a lot of the Mars landscapes, creating the exterior landscape miniatures. We also built these giant radioactive cylinders that plunged into the mountainside and created the breathable air on the surface of Mars. A lot of these processes were so new to me, and I thought it was very fascinating and an interesting new realm that I was learning about. *Total Recall* taught me as a practical effects person how to collabo rate properly with visual effects people. Mark Stetson was a wonderful guy and he's still a friend of mine. I'm so grateful to him for giving me an opportunity to work with him on that project."

Right around the same time that he was learning the art of miniatures, Elizalde found out that his services were needed as part of the enormous puppeteering crew that Rick Baker was assembling for Joe Dante's ambitious sequel, *Gremlins 2: The New Batch* (1990).

"*Gremlins 2* was the first time I had ever seen a really big director in person. I was like, *Oh my God, that's Joe Dante right there!* It was so cool. I started working on *Gremlins 2* doing miniature Gremlins that would ooze green stuff and melt into the ground. We did all of that stuff with Mark Stetson's studio."

"But then, I went to work with Rick's massive puppeteering team, which was an immense honor for me. There were three hundred people that were called in to help puppeteer the Gremlin puppets. I had never experienced effects on that kind of a scale before *Gremlins 2*. That ended up being a really busy year for me, because I also worked with Tony Gardner in his studio sculpting some prosthetic pieces for *Darkman*."

"It was more of an entry-level sculpting position," Elizalde reflected, "but it was amazing. It was the first real big sculpting job that I had, apart from what I had done at Dave Miller's [studio], so I was fortunate to have had lots of really cool experiences during that one year."

Elizalde would get the opportunity to lend his puppeteering skills to another franchise when he joined the effects team for Barry Sonnenfeld's *The Addams Family* (1991) movie. Being a fan of the original comic strip and the 1960s television series, Elizalde was especially thrilled to be a part of this new iteration of the iconic clan of creepy and kooky characters.

"I grew up with *The Addams Family* on TV and reading the Charles Addams comic strips," said Elizalde. "I always thought he created such a cool, dark, fun world, and I really fell in love with all the characters. And while I loved all of them, Uncle Fester and Lurch were the two characters that always spoke to me in a special way, probably because of their appearances. On the TV series, Jackie Coogan didn't wear a whole lot of makeup, just some dark circles around his eyes, but Ted Cassidy as Lurch, he was amazing to me. I didn't know if he was wearing makeup or if that's really how he looked. I was blown away by him as a kid."

"So, one of my assignments on *The Addams Family* was to put Carel Struycken in a test makeup for the Lurch character. I was on cloud nine. And what David Miller designed for Carel looked great—I thought it was a terrific makeup. Another thing I did on both *Addams Family* movies was to design the animatronics for the stand-alone Thing hand. I built the hand at Dave Miller's studio and I'm still very proud of how it came out. I never thought I'd get that kind of opportunity, and it was a terrific experience all around."

"On set, I also spent a little time having conversations with Raúl Juliá, who I thought was utterly fascinating. He was such an intelligent, bright, and sensitive man, and I enjoyed my talks with him immensely. He was so engaging and effervescent—a great personality in every way. I also got to meet Christopher Lloyd because of *The Addams Family*, and he was a big hero of mine from his *Taxi* days. And I enjoyed working with Barry Sonnenfeld, as we would go on to work together on three more films after that, thanks to Rick Baker and Dave Miller."

Elizalde kept consistently busy throughout the 1990s, working on films such as *Honey, I Blew Up the Kid* (1992), *Super Mario Bros.* (1993), *Coneheads* (1993), *The Santa Clause* (1994), *The Frighteners* (1996), the first two *Men in Black* (1997) movies, and *Bicentennial Man* (1999). In order to keep up with the high demand, in the mid-1990s, Elizalde and his wife, Mary, launched their own studio, Spectral Motion, and by the early 2000s, Elizalde found himself standing shoulder to shoulder with two of his personal heroes while on the set of *A.I. Artificial Intelligence* (2001).

"I was hired by Stan Winston to come and work with the team on *A.I.*," Elizalde said. "I was assigned a specific Mecha character, so I had to build my own designed character, and I was also assigned to go on set to puppeteer some of the Mechas with the team. I had never worked with Stan Winston before, or Steven Spielberg, for that matter, but that experience was a sweeping, epic moment in my life, when I was right in the middle of this amazing situation. It was a dream-come-true moment."

"The *A.I.* set experience was really unique, because it was a Spielberg movie and so, all of a sudden, everything was top quality—even craft services. Watching Steven Spielberg work was really interesting, too. He was always so incredibly prepared. When he arrived on the set each day, he

Mike attends to Ron Perlman on the set of *Hellboy II: The Golden Army* (2008). Photo courtesy of Mike Elizalde.

had all of his shots worked out, and they were able to move from one set to the next very quickly because he planned every little aspect out ahead of time. It was a well-oiled machine and we rarely ran into problems."

"I was a little nervous being around Spielberg," Elizalde admitted. "The first time I knew I was going to be seeing him, I wasn't really sure how to act. But somehow, I managed to pull myself together and then I was fine. Working with Stan was phenomenal, too, because he was such a legend. I learned a lot and made a lot of new friends and colleagues on that set."

A year later, Elizalde met another visionary filmmaker who would have a profound impact on his life both personally and professionally: Guillermo del Toro. The pair first collaborated together on *Blade II* (2002), and they continued their working relationship through various other productions, including *Hellboy* (2004), *Hellboy II: The Golden Army* (2008), *Don't Be Afraid of the Dark* (2010) (which del Toro produced), and *Pacific Rim* (2013).

"I was working at Steve Johnson's studio for *Blade II* when I first met Guillermo. I was designing the animatronic Reaper puppets that were used in the movie, and I was also the lead puppeteer on set, so we got to spend a lot of time together working on *Blade II*. One of the first things that happened when I met Guillermo was that he hugged me immediately. I remember thinking to myself, *Oh, this is terrific!* Because you don't often meet too many people who're that warm, friendly, and so willing to welcome you that way as a collaborator. Guillermo and I hit it off right away. We became good friends, and the work we did on set together was really fun. We had a great time working and making movies together for years."

"We still call each other up and say, 'What's going on? Let's go to lunch,' when he's in town. I do miss working more closely with him, because he moved his operation to Vancouver a few years ago when he began working on *The Strain*, so we don't see each other that often. But all those experiences that I have enjoyed with him over the years are priceless."

"I have so many funny Guillermo stories that I took away from those experiences, and being able to create these amazing characters that came out of his scripts and projects, which in turn helped our company's career, was a real blessing. I'm very grateful to him, and I always will be."

Another landmark effort for Elizalde and Spectral Motion was their work on Joe Cornish's sci-fi actioner, *Attack the Block* (2011), which introduced audiences to a brilliant creature design devoid of color and detail,

Mike examines the animatronic Sammael from *Hellboy* (2004).
Photo courtesy of Mike Elizalde.

adorned only with glowing fangs that made for an unsettling snarl and a practical monster truly unlike anything that had graced the big screen before.

"The look of those creatures and the design was very much driven by Joe Cornish. He had a very specific idea, a very specific notion about what these things would be like. When we first started designing the creature suits, we would go to a little shooting stage and film them in shadow. We would film shadows of the creatures so that we could study what they looked like in various environments."

A maquette of the alien monster from *Attack the Block* (2011), created by Spectral Motion. Photo courtesy of Mike Elizalde.

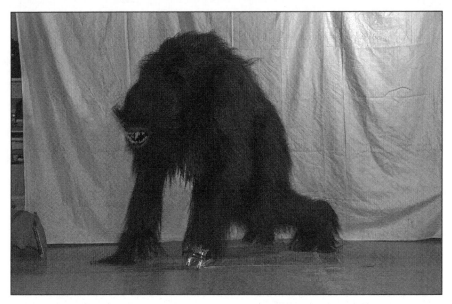

Spectral Motion tests the creature suit mobility for *Attack the Block* (2011).
Photo courtesy of Mike Elizalde.

"Joe's conceit with the design was that because these things come from another planet, or even another dimension, they should react differently to environments than anything from our planet does. They reflect no light, and they completely absorb all of the light around them, so that made them into these weird and mysterious creatures. They almost look like these weird space baboons, but they don't have eyes and their teeth glow."

"We created the creatures out of fur suits and then we rotoscoped every single creature to create all kinds of absence of light, so there's no contour to them at all in the film. If you watch *Attack the Block* again, and you watch carefully, you'll see that there isn't any reflective quality to these monsters at all. It was all Joe's brilliant idea. He did amazing things with that film on a very modest budget. It's a masterpiece."

Another film that Spectral Motion and Elizalde left their indelible imprint on was *Hansel & Gretel: Witch Hunters* (2013), not only designing stunning practical witch effects, but also giving new life to the memorable character of Edward the troll.

"The Director, Tommy Wirkola, was great to work with on *Hansel & Gretel* because he came in with the same idea that we had, saying, 'What we need to do is create as much of this movie practically as possible, because that's what I, Tommy, find amazing and incredible as a fan.' He really went to bat for us on that movie, especially with the Edward character."

"The studio was insistent that that character couldn't be done with animatronics, or as a practical character. Tommy said to them, 'Look, I know that these guys can pull this off. I've seen their work, and they're going to do a great job with this. We need to give them a chance.'"

"But it became a struggle, a daily testing ground for us. Every single day that we were filming, we had to prove ourselves. We had to show that it could work in the dailies. I don't want to speak for them, but I think they were hesitant to adjust to the idea of doing it practically, and so I suspect they were creating a digital version just in case. But at the end of the day, we won them over, and Tommy was a big part of that. It's always great to know that the work you created influenced somebody into believing in your work, and that what you told them was a viable solution would really work."

Since *Hansel & Gretel: Witch Hunters* (2013), Spectral Motion has consistently stayed hard at work over the last few years, bringing to life more iconic characters in films like *R.I.P.D.* (2013), *Anchorman 2: The*

Mike makes an adjustment to Famke Janssen's witch makeup for *Hansel & Gretel: Witch Hunters* (2013). Photo courtesy of Mike Elizalde.

Legend Continues (2013), and *Dead Snow 2: Red vs. Dead* (2014). Elizalde even contributed his creative talents to the Oscar-winning film *Birdman or (The Unexpected Virtue of Ignorance)* (2014), on which he served as a Specialty Costume Supervisor for Director Alejandro G. Iñárritu. And while he doesn't necessarily have a secret to why he's been so successful in the world of special effects for over three decades, Elizalde does say that there is one key element all artists need to sustain themselves and thrive: adaptability.

"The biggest requirement to be successful in anything is to be adaptable. You have to understand the landscape in your field and you have to be willing to change course if necessary. It's very challenging, especially in the last ten years, things have really changed in how our contributions are perceived by the productions we're working with. Back in the heyday, when it was Rick Baker, Robert Keen, and Stan [Winston], they were viewed as incredibly valuable assets to the production, and they were treated very respectfully. They always had all of the resources that they could possibly need."

"But as time has gone on, the industry started pulling back the resources and asking much more to be done for a much smaller budget. The work that those guys did in building up that respectable image for our industry has suffered because of that, unfortunately. So you have to become adaptable. You have to understand that maybe there are other avenues to pursue outside of film, and that's something we've done at Spectral. We've done work with Disneyland and Universal Studios over the last few years, so we're continually expanding our base so we can always stay diversified as a company."

"The film business is a changing landscape," Elizalde added, "and it's not always going to support the efforts that we'd like to keep doing or the quality that is paramount to us. We don't believe in skimping. We don't believe in hiring less experienced people when we know there's really only one right way to do it. That's a challenge. It's a very difficult challenge to negotiate, but in the end, it's something that you have to do. You have to be able to focus your energy a little more sharply so you can lead your team to fight another day."

Someone else Elizalde credits for the success he and Spectral Motion have had is his wife, Mary, who has been heavily involved with the company since it launched back in 1994.

Mike poses with "Wink" on the set of *Hellboy II: The Golden Army* (2008).
Photo courtesy of Mike Elizalde.

"Mary is definitely a driving force in our company who has carried us through thick and thin. She's a salt of the Earth person, very wonderful, and has always been a supportive partner. She even supports me in my follies and foibles into magic, and a lot of partners might not understand why anyone would waste their time like that."

"She's always been there for me," Elizalde emphasized, "and she's always believed that we can succeed at what we try. She's a very dearly loved and essential member of our company, and she's been a terrific wife and best friend to me for years and years. I couldn't have done any of this without her, so it's important that I mention her, because I wouldn't be here talking about my career today had it not been for her support."

9 Bart J. Mixon

FOR OVER THIRTY-FIVE YEARS NOW, Texas native Bart J. Mixon has paved his way in the world of special effects, tirelessly lending his talents on over one hundred films and more than twenty different television series since 1980. A multiple Emmy Award nominee, Mixon has helped to create compelling and unique makeups for almost every cinematic sub-genre in horror and science fiction, overseeing crews on some of the most ambitious productions in modern film history.

"I guess I've always been artistic," Mixon said. "I started collecting comic books when I was about five or six. My brother, Bret, and I would draw our own comics and that sort of thing. I was always interested in comic books, monster movies, science fiction, and that's how I learned about makeup and stop-motion stuff. There was a member of this comic book club in Houston I was in that knew a little bit about makeup, so he would give me pointers on how to do things. Not that they were necessarily the right ways, but it was at least something that made me familiar with things like how to make a mold or how to pour latex into it."

"There was also the *7 Faces of Dr. Lao*, which was the first makeup-type movie I can remember—there was one actor playing all these various characters, and I re-

Photo courtesy of Bart Mixon.

139

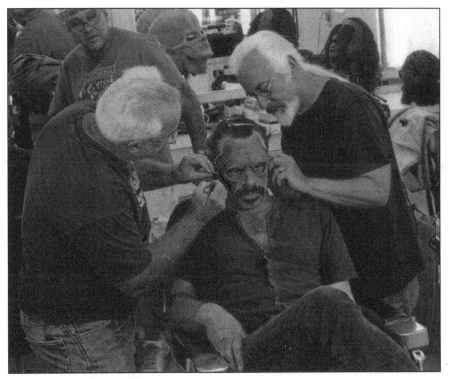

Bart Mixon and Rick Baker prepare the character of Boris (played by Jemaine Clement) for *Men in Black 3* (2012). Photo courtesy of Bart Mixon.

alized there was a makeup artist that was behind it all. Then there was *Planet of the Apes*, which fueled my interest in makeup even more. I started making my own Super 8 movies, where I was trying to do makeup effects and stop-motion, but it was pretty difficult because I didn't have the proper cameras and equipment. But I was able to sculpt and mold, and I was pretty good at making masks and prosthetics. I just didn't know where that would all lead me."

"Where it all changed for me, though, was reading about Rick Baker in *Famous Monsters of Filmland* sometime around 1970. Seeing him in there made a career as a makeup artist seem a little more attainable. Before, you'd always see guys like John Chambers and Jack Pierce in articles, but they were all these older guys. Rick Baker was eighteen, essentially still a kid, so it was like, 'Well, if this guy can do it, maybe I can, too.' Of course, the hurdle of living in Houston still had to be overcome, but at least the dream felt like it wasn't a complete impossibility."

The professional world of makeup effects became even more attainable for Mixon in the late 1970s when he discovered an annual comic book and sci-fi convention in Houston. That's where Bart met Rick Baker in 1977, striking up a friendship that would continue over the next forty years.

"When I met Rick, I had done a few things, but nothing very good and, quite frankly, most of the stuff I had to show him was pretty bad. I'm surprised he even talked to me in the first place. He gave me his address and phone number and invited me to correspond with him, and I used to send him a list of questions and a cassette tape. Rick would sit there and record his answers and mail the tape back to me, because that would be easier for him than writing everything out. So that was a huge help to me as I was figuring things out."

"A funny coincidence: the same convention where I met Rick was the very same one where both Steve Johnson and Matthew Mungle met Rick, too. In fact, Steve grew up a half hour from me," Bart added, "but I didn't know him until then."

A zombie sculpture from early in Bart's career. Photo courtesy of Bart Mixon.

Baker wasn't the only contact Mixon made early on in his career as an aspiring artist in Houston. In fact, he found a few legends who weren't all that far from his very own backyard.

"I knew Ernie Farino, who lived in Dallas, and he was doing stop-motion effects up there. He ended up becoming the effects coordinator on *The Terminator* and worked on *The Abyss*, too. I made a few more contacts in the area and then I started working on local projects, not that there were that many. I was still going through *Famous Monsters* as my resource, and I came across a photo for *The Alien Dead*, which was done by Fred Olen Ray. He was living in Florida at the time, and I tracked him down and contacted him and ended up doing a few projects for him while he still lived in Florida. When Fred moved out to L.A., I kept in touch with him, too. Basically, I kept looking under every rock that I could while I was in Texas to try and find what little work there might be out there."

"But Ernie was great. When he moved out to Los Angeles to work for New World Pictures, I was sending him pictures of sculptures and makeups and whatnots that I was doing, and he must have shown them to John Carl Buechler, who was heading up the makeup department on

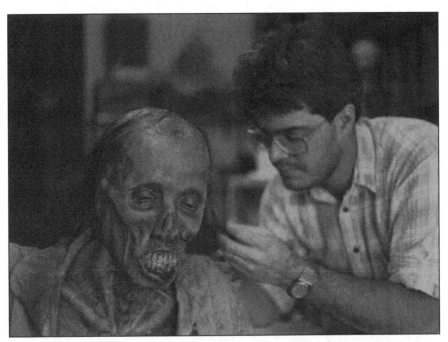

Bart finishes off a zombie for *The Supernaturals* (1986). Photo courtesy of Bart Mixon.

Bart and Mark Shostrom on the set of *A Nightmare on Elm Street 2: Freddy's Revenge* (1985).
Photo courtesy of Bart Mixon.

Forbidden World. I remember getting a call that they needed some extra help, so I flew out for basically a week of work. It was two weeks before I was supposed to get married, so I couldn't stay out there any longer even if I wanted to, but on that job, in addition to meeting John, I met [R.] Chris Biggs and Mark Shostrom, who was the main contact. I stayed in touch with him and even did a few projects with him over the next couple of years."

"I did a show for him called *Raw Courage* in 1983 out in New Mexico, and then in '84 I drove out to L.A. and worked for him on this project called *The Supernaturals*. At this point, my twin brother, Bret, had already moved out there and was doing animation effects at Fantasy II [Film Effects, Inc.], working for Ernie Farino. While I was out there, Ernie had me work on *The Terminator* a little bit and Mark brought me out a year later so I could work on *A Nightmare on Elm Street 2*."

A Nightmare on Elm Street 2: Freddy's Revenge (1985) became Mixon's first taste of a real Hollywood production, a monumental occasion in his up-and-coming career that he still relishes to this day.

"*Nightmare 2* was definitely the biggest show I had been involved with at that point, and to some extent, it was my first real movie. We were all certainly aware that we were doing a sequel to *A Nightmare on Elm Street*, and that it had become a big deal with horror fans and audiences everywhere, so there was some pressure on us, and there was some apprehension, too."

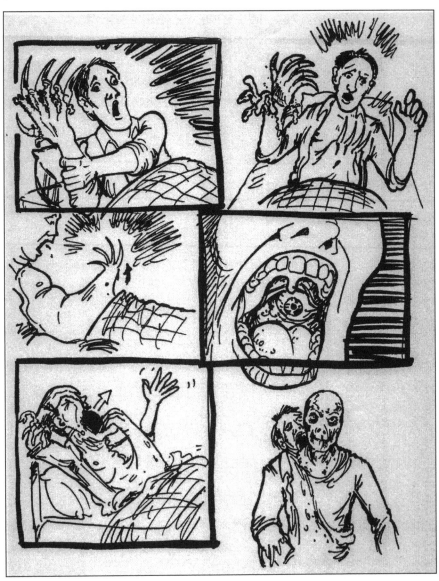

Original storyboard from *A Nightmare on Elm Street 2: Freddy's Revenge* (1985). Courtesy of Bart Mixon.

"There were two effects teams on *Nightmare*," explained Bart. "One was led by Mark and the other was led by Kevin Yagher, and it happened early on in his career, too, so we were all pretty much at the same level experience-wise. Going into it, the producers told Mark that he had to make a choice between either doing all the Freddy makeup or doing the transformation where Freddy rips himself out of Jesse's [Mark Patton's] body. Mark's thinking was that because Freddy had already been done and was somewhat established, that transformation was going to be the showstopper moment in *Nightmare 2*. In that respect, I think he was absolutely right. I was very happy with the work we did on it, too, and that transformation scene ranks up there alongside *An American Werewolf in London* as one of those really cool moments in effects history."

"And if I can toot my own horn for a moment, the one thing I was really proud of on *Nightmare 2* was the shot where Freddy's eye is in the back of the throat, because that was my idea. It wasn't in the script, but I thought it could add something to that whole idea of Freddy being inside someone. What's

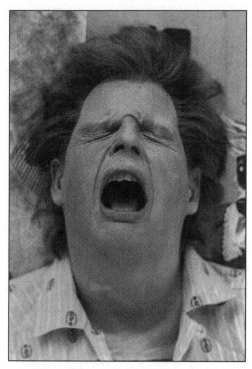

funny is that decades later I worked on *Insidious: Chapter 3*, and they did the very same gag on that, too—although theirs was done digitally and ours was 100% practical."

"Also, I couldn't believe that when we were prepping *Nightmare 2*, the producers came super close to not bringing Robert Englund back. They thought they could just get a stuntman because Freddy was wearing all this makeup, so why would they need an expensive actor for the role? Thankfully, they realized that Robert brought more to that role than just being a guy beneath the makeup, and they brought him back again and again."

A close-up on the Jesse head from *A Nightmare on Elm Street 2: Freddy's Revenge* (1985). Photo courtesy of Bart Mixon.

Seeing steady effects work coming his way in the mid-1980s, Bart decided it was time to make the leap towards becoming a full-time artist.

"It was 1986 when I basically quit my regular job in Houston. I had been working at an oil tool company as a technical illustrator where I would do their tech manuals. But when I got hired to come onto *The Texas Chainsaw Massacre 2*, which was being shot in Austin, I knew it was time to make the leap."

"I was just happy to be working on anything, but the fact that it was a sequel to the first *Texas Chain Saw* was very cool," Mixon continued. "Because my brother had already moved out to L.A., I had known a lot of the guys on the crew secondhand, like John Vulich, Mitch Devane, and Shawn McEnroe, who was an old Rick Baker guy. I was trying to get on the crew with Tom [Savini], and I was calling, but he was always very non-committal. John Vulich finally said to my brother, 'Tom is never going to hire Bart until he meets him face to face,' so I got in my car and drove to Austin to meet Tom. And John was right, because I started working a day or two later."

"It was great working with Tom. By the time I came on, they had already been prepping it for a couple of weeks, so everything had pretty much been assigned already. Mitch Devane was doing the Leatherface mask, Shawn McEnroe did Chop-Top, and John Vulich was doing Grandpa. There was a severed hand that I got to sculpt, but it never made it into the movie. We did it on an amputee and the guy had recently lost his hand. I remember when I was taking the mold off his stump, I asked him, 'Hey, are you sure you're going to be okay with this?' He said, 'Oh yeah, it's going to be great. I mean, it's *Chainsaw 2*, so this is going to be so cool!' So we thought everything was great."

"But then, on the day we had to shoot the effect, John Vulich was doing the makeup on him and as he applied blood to the stump, the guy freaked out and he just bolted. We never saw him again. And I was like, *Ah, great. There goes one thing I sculpted for the entire movie and now it's not even going to be in there.*"

"But I did do a lot of lab work on *Chainsaw* [*Massacre 2*] and ran a lot of foam latex, too. I remember one last-minute thing that came up was when Chop-Top was beating the guy at the radio station and Tobe [Hooper] wanted some hammer wounds on the guy's head. It was a spur-of-the-moment thing, so we didn't have anything prepped for it. I just had

Peter Weller being transformed on the set of *RoboCop* (1987).
Photo courtesy of Bart Mixon.

to do stuff out of the kit very quickly. Thankfully, Tobe was happy with that, so I was happy I was able to give him what he wanted right there on the spot. The thing I will always remember about that shoot was how Tobe told me that I looked just like Stephen King," Bart added, "which I took as a compliment (and hopefully he meant it that way)."

As it turns out, quitting his day job to pursue makeup was the right call for Mixon. Shortly after completing work on *The Texas Chainsaw Massacre Part 2* (1986), he was contacted to come on board what would become one of the most iconic sci-fi films of its era, Paul Verhoeven's *RoboCop* (1987).

"Shortly after *Chainsaw 2*, Rob Bottin called me to work on *RoboCop*, which was shooting in Dallas. We had met years prior through Rick Baker, and Rob knew that I lived in Texas. So when an opening came up last minute on *RoboCop*, he reached out to me. I remember that he called me up at midnight on a Saturday night, I flew up there on Sunday, and started working by Monday, so it all was a very quick process for me."

"With *RoboCop*, it had all been built in L.A. and shipped out to Dallas, so what we were working with was all this finished stuff, and all of it was so cool. The suit that Rob Bottin designed was brilliant, and he had already done *Legend* and *The Thing* [1982], so he was the biggest-name effects guy that I had worked for at that time. I remember on the first day, I was helping suit up Peter Weller, and the suit itself was a little tricky to put on. You had to do certain things in a certain order and it was a very different process for me. Peter didn't know what to make of me at first, but by the end of the week, I was the only guy that he wanted to suit him up. I also think it was because I was the only one with the upper body strength to get him in there properly, too."

"*RoboCop* was also the first time I had ever applied prosthetics on set. Stephan Dupuis was doing the right side of Peter's face and I was doing the left, and I remember on the first makeup test it was Stephan on one side, myself on the other, and then Rob's face was right between us the entire time. It looked like the opening of *The Three Stooges* or something, where you've got the three heads lined up. But there was a little bit of pressure with Rob watching me as closely as he did that day, and I would have to say that *RoboCop* was a really great learning experience for me. *RoboCop* also ended up being a career highlight for me, so when the film

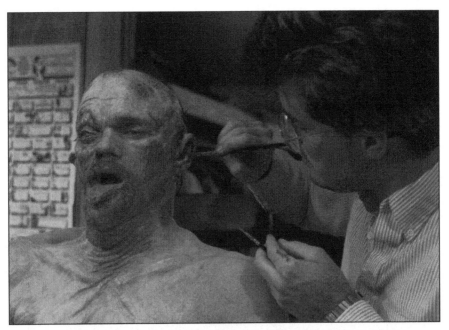

Bart applying makeup to Paul McCrane for his melting scene in *RoboCop* (1987).
Photo courtesy of Bart Mixon.

turned out as well as it did, it became a good calling card to use when I moved out to Los Angeles shortly after that."

In March 1987, Bart decided it was time to take his career to the next level, which meant he needed to get himself out to Hollywood to be in the mix of everything happening in the makeup industry. Having already established relationships with many of his peers (and legends in the business who were running their own shops back then), Mixon was able to find work rather quickly after transitioning to the West Coast.

"Within two weeks of moving out here, I was working during the day at Rick Baker's [studio] on *Gorillas in the Mist* as extra help in the mold shop," reflected Mixon. "I was just doing whatever menial stuff they needed done on that show. I thought it was great, as I didn't care what kind of work I was doing; I just wanted to keep working. At night, I was working at the Chiodos' [Stephen, Charles, and Edward's] shop, which was literally around the corner from Rick's shop. They were busy prepping for *Killer Klowns from Outer Space*, and I worked over there for a few days on an oversized hand gag they were using in the movie. I would come in at night and I sculpted up a couple of generic skin texture shapes, then I molded those and ran a lot of latex skin pieces that I applied to the hand so that it was ready for painting."

"At that time, my brother was still working over at Fantasy II Film Effects, which is Gene Warren Jr.'s company, and Gene knew that I was a makeup effects guy. They had been doing mostly opticals and miniatures, so he thought I could help them out by doing some practical effects. There was a show called *Dracula's Widow*, where I made a plaster head that we rigged with a chamber behind it to pump blood out of it on cue, that could then be matted onto the vampire's face. It was a quick job, but I enjoyed working with Gene. And because of him, that's how I ended up working on *Fright Night Part 2*."

"When *Fright Night Part 2* came along, Gene had put in a bid for the visual effects, and I think he went to the producers and asked to do the practical [makeup] effects as some kind of package deal. Initially, there were some debates about who was going to handle certain aspects of the effects, but the feeling was that because Greg Cannom had just done the *Werewolf* TV show, it made sense that he do the werewolf character that was in [*Fright Night Part 2*]. I'm not sure how Greg ended up with the bug guy [Brian Thompson's character, Bozworth], but I think he was something that came along later on. I ended up with the rest of the characters

Bart on the set of *Fright Night Part 2* (1988). From left to right: Mixon, Carol Rees as the "Regine Monster," Jim McLoughlin, and Aaron Sims. Photo courtesy of Bart Mixon.

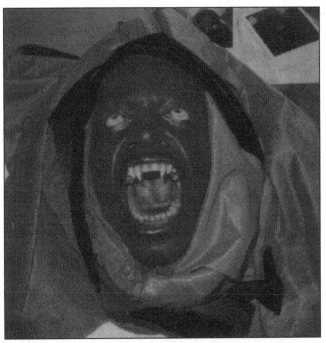

The "Belle's Head" sculpture from *Fright Night Part 2* (1988). Photo courtesy of Bart Mixon.

on *Fright Night 2*, which was mainly Julie Carmen's Regine character and her various incarnations, as well as the androgynous roller-skating vampire [Belle, played by Russell Clark] and Charley's friend Richie [played by Merritt Butrick], who becomes a vampire."

"*Fright Night 2* also ended up being the first show that I supervised on, too," Bart added. "I was still under Gene, but he wasn't applying the makeup or anything, so he mostly just let us do our thing. That was cer-

tainly a huge stepping-stone for me, and a lot of responsibility, too, especially since I knew our work was going to be on-screen next to Greg Cannom's. Those are some high standards to have to meet, and I feel like I assembled a great crew with Brian Wade, Norman Cabrera, Aaron Sims, Joey Orosco, and Matt Rose, who did a little bit, too. I'm sure I'm forgetting some other people, but our team created some amazing effects on *Fright Night 2* that were of a comparable caliber to the fine work that Greg did, so it's a show I'm still very proud of."

After *Fright Night Part 2* (1988), Mixon spent the next few years contributing to several other notable sequels, including *A Nightmare on Elm Street 4: The Dream Master* (1988), *Predator 2* (1990), and *Gremlins 2: The New Batch* (1990), which provided him with another opportunity to flex his creative muscles in an advisory position.

Regine's corpse from *Fright Night Part 2* (1988). Photo courtesy of Bart Mixon.

"Rick [Baker] brought me onto *Gremlins 2* as the shop foreman, and I think we had a crew of seventy-five people on that show. I did the initial script breakdown, which was very involved because of the amount of work we had to do on that show. Usually, Rick would just have one guy running things, but for *Gremlins 2*, he had three—one in the office, one in purchasing, and me on the floor in the shop."

"There were a lot of headaches on *Gremlins 2*, and I remember that I'd wake up sometimes at two or three o'clock in the morning, thinking, *Well, what are we doing today? Are we going to get this done? We can't forget about that, either.* I was constantly going back over our schedules. It was a lot to keep track of and sometimes I had to be the one to make the unpopular decisions, like moving from an eight-hour workday to a ten-hour day. We had the best people in town working on *Gremlins 2*, and I brought all my *Fright Night 2* people over that weren't already working for Rick themselves."

"When it came time to create the Gremlins themselves, we were all following Rick Baker's art direction. On the first *Gremlins*, it's all a standard design other than Stripe, so they all came from the same mold. One of the things that Rick wanted to do with this one—which, obviously made more work for us—was to create eight distinctively different Gremlin looks even before you got into the genetics lab, so we started having all those wild designs of Gremlins: the Vegetable Gremlin, the Bat Gremlin, and all those crazy creatures."

"Rick's inspiration came from a project he almost did back in the early '80s called *Night Skies*," Bart explained, "which was being produced by Steven Spielberg, and Ron Cobb was going to direct it. It was based on a famous UFO case in the 1950s, where some guy on a farm was supposedly terrorized by aliens for a weekend after a UFO landed nearby. John Sayles wrote it and Rick was building the aliens for it. While he was prepping it, Spielberg was off doing *Raiders* [*of the Lost Ark*], and he decided he didn't want to make an evil alien movie, so he came up with *E.T.* [*the Extra-Terrestrial*]. So, when he got back from *Raiders*, he said, 'We're not going to do this *Night Skies* thing anymore. We're going to do *E.T.* instead.' And Rick knew all those designs for *Night Skies* wouldn't work for *E.T.*, either. But then Rick got onto *American Werewolf* and had to quit working on *E.T.* because he didn't want to screw [over Director] John Landis."

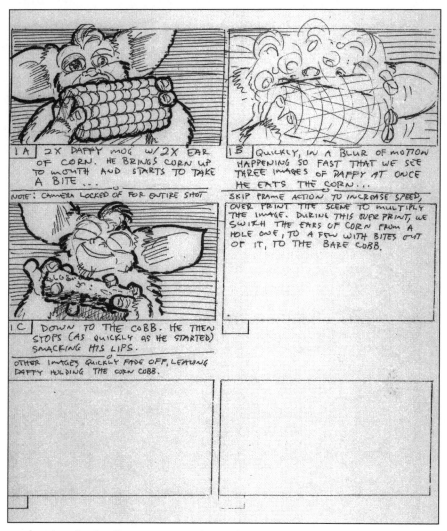

Storyboards of Daffy eating corn on the cob from *Gremlins 2: The New Batch* (1990).
Courtesy of Bart Mixon.

"The point of bringing that up is that he had one basic alien he had created for *Night Skies*, and then there were, like, six different designs, so when you would look at them, you knew, '*This is the smart one, that's the mean one, that's the stupid one,*' and that brought out their characteristics. So that's what Rick ended up doing with *Gremlins 2*, where you had your basic Gremlin look, but then you've got the George Gremlin, the Daffy Gremlin, the Mohawk Gremlin, and other than Lenny, they're all the same body. So I just thought it was interesting that Rick hung on to that idea for eight years. We probably ended up making four to six different puppets just of those initial characters, which was around fifty puppets right there. Once all the other Gremlins took over, *Gremlins 2* became a huge undertaking, where I would say we ended up making something like five hundred puppets on just that show alone."

Even though the final version of *Gremlins 2: The New Batch* (1990) boasted an unprecedented amount of practical effects, several ideas were scratched during production.

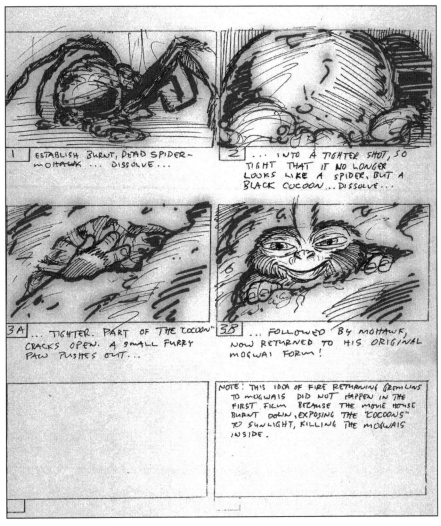

Bart's recovered Spider Gremlin storyboards for *Gremlins 2: The New Batch* (1990).
Courtesy of Bart Mixon.

"Because [Director Joe] Dante was so open to ideas, I remember he was always fielding our suggestions for gags we could do in the movie. I had storyboarded out a transformation sequence that I thought would be interesting story-wise, where there was a cocktail of something in the genetics lab that would turn a Gremlin back into a Mogwai. I did a shot-per-shot sequence based on the *American Werewolf* transformation, where a Gremlin is horrified that he's turning back into a Mogwai, with all the same angles and all the same cuts as [*American*] *Werewolf*."

"I remember Dante asked me, 'So, what would he drink that would make him change back, then?' I honestly had no idea. I guess that maybe I didn't pitch it enthusiastically enough, or maybe I should have based it on *The Howling* transformation, but he didn't go for the idea I presented. I thought it was a pretty good idea, though, even if it would have been an enormous amount of extra work."

"Recently, I found these storyboards that I had forgotten about involving the Spider Gremlin. We had played around with the idea of having this little tag at the end of the film, where the husk of the burned Spider Gremlin would burst open and his abdomen would split like an egg. It was going to be filled with little Mogwais that would spill out, almost like spider eggs. There was something discussed where it would be implied that fire would turn them back, but because they were in the movie theater that burned down in the first *Gremlins*, I don't know if it made much sense with the mythology. I don't remember if we ever even showed that to Dante or not."

After surviving eighteen months on *Gremlins 2: The New Batch* (1990), Mixon moved on to another project that was ambitious, albeit for very different reasons, as he was tasked with bringing to life the nightmarish world of Stephen King's best-selling novel *IT* (1986).

"When you're in this business, it's nice if you can get one character that truly becomes your calling card, and Pennywise became mine. Working on *IT* in that respect was very gratifying because it's something that has endured with fans to this day. Go to any horror convention, or any store that sells Halloween stuff, and Pennywise's face is everywhere."

"I was certainly aware going into *IT* that it was so popular, but I honestly wasn't a huge Stephen King fan myself. I didn't dislike his stuff, but I hadn't read a lot of his books up to that point. I had read *Pet Sematary* and one of his short story collections, but my twin brother, Bret, was a huge fan, and he helped get me familiar with the book. Then I decided to read

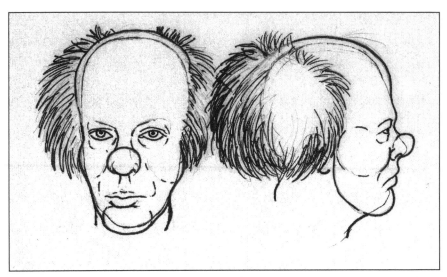

Original Pennywise sketch for *Stephen King's IT* (1990). Courtesy of Bart Mixon.

IT for myself, and between Stephen King's vision and what we were given in the script, I had to find the best way to represent the character of Pennywise. Story-wise, the clown is an illusion; it's not a real manifestation. So, to me, it made sense that it would look like a friendly clown, especially since he was trying to lure in little kids. I almost wanted him to look like a live-action cartoon, and at one point, we were going to do blue contact lenses that would almost look like an animation drawing."

"I was also thinking of giving him pure white teeth that would match the clown-white paint on him. I just wanted to see him pure white, because

Bart touches up Pennywise's makeup on the set of *Stephen King's IT* (1990). Photo courtesy of Bart Mixon.

a lot of clown makeup goes gray since you can often see the skin tone underneath it. The colors had to be real stark, and I wanted to use primary colors like the red and yellow against these clean lines. I just thought that would all be horrific to see as It brought about suffering on these innocent kids."

"My intention was to have two looks for Pennywise: the

Tim Curry poses as Pennywise on the shower set of *Stephen King's IT* (1990).
Photo courtesy of Bart Mixon.

clean version, because that makes sense when you're dealing with kids, and then a monstrous version that is there taunting them as adults, because they all know at that point that he's a monster. Originally, I had wanted to continue using the battery acid look, where half of his face is disfigured, but for different reasons, Director [Tommy Lee Wallace] didn't want to go that route."

One of the more interesting "what if?" scenarios on *Stephen King's IT* (1990) concerned the miniseries' casting of its now-iconic villain. Looking back, Mixon reflected on how it was down to three brilliant actors for the role, and how much he enjoyed collaborating with Tim Curry, who would end up playing Pennywise.

"Originally, Tim Curry, Roddy McDowall, and Malcolm McDowell were the three names that were mentioned to me when I first came on. It was going to be a three-part, six-hour miniseries, too, which I don't think a lot people know, either. Any one of them would have been a very cool Pennywise, but Tim really made this character his own. Just coming up with the Pennywise makeup was certainly a collaborative effort between Tim, me, and Tommy. They both would give me their feedback on my drawings or sculptures, and I would fix anything they didn't feel was right."

"Tim was so great to work with, too. What I liked about him was that you could do a clown makeup on him and he could look like a nice, friendly clown, and then with just his eyes or a twitching of his mouth, he suddenly looked evil. It was so subtle. I do remember that there was some controversy surrounding the battery acid look of Pennywise, though. It was decided at that point in the script that he would get that disfigured makeup, but when we shot the movie, we ran out of time up in Vancouver and we never got to the battery acid look. They just kind of shot around the kid spraying Pennywise, and then Pennywise jumping in the drain. They never did Pennywise's reaction shot, so I figured they would just be picking that up on inserts later on."

"But we had to make a miniature of Pennywise for the shot of him going down the drain. It's an eighteen-inch stop-motion puppet, and up until the time that I molded it, they weren't going to use the disfigured look for whatever reason. So I said, 'Well, all right. Sculpt it with the normal face.' And literally the day that I molded that half of the puppet—the front half—they came and said, 'All right, we decided Tim's going to wear

Bart touches up Pennywise's disfigured face during production on *Stephen King's IT* (1990). Photo courtesy of Bart Mixon.

the disfigured makeup, so now we're going to shoot that sequence.' What that meant was that I then had to make a little miniature prosthetic to put on the stop-motion puppet to change its appearance to look like the disfigured one. I'm so grateful they finally changed their minds and that Tim was willing to wear that piece, because that sequence would have played out very differently had Pennywise just had a normal face."

"Also, the sequence where they hit Pennywise in the head with the silver and it punches a hole in his head where the deadlights shine out originally played out differently in the script," added Mixon. "It was supposed to be spider hairs sticking out of his head, and to me it just seemed too literal because the spider isn't what he really looks like, either. It's the deadlights that are the true representation of what this character is. So at least Tommy agreed with that and they ended up rewriting the script. Dynamically, I thought it would be more interesting to present it that way, and I think that scene turned out great."

Right around the time that he was wrapping up on *Stephen King's IT* (1990), Mixon also did some work on James Cameron's *Terminator 2: Judgment Day* (1991) making models and a stop-motion puppet of Arnold Schwarzenegger. While the writing on the wall regarding the need for computer-generated imagery (CGI) in modern filmmaking was becoming slightly apparent on that project, he explained how it was *Jurassic Park* (1993) a few years later that sent many of his peers into a frenzy.

"There was this feeling once *Jurassic Park* came out that it was all over for special effects. Everyone went into this doom and gloom mode, but I realized that there were just certain things you were never going to be able to afford to do with a computer, so I wasn't panicking myself. Besides, look at all the big special effects shows that still came out during that time: *Men in Black*, *The Grinch*, *Planet of the Apes*, *Hellboy*, or even more recently, you have movies like *Oz the Great and Powerful* or *Guardians of the Galaxy*, where almost every character is under some type of makeup. Things may have slowed down, but makeup effects weren't going anywhere, at least in my mind."

Mixon was right. Throughout the 1990s, he continued to stay busy working on a number of films, including *Ernest Scared Stupid* (1991), *Return of the Living Dead 3* (1993), *Necronomicon: Book of the Dead* (1993), *Ed Wood* (1994), *Fargo* (1996), *Men in Black* (1997), and *How The Grinch*

Bart adds some goo to Dr. Madden (played by David Warner) on the set of *Necronomicon: Book of the Dead* (1993). Photo courtesy of Bart Mixon.

Stole Christmas (2000). In 2000, Bart reconnected professionally with Rick Baker when the effects legend hired him as a Project Supervisor on Tim Burton's remake of *Planet of the Apes* (1968).

"I think every single person on our crew was influenced by the original *Planet of the Apes*," Bart said. "There's no denying the historical significance of the original film, so it was cool from that respect to be involved. Plus, with Tim Burton directing, that aspect of it had its own potential, too. What made this something of a dream project to me was just Rick Baker himself. Nobody does apes like Rick, and him being the guy to create these apes made it all that much cooler. One thing I do admire and appreciate in the new [*Planet of the*] *Apes* was that previously, whenever someone would do an ape or a monkey type of character, they would do it just like [makeup artist] John Chambers did in *Planet of the Apes* [1968]. Nobody was really looking at it and trying to rethink it or improve it in any way. It was just an industry standard."

"But Rick was like, 'No, we can definitely do something to improve upon that look,' and he came up with the idea of using dentures where the teeth were to push the lips so far forward that the actors were able to manipulate the lips in ways that they couldn't do in the original *Planet of the Apes*. It was an innovative way to take that classic makeup to another level. I can remember doing a press event for *Planet of the Apes* over a weekend, and everyone kept remarking that the makeup looked so great because of all the advancements in the technology that had occurred since the original *Planet of the Apes*. I had to point out that our approach was all foam latex, hair, and dentures—stuff that has been around since *The Wizard of Oz*—so it wasn't anything with technology. It was all due to Rick Baker's art direction."

"The makeups were originally designed to have contact lenses to complement the look, so we could get bigger, more ape-like eyes because their irises are larger than a man's. But production didn't want to spend the extra money to have a couple of lens technicians on set to handle all the contact lenses, so that was a design element that got dropped early on. I know there are a couple of test makeup photos floating around that *Make-Up Artist Magazine* had in one of their issues featuring the makeup with the contact lenses, and they really just take it that much further."

"Something else that elevated the work we did on *Planet of the Apes* was the fact that we had a great group of actors behind the makeup who put in the extra effort with their performances to make it all look so be-

Bart touches up Michael Chiklis as The Thing on the set of *Fantastic Four: Rise of the Silver Surfer* (2007). Photo courtesy of Bart Mixon.

lievable. I remember Paul Giamatti was watching the Roddy McDowall interviews for the original [film] to help with his performance, and that extra effort shows. There were some guys on *Apes* that really embraced their look, and it shows when you go back and watch it now."

"The same thing happened when I did Michael Chiklis as The Thing on *Fantastic Four* [2005]. On the first day we put him in the prosthetics, he sat there in front of the mirror for a half hour and just explored what it took to make the face do what he was imagining it was doing. He saw that he had to exaggerate certain things, and it's always great when you have an actor that really embraces the makeup like that. It doesn't always happen."

While Mixon spent several more years collaborating on other Baker-led makeup movies, he was also forging a creative relationship with the likes of Rob Zombie and fellow effects artist Wayne Toth, who hired Bart to come on board the musician's directorial debut, *House of 1000 Corpses* (2003), and would also bring him back for several of the rocker-turned-director's subsequent cinematic projects over the next fifteen years.

"I thought *Corpses* was fun just because Rob was trying to do something different at the time, and he's always trying to do that with all his movies. You can debate whether or not it's successful, but at least he's trying.

I like that with every film, he firmly puts his own unique stamp on it. I've had a great experience on all of them with him, and with Wayne Toth, too. Wayne had created a lot of the stuff for Rob's stage shows, and for *Corpses*, he brought me in to help apply the burn makeup to Tiny, who was played by Matthew McGrory. I was only on most of the days that he worked, so it was low pressure. There was a lot of pressure on Rob on that one because it was his first film, so I didn't really bother him much on *Corpses*."

"But by the time they did *Halloween II* (2009), which was his fourth film, he was more comfortable as a director and I was there for the whole show, working with Wayne. I was in the inner circle by that one. I was in our makeup trailer that Zombie would come hang out in when he couldn't stand all the crap, so he would just come in and sit down and hang. I got to know him and his wife [Sheri Moon Zombie], and what's funny is that after the *Paul Blart* movie came out, they both would call me 'Blart' instead of 'Bart.' The cool thing about Rob is that he's a fan and he's always open to everything. There aren't a lot of directors who are as open as he is."

"We were talking one day when we were working on *31*, looking at all his tattoos, and on one of his wrists he's got a tattoo of the Jack Kirby version of The Thing from *The Fantastic Four*. That meant a little bit more to me because Kirby's my favorite comic book artist and Kirby did my favorite run on *Fantastic Four*, so that was an extra level of cool to me."

"And Wayne and I have been friends for a while. He's one of a handful of guys that whenever they call, if I'm available, I'm there. It's always fun to work with either of those guys, and I've enjoyed our working relationship over the years."

Shortly after being a part of Zombie's *House of 1000 Corpses* (2003), Bart got the opportunity to work with another passionate filmmaker making his mark on the landscape of horror and sci-fi cinema: Guillermo del Toro. While working for Rick Baker on *How The Grinch Stole Christmas* (2000), Mixon was brought into the creative mix as del Toro was beginning to gear up for his adaptation of Mike Mignola's cult comic book series, *Hellboy*.

"We had our first meeting at Rick's back in 1999 when I was doing *The Grinch*, and that was about four years before we got around to actually doing it [*Hellboy*]. Coincidentally, when Matt Rose did his first clay sketch of Hellboy, he just went into Rick's archive and pulled out a Ron Perlman bust because he thought, *'Oh, this guy has got a good face.'* So he

Ron with actor Ron Perlman on the set of *Hellboy* (2004). Photo courtesy of Bart Mixon.

picked Ron completely independently and without any direction from Guillermo. As it turns out, Guillermo and Mike Mignola were talking about who they would want for the character and they both, at the same time, said, 'Ron Perlman.' So I always thought it was interesting that they all came up with Ron on their own."

"The main reason the *Hellboy* films are so great is because you have Guillermo at the helm. He's a real fan of the source material, and he's also a fan of makeup effects, because that's the world he used to work in. He's a guy who knows when to be practical and when to be digital, and both *Hellboy* movies were good examples of how to properly marry the two techniques."

"*Hellboy* was a passion project for everyone involved, too. Rick was doing *The Haunted Mansion* [2003] at the time, and he just took *Hellboy* because Matt and Chad [Waters] were so passionate about it. In fact, I quit *The Cat in the Hat* [2003] to work on *Hellboy* because I was a *Hellboy* fan. I remember I was prepping *The Cat in the Hat* over at Steve Johnson's, and people on the crew were jumping ship to go work on *Hellboy* because they were so excited. The great thing with the *Hellboy* films was that Guillermo was the only guy that you had to make happy. He had the final word on everything. Other shows, you usually have to run the stuff up the ladder, but with this, it all began and ended with him."

"On the first *Hellboy*, I got to do Ron's makeup for a couple of days, but I was mainly doing the photo double, who was wearing the same prosthetics. On the second film [*Hellboy II: The Golden Army*], I started co-applying Hellboy's makeup with Mike Elizalde. Early on, the guy that was doing Luke Goss' makeup quit kind of unexpectedly, so they were scrambling around trying to find somebody who could take over Luke, and so I volunteered for that. That schedule was twenty-seven days long, and I ended up doing him, like, fifty-three times. It was pretty crazy."

"I also remember going by Spectral [Motion] when they were sculpting all this stuff for Luke's character [Prince Nuada], and I saw how thin the appliances were, so I was like, 'Man, am I glad I'm on the Hellboy team.' Then, a few months later, here I am working on Luke. Should have kept my big mouth shut, right? But Luke was just cool and we got along great on *Hellboy II*."

Throughout a career that now spans over four decades, Bart Mixon has been a part of over one hundred film projects, has two dozen televi-

Guillermo del Toro looks on as Bart touches up Luke Goss on *Hellboy II: The Golden Army* (2008). Photo courtesy of Bart Mixon.

sion credits to his name, and he's not slowing down just yet. When asked about the secret to enjoying longevity in such a demanding profession, Mixon credits his willingness to always lend a hand as a big factor in why he's stayed so busy over the years.

"I don't want to say, 'Oh, I'm a great guy and people love me,' but there are a lot of very talented people that burned their bridges for whatever reason over the years. So a lot of it comes down to not being a jerk and just being the guy who always wants to help. You have to be a team player in this industry. There's no way around it. I'm sure there are a number of factors behind my career, but all I really know is that I've been very fortunate. I'm grateful I got to work with guys like Rick [Baker] and Steve Johnson, and I'm thankful that people continued to hire me and still hire me today."

"When I was a kid, all of this seemed like a million miles away because I was out there in Texas. When I was first even thinking about doing effects, it was like, *Ah, what are my chances?* But then some smaller projects came my way, which led to some very high-profile, memorable projects, and then suddenly I'm getting to work on films like *RoboCop* or *IT* or

Bart attends to Kelsey Grammer as Beast between takes on the set of *X-Men: The Last Stand* (2006). Photo courtesy of Bart Mixon.

Bart transforms his son into Frankenstein's monster for his fifth birthday.
Photo courtesy of Bart Mixon.

Gremlins 2. I've gotten the opportunity to apply a Rick Baker makeup for the main villain in *MIB³* [*Men in Black 3*]. There's a part of me that thinks about that and it still makes me giddy. The fan in me is still excited about the work and getting to be a part of all these incredible movies. I grew up loving all this stuff, and now, to be able to do something like create The Thing for *Fantastic Four* [2005], or work on *Planet of the Apes* [2001], or even create Vision for *Captain America: Civil War*—how cool is that?

"I don't know if there's a real secret or anything, but I'm very thankful for all I've done," Mixon enthused. "I'm happy that I can just hang on in this world for a little longer. It's been a great ride."

10 John Goodwin

WITH OVER FORTY YEARS in the film industry, makeup artist John Goodwin has experienced many milestones throughout his career: being mentored by his heroes, major studios closing up shop, the ushering in of digital effects, and more. He's worked on several landmark films in the world of special effects, including *The Thing* (1982), *Legend* (1985), *Spaceballs* (1987), and *Men in Black* (1997). He's handled makeup on over 150 episodes of *CSI: Crime Scene Investigation* (2000), and its spinoff, *CSI: NY* (2004), and has even pursued his love of acting in projects like *Tremors* (1990) and *Heart and Souls* (1993). For Goodwin, the spark that ignited his love of monsters and makeup started at the cinema in his hometown of St. Louis.

John Goodwin (on the left) with actor Ernest Borgnine. Photo courtesy of John Goodwin.

"My love goes way back," Goodwin said. "It all started with movies— I loved the movies. I was a pretty shy kid, so they became my escape. Movies first got me interested in dinosaurs in kindergarten, and monsters were a big thing then, too, especially the Universal Monster movies. Those would be on television a lot, and I remember thinking that even though The Wolf Man scared me, the monsters were actually pretty neat."

John dressed as Boris Karloff's character from *The Raven* (1963). Photo courtesy of John Goodwin.

"When I got to high school, Hammer films were still playing, where you were seeing blood on the screen and horror movies in color—the whole thing. Those Hammer horror pictures never played an indoor theater by me. They were usually at the drive-ins, so I started going to the drive-ins when I went to college in Indianapolis just so I could see them. I remember seeing *Horror of Dracula* and *Curse of Frankenstein* on a double bill, first run. And you had Vincent Price and Boris Karloff still making films back then, too; I don't think I missed a single movie of theirs, either."

"Because I was so taken with the movies, I initially thought I wanted to be an actor, but I was already playing around in monster stuff by then, so I was very taken with the world of makeup effects. I had discovered *Monster World* and then *Famous Monsters of Filmland*, and Forrest J. Ackerman created both. I can't overemphasize the importance of both publications, because it made you realize, *Hey, I'm not the only one*. They felt like vindication."

"That's how I discovered Dick Smith's workbook [the *Do-It-Yourself Monster Make-Up Handbook*], because it was being advertised in *Famous Monsters*, and I bought that immediately. I still have it, in fact; it's so dogeared now that you can hardly read it. It opened up a whole new world for me. I did every makeup in that thing, and there are still techniques in there that you can go back to today and go, 'Hey, that might work for something.' Dick was not only a very practical artist, but he was a wonderful artist, too. His techniques worked well."

As he entered his college years, the world of movies was still very much on Goodwin's mind.

"I became a film major at USC [University of Southern California] after I transferred there from Indianapolis. When I got out here, I knew

I wanted to do something in movies. I discovered that Bill Tuttle taught a course on Saturday mornings, where he would come in and teach what actually was on the makeup union exam, but I didn't know that at the time. He wouldn't do prosthetics until you had learned everything else first."

"Over time, I became his teacher's assistant. I would set up for him and then he'd do his class. One day, Bill said to me, 'You know, John, you can make a living doing this.' I wasn't a member of the union, so I didn't even understand what he was talking about in those days. But one day, he called me up and said, 'Listen, they need a makeup artist up at Universal [Studios] for the tours. All you do is pick somebody out of the audience and make them up.' So I made the call and was hired. And later, when I did get my days in, I was very grateful because Bill had taught me everything I needed to know to pass the union exam."

"When I started up on the tours, Universal sold a makeup line called Cinematique, which wasn't bad makeup—it was just more glamour stuff than anything. I'd pick a lady out of the audience and we had nine minutes to do an entire makeup with artificial lashes. I really hated it, but I figured it was still a good experience because I was out in front of people and I was getting to work at Universal, so I appreciated the opportunity."

"Then, they brought in this guy named Verne Langdon to put together a monster show because everybody had been asking for it, so Universal finally did it. They called it *The Land of a Thousand Faces*. They would pick two people out of the audience, usually a couple, and make them into Frankenstein and the Bride of Frankenstein. They didn't see each other until we turned their chairs. It was a lot of fun. I did that for a couple years, but then I could see they were going to close that because they were putting in another show. So I went down to the lower lot to see if I could get a job."

While working at Universal, Goodwin realized that as much as the performer inside him relished being in front of audiences, he was growing even more passionate about the world of makeup effects, and eventually, the time came to pursue a full-time vocation in the industry.

"Nick Marcellino was head of the makeup department at Universal, as he had taken over after Bud Westmore died. I had done a favor for him on one occasion when they needed an extra non-union makeup artist, so he remembered me right away when I came down to speak with him. I ended up getting my days in for the union at Universal because of Nick.

He was a wonderful guy; he actually kept that department open for years after Universal probably wanted to close it. He was a very good makeup artist and a very good executive, too. I loved working with Nick."

"One of the first things I worked on was a TV movie called *The Munsters' Revenge*, where they were bringing back the Munsters. Sid Caesar was in it, too. There was a scene where they're in the wax museum and all the great monsters were supposed to be in there. They wrote in the Gill-man from *Creature from the Black Lagoon* for the scene, but then we were told they decided to cut him because production thought we didn't have time to make it. So Kenny Diaz and I decided, after we finished the day's work getting the other stuff ready in the lab, that we would clock out and come back up to do him ourselves."

"So, we took the *Creature from the Black Lagoon* mold that was still at Universal and we started doing a latex creature out of that. Well, Nick comes around, turning out all the lights and he sees us there. He initially thinks this is all on payroll and I could see the panic on his face. I quickly assured him that we clocked out, and we just wanted to finish the creature because you gotta have Gill-man in there. And all he said was, 'Oh,' and then he disappeared."

"But when Nick came back, his tie was off and he had beer and pizza for us, too. He sat down and started talking to us, and it was just magic. He told us about making up Orson Welles on *Touch of Evil* and stuff like that. I will never forget that night."

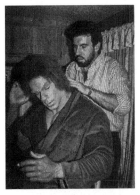

John working on actor Lou Ferrigno for NBC's *The Incredible Hulk Returns* (1988) TV movie. Photo courtesy of John Goodwin.

After being a part of the Universal family, John had the opportunity to work for another legend in the makeup industry, Bob Schiffer, when he transitioned over to Disney's studio to lend his talents to their makeup effects department.

"I just loved working with Bob. He was a rogue, there's no question, but he was a loveable rogue. After the end of the day, I'd get him talking because I loved hearing the history behind movies. He was, among other things, best friends with Burt Lancaster, and he did Rita Hayworth's makeup, too. He was a great raconteur."

"A great thing about the way Bob ran the department was that he was a great buffer to all of us. If a star or a producer didn't get along with a particular makeup person, he would put you somewhere else, or put you with somebody else entirely. There was kind of an in-between place where the head of the department took care of all the grievances. Schiffer was a great buffer zone for all of us, even Stan Winston, who was the last one to come through the apprenticeship program. Bob would always help out when things weren't right, and he actually did a lot of work on a lot of those shows—especially *Something Wicked This Way Comes* [1983]—where other people were getting all the credit. Bob was a great boss and worked very hard on everything that came through our department."

As John continued to earn his days to take the makeup union examination, he was called in to work on a highly ambitious project for Universal: John Carpenter's *The Thing* (1982), with makeup effects spearheaded by the now-legendary Rob Bottin. Not only would the remake of *The Thing from Another World* (1951) become one of the most audacious practical effects films of its time, but it also helped Goodwin finally make his way into the makeup union, which wasn't an easy achievement.

"There will never be another movie like *The Thing*," said Goodwin. "What's so interesting about how they made it, is that they shot the entire film up in British Columbia without the effects, which were all done at the Hartland Studios in North Hollywood. We worked on it for almost sixteen months, and both John Carpenter and Rob were really just on the same wavelength throughout the entire process. Rob could pitch an idea and they had the budget on that film to come back and incorporate it. Having that kind of creative freedom is rare, especially these days. I would say that 50 to 60% of the things we shot never made it into the final movie, but Rob was always given the freedom to try new things. It's a remarkable movie."

"Going into *The Thing*, Rob wanted it to be more like John Campbell's original story, *Who Goes There?*, which was what Howard Hawks had wanted to do on *The Thing from Another World*, but the Hays office gave him grief over it. I guess they even had this monster designed by Harper Goff, who was the designer that did *20,000 Leagues Under the Sea* [1954], and the office just said, 'No way.' Howard got mad about it and then got so tired of trying to get those designs through the office, so he finally said, 'Just make it look like Frankenstein and we'll shoot it in shadow.' Lee Greenway did a wonderful job with what he had to work with on that movie, but the makeup really does look like Frankenstein['s monster]. Had they been able to do what Howard originally envisioned, *The Thing from Another World* would have been ahead of its time."

"Rob and John both thought that because Howard couldn't do it in the '50s, they could do it in the '80s. We spent a lot of time making stuff and trying things out where we'd shoot tests, and they'd never allow that kind of time today. All the effects sequences were really planned out filmically, too. For example, there must have been twenty-five to thirty setups alone in just the scene where [Vance] Norris' chest bursts open. Rob did something that I had never, ever seen anybody do, which came from his love of cartoons. Rob was taking animation techniques and lending them to the world of practical effects. It was brilliant."

"I also owe a lot to Rob," Goodwin added, "because he got me the rest of my days that I needed on *The Thing* in order to take the union exam. I will always appreciate that. What some people might not know about the union was that back then, it wasn't very friendly to makeup effects artists. Howard Smith initially tried to push Rick Baker out, and he's probably the most famous makeup artist in the world now. There were three of us at that time who were ready to take the exam, but they didn't want to give it to us. So it was Nick Marcellino that called up and made the union give us the exam. I owe him and Rob a lot for that."

Before reteaming with Bottin for Ridley Scott's *Legend* (1985), John found an unusual opportunity to utilize his makeup skills—as well as his love for performing—in a completely new environment when he joined The Groundlings comedy troupe in Los Angeles during the early '80s.

"I got into The Groundlings around the same time when Phil Hartman and Pee-wee Herman [Paul Reubens] were in there. I did that for about three or four years, and I was the guy always sticking stuff on my face. I even did Princeton Vice, who was the Vincent Price character, and that was a lot of fun. It gave me

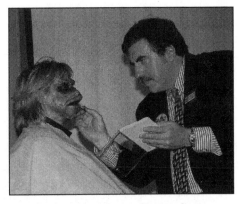

John does a makeup application during a tutorial session. Photo courtesy of John Goodwin.

a better appreciation for what actors go through, which is a big part of the job, and it absolutely helped me in the future as I worked on more makeup jobs."

"During that time, I went onto *Legend*, which was another interesting project. I knew we were kind of doing brilliant stuff for something that was eventually going to sink at the box office. First of all, it was supposed to be made at [20th Century] Fox here in the States, which would have helped all of our stuff, but we ended up having to send it over to England, where they wound up shooting the show. The artists there were wonderful artists, but something was always getting lost in translation, so that was tough."

"Another problem on *Legend* was that people who were high up in the studio echelon started re-cutting the film and tried to make it into all these different things it wasn't, and they should have let Ridley just make his own movie. The pig characters were major characters originally. They had a lot of Laurel and Hardy-type material that was really funny, and we made more pig masks than we made of anything else because they shot them almost every day for months. But none of that's in the film."

"Rob came in one day and told me they got Jerry Goldsmith to do the music, which I thought was great because his work elevates the movies he's contributed to quite a bit. But then, some time later, Rob comes in and tells me, 'Oh, they fired Jerry. They're gonna have Tangerine Dream do the score now.' They're wonderful musicians, but their style didn't really fit this film in particular—at least to me. I still think it would be interesting to hear the Jerry Goldsmith score if they ever do decide to release it."

"But *Legend* was the studio system at its worst," John continued, "because you were dealing with people that were not real producers, but had a lot of say-so. They'd go and see what the latest hit was at the box office, and then they would come back and try and make whatever movie they were making into the same thing. It just doesn't work. A lot of what happened on *Legend* was similar to what happened just a few years ago to Tom [Woodruff, Jr.] and Alec [Gillis] at Amalgamated Dynamics on the [2011 prequel] to *The Thing*. To see your hard work replaced with digital effects without ever being told—that's heartbreaking."

After Goodwin finished working on *Legend* (1985), Ken Diaz brought him on board Mel Brooks' *Spaceballs* (1987), the now-beloved spoof of the original *Star Wars* (1977) trilogy featuring numerous practi-

An all-body makeup application created by Goodwin. Photo courtesy of John Goodwin.

cal effects and performances by the likes of Rick Moranis, Bill Pullman, John Candy, Daphne Zuniga, and Joan Rivers as the voice of the film's robot character, Dot Matrix. Because they were working in some "familiar" territory when it came to the movie's various tributes and homages, Goodwin saw things change quite a bit on *Spaceballs* (1987) from the original script to the finalized film.

"For *Spaceballs*, I have to admit that I thought the original script was a lot funnier than the movie. It should have been more of a generic satire of science fiction, but Mel made it so specific to the *Star Wars* universe, and those films had already been out for some time, so it felt like it came along a little too late. The script had some fantastic gags in it that we never see. Here's an example: there was a scene—and they shot it—where you have these guys in a hovercraft, and then suddenly everything gets really bumpy and one guy says, 'Wait a minute, we gotta stop. We got a flat tire.' Obviously, you can't have a flat tire on a hovercraft, but he gets out and the scenery underneath the hovercraft is just painted-on metal, so he lifts up the metal and you see the tires underneath it. That was a great visual gag that got lost along the way."

"Also, in the script, there's the final scene on the ship when somebody says, 'It's like a circus in here,' and everything becomes circus-y stuff. It was originally supposed to be all aliens, but Mel was afraid of being sued, so they changed it. And we had made a lot of stuff for that scene—somebody had big Spock ears, and we did a lot of other looks that were tributes to other great sci-fi movies, like what KNB EFX [Group] did for the *Looney Tunes* movie [*Looney Tunes: Back in Action* (2003)]. All of those general science fiction nods in the film got talked away at some point."

"But I'm so thankful to Kenny for bringing me onto *Spaceballs*, because we all had a great time working on it together, regardless of whatever changes were being made," Goodwin said. "I already knew John Candy, as I had wound up doing a life mask of him in his pool house for a stuntman in *Armed and Dangerous*, and he and I got along famously. He was a very funny man, and I remember the day I was doing the life mask was right after he'd just moved into this house that had been owned by a composer. All the doorbells would play music instead of a normal doorbell ring, and as I'm starting to do the alginate to make his head, this music starts going off and he's panicking, saying, 'I don't even know which one that is!' It was hysterical."

"It was fun to see him on *Spaceballs* playing the Chewbacca character [Barf]. Initially, we sculpted a lot of different slight satires of the Chewbacca look—Kenny had done some, I had done a few, and Screaming Mad George, who was also sculpting on *Spaceballs*, had made some, too. But it became apparent to Ken and I that they were going to go in a different direction because Ben Nye, our department head, wasn't an appliances guy. He wasn't very into prosthetics, so it eventually trickled down that they wanted to see as much of John's face as possible in the design."

"The other big problem was that it was going to take too long to make him up every day. Originally, they had this dog makeup, where they were laying the little individual hairs on him for about three and a half to four hours, and none of that was even going to read on camera. It was all a process. But Rick Lazzarini made those wonderful ears for John, and I still think those ears are the best things in the movie. They had a personality to them all their own."

"I also remember when we did the headpiece for Yogurt [played by Mel Brooks]. We had just pulled the foam latex head out of the mold, and Mel ran in and grabbed it while it was still hot. He put it on anyway. It wasn't even painted at that point, but he was so excited that he had to run up and show everybody in the office."

"My most memorable day on the set of *Spaceballs* was when we heard all this noise outside in the alley. Mel stopped shooting so we could run out and see what was going on. We got out there and they were taking down the MGM sign. *Spaceballs* was the last film released as an MGM picture, so them removing the sign, which in itself was a Hollywood landmark, was very sad. As we watched the sign come down, Mel stood there and very seriously said to us, 'I just don't know why they have to do that,' and we all just went back to work. We knew that day was the end of an era."

Throughout his career, Goodwin was fortunate to work with one of the unsung heroes in special effects, Mike McCracken, who brought John in on a variety of projects, including *Heartbeeps* (1981), *Poltergeist* (1982), *Fright Night* (1985), and *Communion* (1989), Philippe Mora's adaptation of Whitley Strieber's controversial alien abduction novel.

"Craig Reardon was in charge [of special effects makeup] on *Pol-tergeist*, and he had hired Mike

The Phantom of the Opera (1925) tribute makeup designed by John. Photo courtesy of John Goodwin.

McCracken, who had studied directly with Dick Smith. I worked with Mike on a lot of things, and I learned a lot from him. He was the artist behind the artists, similar to when in the earlier days, before I was around, there was a sculptor by the name of Chris Mueller, and he sculpted everything, including The Creature [in the *Creature from the Black Lagoon* (1954)], and he worked on *20,000 Leagues Under the Sea* [1954]."

"*Communion* was an interesting show because Mike was able to take things that were not really sculptable entities and really make them look nice, and he was always talking about Whitley Strieber. He liked the guy a lot, and they really hit it off. Mike was the one that actually sold Whitley on the idea of seeing this alien visage, but also something else behind it. There are some shots in the film where it's implied, and Mike sculpted this inner part so it looked like something that had just taken shape. That really helped the film, but I will admit I've actually never seen the full film."

"Looking back now, perhaps if I had worked more with Rob [Bottin] or Rick [Baker] over the years, I might have worked on some bigger shows. But I got to work with Mike [McCracken], and he's such a pure artist that I feel grateful I was able to work with him and learn the fine art side of effects, especially at that time in my career."

Following *Communion* (1989), John got the opportunity to flex his acting muscles for the comedic creature feature *Tremors* (1990). Although he was initially supposed to play a more prominent role, a last-minute decision by Universal Pictures forced fate's hand on the project.

"For a while, I really began pushing my acting career, and I even auditioned for Robert Aldrich once, who was very nice to me, but told me I was too mature for my age. *Tremors* was written by my friends, Steve [S.S. Wilson] and Brent [Maddock], who I knew from film school, and Ron Underwood was going to direct it. I was supposed to play Burt Gummer, the role that Michael Gross plays, and Steve even told me that he wrote the part specifically for me because Burt's a gun nut, but he has to be a nice guy, and they thought my personality fit the more heroic aspects of Burt's character."

"I went in and read for [Executive Producer] Gale Anne Hurd, and I knew the part inside out. But three days before they began filming, they called me up to say that Michael had really wanted to take on the role, and Universal agreed. It was unfortunate, because that's the kind of role you get noticed with, but they did still give me a small role as one of the workers on the road. I really give my humble thanks to Brent, Steve, and Ron, because I know they hung in there as much as they could for me."

"They actually cut another scene I was in on *Tremors*, and that happened to me on another film I worked on with Ron, *Mighty Joe Young*. In that one, I was playing a professor who sees Joe run across the highway. They ended up scrapping that scene for the helicopter chase, so Ron always joked about having me in his movies, but then cutting me out."

While John continued working on feature films for many years, he found great success in the world of television when he joined *CSI: Crime Scene Investigation* (2000)—and later *CSI: NY* (2004)—to bring the series' groundbreaking, re-

A mummified victim from *CSI: NY* (2004).
Photo courtesy of John Goodwin.

alistic practical effects to life. His exemplary efforts on both series wouldn't go unnoticed, either, as Goodwin earned six Emmy Award nominations and one win for his seven years of work on the shows.

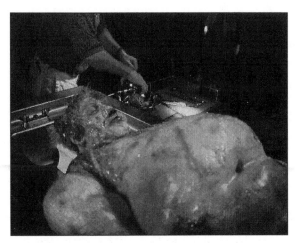

A bloated victim designed by Goodwin for *CSI: NY* (2004). Photo courtesy of John Goodwin.

"I took on *CSI* right as it was beginning," reflected Goodwin. "I had done television series before, but for years I was mainly working on theatrical projects. So, here I was back in the world of television. That was a turning point for my career, too, because Anthony [E.] Zuicker sold this whole thing to the press that this was a show where you were going to see everything. There were no 'talking heads' segments with people discussing different aspects of a crime. He was going to show audiences everything. In the first year, I made everything they needed for the show, but a lot of times it never made it into the episodes. CBS censors were a big part of that."

"By the second season, we had an episode where there was a body on an autopsy table whose head had been crushed in, and that director did a moving shot around the entire table, following the coroner, and you couldn't cut into the shot at all. It played out and nobody said anything, so the cat was out of the bag. I was now doing work on a television series that I would have been grossed out doing for a movie. Now they show everything on TV."

"I was part of that world for seven years, between *CSI* and *CSI: NY*, and when you're someone who does something creative for a living, if

Makeup designed by John Goodwin for Tyler, The Creator. Photo courtesy of John Goodwin.

you do the same thing for long enough, you begin to be known only for doing that thing in particular. I loved the work I did on those shows, but it was time to do something new."

John continues to work in the makeup effects industry to this day, spending time teaching new generations of artists the essential skills they need to make it as technicians. Despite more than four decades in the business, Goodwin is still a big monster kid at heart (who also has a penchant for trains) and has come to recognize that while a lot of things have changed throughout his career, there are some constants

John poses with his handiwork behind the scenes on *CSI: NY* (2004). Photo courtesy of John Goodwin.

that will always remain tried and true in his profession.

"The only way you learn in this business is by experience, and a lot of times it comes down to just picking the right materials. In film school, the biggest lesson we were taught was that we were in an industry where everything was about thirty to thirty-five years out of date. It was always said that it doesn't matter what the technique is. If the film is a big hit, that's going to be the technique that you'll be using on your next several movies. If *Jaws* uses foam latex for an artificial head in the water, you can bet that you'll be using foam latex for your next artificial head in the water. That's just the way it is. I've seen a lot of things change, but some things will always stay the same, and there are techniques and materials I was using when I first started out that are now suddenly in vogue again."

11 Michèle Burke

FOR MULTI-AWARD WINNING ARTIST Michèle Burke, paving her way in the world of special effects came out of necessity. Growing up in rural Ireland as the second oldest of ten children, Burke was encouraged to blaze her own trail into adulthood after finishing school—even if she didn't exactly know what it was that she wanted to do for a living at that time.

"My father was in the horse racing business," Burke explained. "At one point, he was doing very well, but by the time I was fourteen or fif-

Photo courtesy of Michèle Burke.

teen, it dawned on my poor mother that he had pretty much drained the family of their money because of gambling, drinking, and other shenanigans, as they say. Suddenly, our world became very different."

"At the time I was in a boarding school in France for a year and my brothers were in a great Jesuit school. That all ended abruptly due to lack of funds. My mother began to panic, and it was very hard on everybody because she couldn't hold the family together. She opened up an antique shop, because we lived in this old hotel that was a 'guest house by the sea' type of house."

"I helped her for my last two years of school, but after that she said to me, 'You've got to get out there. We have no money. You've got to seek your fame and fortune by yourself, because we have no money and I can't afford to keep any more people in the house.'"

Realizing that it was time to forge her way into the world, Burke set out to begin a career as an interpreter, but an undiagnosed ailment would force her to reconsider her choices.

"I went to Spain for three years and studied Spanish at the University of Madrid, because I thought I wanted to be a UN [United Nations] interpreter. I supported myself by giving English classes, but I didn't realize that all through my childhood, I had dyslexia. No one knew, because no one knew about that stuff. So I never quite understood how I couldn't get certain things, yet on other levels I was quite brilliant, like art. And I am great at languages, too, and yet I couldn't add two and two."

"I decided, then, that the only solution after Spain was that I would emigrate to Canada, because Canada was this brand new frontier. At the same time that I applied to Canada, I applied to Australia because I figured, *Okay, it'll be the luck of the draw. Whichever country takes me first, I'll go to that country.* I was in my early twenties and had never been to these places, so I didn't know anybody. Think about how nuts it was to do something like that, and probably a little naïve, too. My older brother came with me, because he was in the same boat as I was. Canada replied first, so we said, 'Okay, that's an omen,' and off we went."

"The idea was that we would go first, then once we got established, my mother would follow with my other siblings, and we could save the family. But that never truly happened, as even though my mother came over, the rest of my brothers and sisters returned to Ireland after rather short stays."

Michèle picked Montreal as her new home based on her linguistic skills, but a lack of solid job prospects left her less than enthused ("most jobs I was offered were for being a secretary"), and so she decided to work as a cocktail waitress, which eventually led to her falling in love with the world of makeup.

"I ended up getting a job at this place called the Rainbow Bar and Grill, which was a very hip, arty, musician place. I began to meet a lot of people, plus I made great tips, so it was a perfect opportunity. I met a girlfriend there whose family was in the fashion business, and she asked me to do some fashion shows. I was completely naïve as to what I would be doing, but I agreed to it."

"So, I began to help her and I even modeled in a few fashion shows, too, but it didn't last long. But through fashion I realized that makeup was really interesting and had the potential to transform people in such a way that was, to me, mind-boggling. I couldn't get over how I'd never seen anything like this. There was this makeup artist who came in one day to do the models for this show we had organized, and he asked if I wanted to see his portfolio. I didn't really know what that was, but as he started showing me the pages, I could see the faces and they were all so stunning. This was all fashion makeup, but it was like this big gong hit me in the head, and I said to him, 'I never knew you could do this.' It was a complete revelation; how come I didn't know about any of this?"

Burke was immediately drawn to the world of makeup and all the creative possibilities that awaited her, and after borrowing two hundred dollars from a credit card, she enrolled in a six-week course that taught her the basics of beauty makeup.

"When I took the course, I thought it was something that I could do for a hobby," reflected Burke. "But I was completely into it. It was like I found my true love. And through that, I got a job as a demonstrator for Revlon cosmetics in the department stores doing demos and promotions."

"The great thing about that job was that I got to do hundreds of women's makeovers, because it was the time when people were changing over from that heavy '60s look with the blue eye shadow and heavy eyeliner into a natural look, so I was very busy either giving them a transitional look or giving them a whole new face. They were loving it. People were lined up and all I did all day was work furiously. I learned not only how to work very quickly, but very quickly I learned the face and how to maneuver around it."

"From there, I got a job with a couple named Electa and Corrado [di Genova], who were the top fashion makeup artists in Canada. They were the precursor to MAC [Cosmetics]. They did all the fashion shows in New York and fashion spreads—anywhere you saw *Vogue* covers, everything—they were the go-to couple. And they had a little boutique in the center of town that sold their brand of makeup and also did makeovers by appointment when we weren't being sent out on photo shoots and doing fashion shows. I was with them about three years as their top makeup artist and I loved it. It was just fun, and very exciting, too."

As she was honing her skills as a cosmetic artist, Burke came across a publication that would steer her career in a new direction.

"Right around then, I found Richard Corson's *Stage Makeup* and suddenly it dawned on me, where I felt like a deflated balloon: I'm not a **true** makeup artist. I don't do the character work or all this prosthetic work, either. I wanted to be doing that work, but it was something that I thought was only happening down in Hollywood, which I'd never been to, so I had to figure out how to do all of this new stuff I was now falling in love with."

"Now, this was towards the late '70s, when films began to come into Montreal that were tax break films, and of course they were all low-budget horror projects. But the bonus part was they didn't have anyone to do the work, so that afforded me a lot of opportunities. I approached this old-timer makeup artist, Micky Hamilton, who came from the theater and really knew her stuff."

"I literally cold-called her, knocked on her door, and asked her, 'Here I am. Do you want to see my work? Because I want to work with you.' She was older and she was a tough nut, too. And she said to me, 'Yes, you can, but you'd have to work with me for nothing.' And I agreed, because I knew that if I worked on a film, then I could learn how to work on a film and eventually apply to work on more films down the line. But if I never worked on a film, how could I apply to work on anything at that point? I knew I had to pay my dues."

"So I worked with Micky for three films, and I learned a lot. I learned all about the set, how to maneuver, how everything happens during production, and also a lot of her techniques and how they worked together. After working for her, I began to get my own little films, which was great.

They were low-budget films, and I was learning on the job, really, but no one cared because everyone was in the same boat, and it was a happy group of people creating art the best that they could with the resources we had. It was great."

Shortly after venturing out on her own, Michèle met another fellow up-and-coming effects virtuoso in Canada, Stephan Dupuis, who would also go on to become an award-winning artist during his career.

"Stephan and I hooked up because we were kind of newbies to everything, and so we opened up a lab together. Suddenly we began to get called for all these horror films that were happening up there in the late 1970s. He was very experienced on the sculpture end of things and I was super experienced on the makeup side, so we made a great team. He learned from me and I learned from him, so between the both of us, we learned a lot of the lab stuff while we worked together."

"One day, Stephan and I got a call that Dick Smith was coming up to do *The Hunger* and he wanted to know if he could borrow our studio for the time he was there. We were like, 'Oh my God, it's Dick Smith!' Meeting him and him sharing a lot of stuff with both Stephan and I pushed us to learn more, to do more things, and to make molds in a better way. Our molds were like pudding; he showed us how to make circular molds and overlapping pieces and much more sophisticated things. We were doing foam latex at the time, but Dick had a formula that was much better than ours."

"So, little by little, Stephan and I began to get better and do a lot of prosthetic work—fake heads and slasher films, stuff like that. I began to branch out more and more on my own, heading up departments, and so did Stephan, because we didn't want to always be a team. We wanted to forge our way ourselves, and so we did."

After a few years of continuing to hone her craft and techniques in the late 1970s and early 1980s, Burke received a call that would forever change her life.

"When I got called for *Quest for Fire*, it was one of those 'wow' moments for me. But the reason why I was called was by default. It was a film that had been picked up as a French/English co-production, and the film would only get funded if they sent over a certain amount of technicians from Canada to Africa, where it was going to be filming. So I was filling a quota, really, but it hardly mattered to me at the time."

A sketch done by Michèle for *Quest for Fire* (1981). Courtesy of Michèle Burke.

"They had called all around the city looking for makeup artists, and most refused because it was a movie about Neanderthals and no one knew what a Neanderthal was back then. Another reason was because of the timing. When they called me, they said, 'If you do this, you have to leave in three days and it's shooting in Africa.' Most people were either busy or couldn't go—or maybe they didn't want to go. Not me. Right away, I said, 'Oh, great! Yes! Put me on the plane!' Of course, I didn't ask about how much money the job was offering, I just wanted to get on that plane."

"So, I went off to have the adventure of a lifetime, and I learned so much. The first part of the shoot was headed up just with one of the tribes, mainly with the three leads [Everett McGill, Ron Perlman, and Nameer El-Kadi]. Sarah Monzani headed that department and we shot it in Kenya. Then, we broke for Christmas and finished the rest of the film, which had two other tribes, and I was asked if I would head up the department, because production's budget was tight. So that's how I ended up sharing the [1983] Oscar [for Best Makeup] with Sarah."

"The most amazing part about the film, apart from it being horribly exciting to be a part of, was that it was very difficult. It was like swimming in deep water every day, way above my head, where I felt like I was constantly gasping for air. It was a huge amount of responsibility and the work never seemed to end. I had huge film crews and we had to set up new techniques, and it had never been done with this amount of people all doing these special makeups on these big tribes all at once."

"Back then, there weren't a lot of wig specialists, so when we were in Montreal, I went to a Korean wig shop and found these women who could hook wigs really well, and they did a lot of the hair work for me. I even

Michèle poses with her first Academy Award, which she won with Sarah Monzani for their makeup work on *Quest for Fire* (1981). Photo courtesy of Michèle Burke.

had to go around to different dentists until I could find a technician who could make me some sets of teeth. We were constantly blazing trails on *Quest for Fire* because this kind of a shoot hadn't been attempted before. There was a lot of pressure, but it put me on the map."

While *Quest for Fire* (1981) was undoubtedly the hardest project Burke had been involved with at that point in her career, she was surprised by how much of an impact her efforts on the film would have, and the attention that came along shortly after winning the 1983 Academy Award for Best Makeup.

"I remember when I was called by the production manager, which was eight or nine months after we finished the film, and he said to me, 'Michèle, guess what? You've been nominated.' All I could think to ask him was, 'Well, what does that mean? Is that good or bad?' And all he did was laugh and say, 'Michèle, this is for an Oscar.' We were up against *Gandhi*, and because that was a super popular film at the time, although it had [almost] no makeup, I honestly thought it was going to win."

"Right around the time of the nominations, I'd been called to do *Iceman*. The producers on *Iceman* told me, because they knew at that point I was nominated, 'If you want to go to the Oscars, you can't take this film because we'll be up so far in Alaska that we can't get you out early enough due to the weather.' Because I still believed that *Gandhi* was going to win, I went off and did that film. And that shows how little I knew at the time, because *Quest for Fire* won. It was hilarious."

"I was later presented my first Oscar by a Canadian Post officer in the post office. When he saw the heavy box, he said that customs had to open it up first. Upon opening the box, he saw the Oscar inside, and he exclaimed, 'This is an Oscar!' My sister, who was with me at the time, said, 'Well, present her with it,' so he did and everyone there clapped for me."

"These things are always bittersweet, because now suddenly I'm 'Little Miss Nobody' being put on the map. I had never even been to Hollywood, and so all these professionals down there are going, 'Who the bleep is Michèle Burke?' Suddenly I'm in the spotlight, but I wasn't sure I was good enough. I just didn't feel worthy. I wasn't ready at all."

"I did a few more films in Canada, but I began to realize I had to go and face the beast. I needed to go down to Hollywood and see if I could make it there, because it was the only way to prove to myself that this was not a fluke. So I did. I went down, and of course, I had to start all over again."

One big difference between the experiences Burke had while working in Canada versus how makeups were handled in Hollywood was the fact that her gender mattered far more than it should have.

"I very quickly realized that down here, the guys were in charge of the 'special' makeups and most of the time, the girls only handled beauty make-ups. Also, because I am self-taught more or less, I had my own techniques and ways to work with color and form. I was the first of many women blazing the trails into special effects at that time—another was Ve Neill. But I had to re-prove myself in the beginning because I was a woman, and it was very hard."

"At times, there were put-downs and people saying things because I wasn't from here," Burke explained. "When I came down, I had already won an Oscar and no one knew who I was at all, which made me highly suspect to everyone else. But I knew I had to tough it out, and because I had six brothers, I knew how to play the 'boy game.'"

"I was also a bit of a loner because I was never quite sure how people would take me and how they would accept me, so I just began to do my own work and do my own thing, and it worked—most of the time. Some-times, I'd hire someone and they'd be nice to my face, but then go behind my back and I'd come to realize that they were actually trying to sabotage me, or they were going to the producer and talking to them as if they were head of the department. I had to learn how to assert myself because I'm not a very bombastic person. That's not how I was raised."

"Over the years I gained more respect because I just kept steadily working. It was complex and I fully understood that, but the only way to keep up with everything that was happening, as a girl in that manly world, was to really be better. You have to truly keep your radar up and know what's going on around you and keep going forward. Instead of trying to keep up with everyone else in the race, you have to cut yourself out of it and run on a lane that you laid clear for yourself. Stay away from the pack and be yourself. I've always just done that because that's how my mother taught me how to do things."

As Burke continued to find her footing in Los Angeles, the opportu-nities to further prove herself as a creative force to be reckoned with kept coming her way.

"I worked with Mike Westmore on *The Clan of the Cave Bear* very soon after arriving in Los Angeles. We were nominated for an Oscar, so that was great. Then, a few years later, I did *Alien Nation* and we got an

Michèle touches up Mike Myers' Dr. Evil makeup between takes on *Austin Powers: The Spy Who Shagged Me* (1999). Photo courtesy of Michèle Burke.

A sketch of Gary Oldman in his human form for *Bram Stoker's Dracula* (1992). Courtesy of Michèle Burke.

Emmy for our work on that, which was very rewarding. After that, I did *Cyrano de Bergerac*, which was another film that we were nominated for [an Academy Award]. It was amazing."

"I just kept on continuously climbing the mountain, making my way up further and further, and folks realized that my early success wasn't a fluke. We got nominated again and again and again—for *Bram Stoker's Dracula*, for *Austin Powers* [*The Spy Who Shagged Me*], and for *The Cell*. What anyone thought about my talent couldn't be disputed anymore, or at least that's how I saw it in my mind. Not that I was trying to compete; I just think my lack of self-confidence, because of my dyslexia, pushed me to always strive to be the best, because I didn't always know if I could be the best."

As Michèle mentioned, the next Oscar statuette she took home was earned from her incredible re-imagining of the beloved bloodsucker in Francis Ford Coppola's 1992 adaptation of Bram Stoker's *Dracula*, starring Winona Ryder, Keanu Reeves, Anthony Hopkins, and Gary Oldman as the titular villain. Even though as an artist Burke is generally confident with her work, there was one day in particular on *Bram Stoker's Dracula* (1992) that made her wonder whether or not she went too far with her wonderfully audacious approach to such an iconic character.

A sketch of Dracula's bold new hairstyle, designed by Michèle for *Bram Stoker's Dracula* (1992). Courtesy of Michèle Burke.

"I remember the first day we shot the old-age Dracula. I had designed this big goofy hair, and he [Gary Oldman] had this regal costume on. Eiko Ishioka was the Costume Designer, so she was very into different stuff, and so was Francis, but the first day Gary came onto set with this hairdo and get-up, the whole crew was like, 'This is not Dracula.' They were used to the traditional Dracula with the widow's peak, the fangs, and the cloak, and we were creating a whole new Dracula."

"I immediately thought to myself, *Oh my God, this could go either way.* I was nervous. This could either be a total flop where the audience will laugh at it and say we failed completely, or they're going to embrace it and love the risks we took. The first day we shot that scene, Francis wanted to do the shadow of Dracula with the hands coming across the wall, so of course, all you see in that shadow is his hair and his hands. I heard snickering all around me, and then I heard the words 'Mickey Mouse.' My heart dropped. I knew that if he looked like Mickey Mouse, the studio was not going to want that, because he's a patented character. So I looked at Eiko and I asked her, 'Is Francis liking this?' She said, 'He **loves** it,' and

Left to right: Greg Cannom, Michèle, and Matthew Mungle pose with their Oscar statuettes after taking home the Academy Award for Best Makeup for *Bram Stoker's Dracula* (1992). Photo courtesy of Michèle Burke.

Michèle and other crew members tend to Lestat (played by Tom Cruise) on the set of *Interview with the Vampire* (1994). Photo courtesy of Michèle Burke.

that's when I learned that as an artist, you don't listen to the chorus. My job was to make Francis happy, and, sure enough, he was."

"I felt redeemed when *Dracula* came out and the look became so talked about. We took some chances and raised the bar with our approach, and I'm still incredibly proud of my work on that film," Burke added.

Just a few years after giving audiences a new take on Dracula, Burke returned to the realm of blood fiends for Neil Jordan's 1994 cinematic adaptation of Anne Rice's *Interview with the Vampire: The Vampire Chronicles*, a project that would lead to a now decades-long collaborative relationship between herself and Tom Cruise. Her approach to vampires this time around was wildly different than what she had created for *Bram Stoker's Dracula* (1992), focusing more on the intricate details and adhering to Rice's vision for the characters from her best-selling novels.

"*Interview with the Vampire* was a much easier project for me, mostly because of Anne Rice," Michèle said. "I was besotted by her books. Her description of Lestat helped greatly, because she talked about the translucent skin, and she talked about him not being noticeable amid people if he was out on the street walking around. And yet, there was still something very striking about Lestat in her descriptions, so we focused more on his skin, his eyes, and his teeth. We gave him veins all over his lovely translucent skin, which became a trend shortly after that, and we decided that for his fangs, we weren't going to use the eye teeth, because that was the standard look, so we went in with one tooth, which made them look a lot better."

"Lestat's nails and hair were also a big deal. It was a makeup of details and a makeup of subtleties. Overall, that's my forte. That's what I do best: real fine, detailed work that's subtle, so that when you're looking at it, you're believing the character. You don't see the actor at all."

While Burke relished the chance to transform a highly recognizable actor such as Cruise into the almost transcendent, blonde-haired, blue-eyed Lestat, there was a lot of skepticism from many who weren't wholly convinced he could pull off the role. In fact, his character's creator, Rice, wasn't shy at all about publicly expressing her extreme displeasure.

Michèle with actor Tom Cruise on the set of *Vanilla Sky* (2001).
Photo courtesy of Michèle Burke.

"At the beginning, a lot of people were against Tom being Lestat," Michèle said. "There was actually a whole movement against him when it was first announced. Anne Rice even took out a full-page ad saying she denounced him being cast as Lestat because Tom wasn't who she saw as Lestat. But when she saw the film and his performance in that makeup, Anne then published another ad saying how she embraced it, how she really loved him as Lestat, and how Tom did a great job."

"Of course, Tom did the acting, but the makeup works in tandem with the actor, and if the two don't mesh, there can be a disconnect. Because if he looks in the mirror and he goes, 'I'm not believing this,' that's not going to work. But Tom was exceedingly happy with what I was able to do with him."

Little did Burke know that *Interview with the Vampire* (1994) would lead to Cruise repeatedly calling upon her expertise over the next three decades on various projects, including Cameron Crowe's *Vanilla Sky* (2001), in which Cruise's character's visage gets horribly disfigured in an automobile accident. Doing the makeup effects on the film tested Burke's mettle as both an artist and a professional.

"After *Interview*, Tom always called me whenever he had challenging looks in a film, because he knew that I would deliver. Working on *Vanilla Sky* was a huge challenge, mainly because the studio didn't want to distort his face. They made it very clear to me and to Cameron that they did not want Tom—an iconic figure and a leading male action hero—to appear grotesque or monstrous, and that they didn't ever want that lasting look of him to be on the screen. So, if what I created was not acceptable by their standards in the makeup tests, they were not going to do the film."

"Cameron came to me and told me, 'If the producers don't like this look, we're shutting everything down,' so I was so stressed. That was a huge pressure. You've got Tom Cruise, you've got Cameron Crowe, and you've got Sony Studios all saying, 'If you fail, we're not doing this.' That kind of pressure was unbelievable."

"When I was designing the look, I drew inspiration from Francis Bacon. I did this thing where one side was distorted but the other side wasn't, so that way, if Tom turned his head one way, you would see the beautiful him that he was, but on the other side you could see the distortion. I thought that might help the issue and would give Cameron a lot of options, depending on how they wanted to play the scene. And sure enough, they did accept it, which was a huge relief for me."

Actor Tom Cruise in his full disfigured makeup for *Vanilla Sky* (2001).
Photo courtesy of Michèle Burke.

Another film in which Burke took huge risks transforming Cruise was the comedy *Tropic Thunder* (2008), when she was tasked with changing one of the world's most iconic movie stars into a sleazy and buffoonish talent agent: a complete 180 from how the world had always seen Cruise on the big screen.

"That was the big challenge on *Tropic Thunder*, to make him completely unrecognizable as himself," Burke explained. "Les Grossman is this overweight character with all this hair, and he's bald, and Tom is none of those things. There was also more pressure on me doing the Les makeup, too, because Tom told me early on, 'You've got fifty minutes to apply this thing,' because he hates being in the makeup chair. He always does stuff like that to me. All the time."

Tom Cruise as Les Grossman in *Tropic Thunder* (2008). Photo courtesy of Michèle Burke.

"So, my only solution was to have many big pieces, where you didn't have to blend the edges as much. Before, it was like, 'Okay, put this piece on, put that piece on,' and so on. But the biggest issue there is that you have to spend a lot of time meticulously blending all the edges. So I thought, *In this instance, let's just slap the whole thing on as one.* The arms were gloves that fastened up into his sleeves, because he needed these big sausage fingers and hair. He had this huge, fat belly suit, and then he had on what we call a 'bib,' with the hair coming out of his chest. It really worked, and he was amazing in that makeup. He really did a great job with that character, too."

Burke later had to evolve her already quicker-than-normal approach to the Les Grossman makeup when Cruise was asked to perform alongside Jennifer Lopez live while in character at the 2010 MTV Movie Awards.

"Everything that I did for the movie, I went even further with it for the MTV Awards. We had even less time than we did on set, so I had to create Les with this wrap that went around Tom's head, almost like a Halloween mask, and then I just blended around his eyes and nose."

"It was super thin and it was really hard to apply, but it worked great. We didn't even have time to test it first, so I was nervous about it the entire time he was on stage. Thankfully, the makeup would only buckle slightly just when he'd tilt his head a certain way, so it really held up."

Burke also lent her creative contributions to two other notable films outside of the horror genre, *Austin Powers: The Spy Who Shagged Me* (1999) and *Austin Powers in Goldmember* (2002), and she was in charge of Michael Myers' characters as well as the makeup for Verne Troyer, who portrayed Mini-Me.

"When I did *Austin Powers: The Spy Who Shagged Me*, the character of Austin was already created when I came on board, so I didn't do much with the design. They had so many cameo characters in that movie—many of them with new looks—that you never felt like you were not designing or creating something fun during that production."

"Plus, I feel like we perfected the look of Austin Powers and Dr. Evil on *Goldmember*," Michèle added. "They both look a lot better than they do on the first sequel, so I was happy to have the opportunity to do something more with those characters. But both films were great fun, and every day you would spend most of your time laughing. [They required] long hours, but I loved working on them—so many great memories."

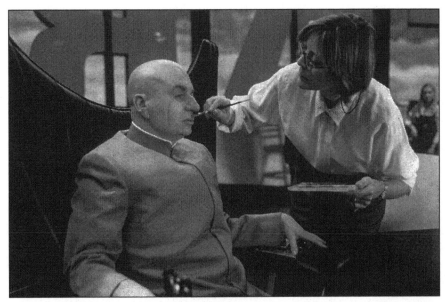

Michèle examines Mike Myers' Dr. Evil makeup on set. Photo courtesy of Michèle Burke.

Some of Michèle's initial designs created for *The Cell* (2000).
Photo courtesy of Michèle Burke.

Shortly after bringing Britain's International Man of Mystery to life for Jay Roach's *Austin Powers* (1997) sequels, Burke found herself collaborating with another up-and-coming filmmaker, Tarsem Singh, who, after directing a string of award-wining music videos in the early 1990s, was transitioning to the world of film with his debut feature, *The Cell* (2000).

"Tarsem Singh is truly something of an individual. He was one of the few directors I've worked with who will literally goad you into doing more, which I love, because directors are usually going, 'Less! It's too much! Do less!' I also worked again with Eiko [Ishioka], who was the Costume Designer from [*Bram Stoker's*] *Dracula* [1992], and she's someone who always embraces the concept of 'more,' too, so right from the start I knew this was something where I would have carte blanche. I knew it would be fun and it was something where I could go a little crazy."

"The biggest challenge for *The Cell* was that it was a low-budget film," Burke continued. "So a lot of the time, he [Singh] would come to me and say, 'Michèle, we have no money.' So I would just tell him that we didn't have a problem and that we'd just do straight body makeup as much as we could. What ate up a lot of the budget was the cape—he was very funny

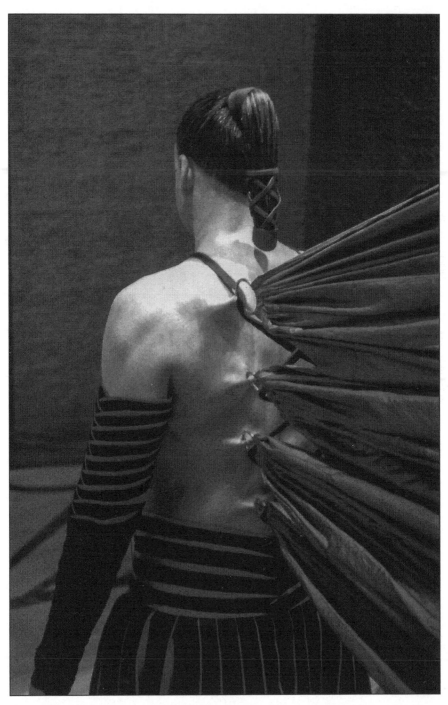

A close-up look at actor Vincent D'Onofrio's back makeup, complete with cape, on the set of *The Cell* (2000). Photo courtesy of Michèle Burke.

like that. Tarsem would do one major piece that cost a fortune and then we'd have to readjust because of the budget. But, in the end, it was so great because it allowed me to help tie the whole thing together with just body makeup, and that approach really made the film's look feel powerful."

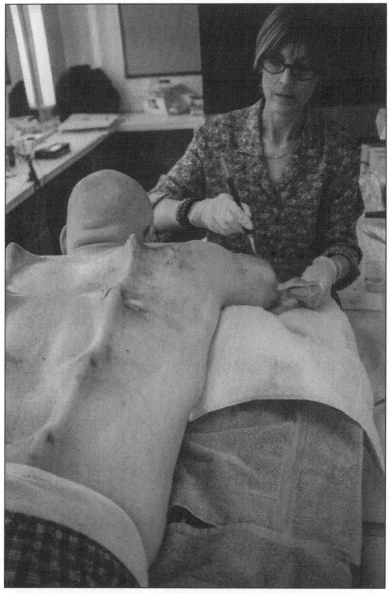

Michèle works on the intricate back makeup on actor Vincent D'Onofrio for *The Cell* (2000). Photo courtesy of Michèle Burke.

"We had another big challenge when we had to hang Vincent [D'Onofrio] by his skin. I remember thinking to myself, *Okay, now we're nearly at the edge of ethically and morally what I like to do on a film*, because we were really pushing the envelope. But Vincent was a nice guy and he would let you do a lot of stuff. He put up with a lot, too. He had to have body makeup and he had rings put on. He was so patient. We did that scene with KNB [EFX Group], and the way it turned out was truly amazing."

In recent years, Burke has continued to stay perpetually busy, lending her design expertise to films of every budgetary level, working in the world of fashion, and honing her skills as a painter as well. The difference

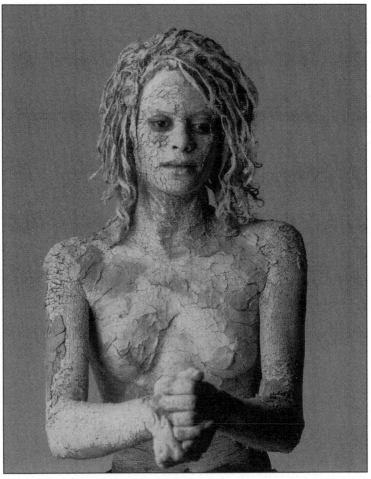

A detailed all-body makeup application created by Michèle.
Photo courtesy of Michèle Burke.

about her workflow now versus when she was coming up in the industry is that she's being creative on her own terms.

"I'm doing stuff, but more at my speed now, and that's the way I like it. It's a nice place to be after so many years. And the thing is, I still love it all. A lot of people have called me up and I teach them stuff, and I still do design work, too. I do whatever work comes in, and sometimes that even includes fashion and photos. I also design applicators for eyes and lips that are sold to some of the top makeup companies, and I enjoy painting, too, which allows me to express myself with no one judging me."

"But the work these days is very different than how it was thirty years ago. All in all, I rode in on the crest of this huge special effects wave in many ways, because when the low-budget stuff in Canada was happening, I was rising with it. And then it became huge here, and I came down and did the same thing. When I look at it that way, I realize I've done all right."

"A lot of people ask me how to do things, or how to make it in this industry, and my response now is, 'You could never walk the path I walked.' Because back then, I was blazing trails. We were all pioneering different techniques during that time, many of which are industry standards now."

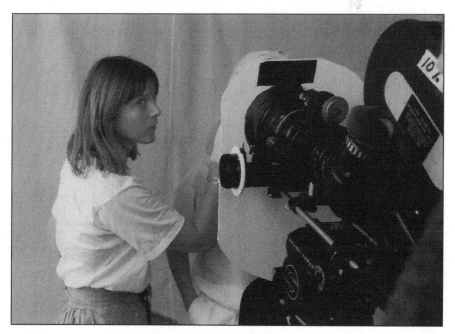

Photo courtesy of Michèle Burke.

There are new challenges to face today. I always tell people to find their own path, because they'll never have the experience that I had. It'll never be that way for them, and I'm very lucky to still be living out my dream after all these years. I still love it all."

12 Steve Johnson

LARGELY DRIVEN BY HIS NEED to constantly create, legendary effects artist Steve Johnson always knew he was destined to follow a creative path, even though he grew up in the shadow of Houston, Texas, more than fifteen hundred miles from Hollywood.

"Stephen King has a famous quote," Johnson said. "People asked him why he writes and he said the answer's simple: because he can't not write. And as a kid, my youngest memories are of making things because

Photo courtesy of Steve Johnson.

I couldn't not be creative. When I started, there were no [special effects] schools [nearby] back then. We're talking about a kid in Cattle Country, Texas, in the '60s doing makeup—it was an impossibility in most people's eyes. But I started figuring out how to do things when I was really young, where I was just making up my own techniques as I was going along."

"I was always doing things, like taking construction paper and old coffee cans and turning them into totem poles, or trying to make a full-size Santa when I was just twelve. I'd seen these little apple mutants and sculptures at county fairs, and I thought, *Well, that's an interesting texture*, so I'd cut the outer skin off apples, put them in the sun, let them wrinkle and prune up, and then I would carefully peel that off and glue them on my friends' faces with Elmer's Glue. I was just making shit up and having a blast with it."

As an aspiring artist, Johnson continued to hone his effects-making skills the best way he knew how, by doing whatever research he could with the resources available to him, and by consuming countless horror and science fiction films and books.

"Around that time, I became fascinated by this stuff. It had started getting in the public eye more, like Dick Smith's makeup on *Little Big Man* and *The Exorcist*, and obviously *The Godfather*, too. People were noticing there was an art to what was being made, like what Rick [Baker] had done with the *Star Wars* cantina creatures, *King Kong* [1976], and even *The Incredible Melting Man*. I began devouring not only the Universal classics and the Hammer classics, but I was also really attracted to reading the works of authors like H.G. Wells, Jules Verne, and Robert Louis Stevenson."

"I was always utterly fascinated and fixated on the macabre and the offbeat, and I didn't know you couldn't not do it, either, so I just started trying to figure out how to make my effects based on what I'd seen in all the horror movies I was watching. I would make my mother drive me to the Galveston County Library, and we'd search through microfilm and old, dusty books looking for anything we could find, but there just was no information out there."

"At first it seemed just so out of reach for a young kid in Texas, but I didn't let that stop me. I mowed lawns. I shoplifted. I did everything I could do to get money for materials. But as I got older and better at my techniques, it got difficult because I wanted to get into dimensional makeup and prosthetics, but I didn't know how to take that next step."

A zombie creation designed by Steve. Photo courtesy of Steve Johnson.

That next step for Johnson would come one fateful day at a mall when he came across the fourth edition of *Stage Makeup* (1983), a guide created by the legendary Richard Corson, who was an expert on live theatrical makeups in the 1940s and was considered the authority on such applications up until his passing in 1999.

"When I found Richard Corson's book, I went absolutely crazy for it, because it was the first time I'd ever seen anything in print that showed actual techniques. A lot of it were some pretty simple stage makeup techniques, but he did get into wigs and prosthetic makeup a little bit, and that kind of information just sent my young mind staggering. Although, that book did result in me doing these deathly experiments in lifecasting with just plain plaster, Saran Wrap, and aluminum foil, which resulted in me almost killing my friends—and myself—repeatedly."

Johnson went on to find inspiration in another form: *Famous Monsters of Filmland*, a horror and sci-fi magazine that began publishing in the late 1950s and has since been revived on two different occasions. The periodical was not only chock-full of pictures that Johnson would spend hours and hours poring over, but he also came across an advertisement in an issue that would forever change his life.

"The second turning point in my young life was when I found an ad for *Dick Smith's Do-It-Yourself Monster Make-Up Handbook* on the back of *Famous Monsters*. In this, Dick was doing more basic techniques that kids could easily do, but it did give me the access to professional techniques from a professional artist that I admired, and also, more importantly, it listed off the materials I needed and where I could buy them."

"So I'd shoplift some more, sell whatever I had off to my friends, mow more lawns, or do whatever it took, and then I'd send off my orders to the Alcone Company and just wait for everything to arrive. Soon enough, I was getting even better and better," added Johnson.

A few years later in the late 1970s, Johnson once again found his destiny altered after an encounter with his longtime hero, Rick Baker, who would go on to become an instrumental figure in his life.

"When I was sixteen, *Star Wars* had just come out and Rick showed up at one of the first horror and science fiction conventions ever in Houston. It was almost a fluke that I found out about it, but my mom drove me down there and with trembling hands, I went up and showed my portfolio to Rick Baker. It was terrifying."

An early burn makeup by Steve. Photo courtesy of Steve Johnson.

"But after flipping through it, he said to me, 'Well, you're not very good yet, but the thing that impresses me is that you're very, very far away from both coasts, about as far as you could be from New York and L.A., where these techniques are in practice, but you're figuring it all out on your own. In doing so, you're exhibiting the most important element of this business, and that is the ability to problem-solve. You're never going to make a vampire the same way. You're never going to make a werewolf the same way. And you're always going to have to find ways to solve new

Steve makes an adjustment on a zombie creation. Photo courtesy of Steve Johnson.

problems in order to keep yourself going as an artist.' The fact that Rick saw my potential was a real bonus for me, and he even gave me his number that day."

That nudge was precisely what Steve needed the most, as he'll be the first to admit that he didn't always have a lot of confidence in himself— that is, until he discovered his burgeoning talents in the realm of special effects techniques.

"Growing up, a lot of how this all happened was because, for me, it was about finally being good at something. I was always bad at sports, I was afraid of girls, I was terrible at math, I was not the best student, and I wasn't very well-liked because I had terrible acne. Honestly, I was painfully, almost clinically, shy as a kid."

"But special effects finally gave people a reason to like me, or at least that's the way I saw it in my young mind," Johnson said, "because I was finally good at something. The days of being chosen last for the softball team were over. I could take my pictures into school and show them off, where even the hot girls in school and the jocks liked me for it. That also fueled my desire to do it, to be good at something and to be kind of idolized."

"After I met Rick, I wasn't just doing makeups for my high school friends anymore; I was doing them to send photographs to Rick Baker, my hero of heroes. He would take a look at them, get on the phone and call me up, and then critique them for me. It was amazing. So, the minute I graduated in high school, I packed up my car, headed out to L.A., and that was the beginning of it all. Of course, I ended up knocking on Rick's door one day, and he was like, 'What the hell are you doing here, kid?' I was like, 'Well, you told me to call you if I was ever out here.'"

Johnson's post-high school transition out to Los Angeles from Houston might have seemed like a daunting risk to take for most folks, but he knew it was the only way to continue to follow his dreams of becoming a professional artist in the industry.

"Many people have said to me over the years, 'Wow, you must have a lot of balls, or nerves of steel, to have just packed it all up at eighteen, not knowing a single soul, and moved out to California with only a thousand dollars to your name,' but it didn't seem like a big deal to me at all. It felt like a natural progression, because when you get out of high school, what are you going to do? Marry your high school sweetheart, get fat, have a bunch of babies, stay in your hometown, and never see the world or chase your dreams? That, to me, seemed infinitely more stupid, and so taking that risk really seemed like the only thing to do. I was never nervous about it. I just did it."

"The support from my mother was the most important thing about being able to take that kind of a risk. Had she not supported me, I would never have followed my dreams and I would have just written them off as the musings of a child. I would have stayed in Houston and studied architecture or plastic surgery or something like that. There's no way I could have done it without her support."

As he settled into his new life in Los Angeles, Johnson immediately began carving out a career path for himself. He spent many of his early years in the business working alongside some of the greatest minds and innovators in modern special effects, and he soaked up as much information and wisdom about the business as he could, while still defining himself as an artist.

"Of course, I wasn't good enough yet to work for Rick, but he did almost immediately recommend that I go work with Greg Cannom on my first film, which I did. It was called *The Galactic Connection*, and it was a very low-budget film that was never released, so I wouldn't say that I learned a whole lot from Greg at that point. But that was because we were all making the most with not a ton of available resources on that project."

"I did certainly learn a lot from watching his progress as an artist throughout the years, because he's an amazing artist who does some of the best work out there. Greg's attention to detail and realism is what I've always been impressed with, because he's brilliant at that stuff. He even received a Technical Achievement Award for developing silicone prosthetics, and that's a huge deal. That's like getting the Nobel Prize in this industry."

"After [*The Galactic Connection*], Rick recommended that I go work with Rob Bottin. I worked with Rob on several films like *The Howling*, *The Fog*, *Tanya's Island*, and *Humanoids from the Deep*. What I learned from Rob during that time was to never, ever stop. To never stop designing, to never give in, and to not worry about impressing the audience, either, because that's secondary. The audience will never be as much of an expert as you are, because this is what you do. So, the primary thing you've got to accomplish is to impress yourself first."

"Rob really taught me to just make your creation the best you can possibly make it, and to just go crazy with it and have fun, too. He shares similar characteristics with Jim Cameron, who I worked with years later on *The Abyss*, and I think they both feel that in every project they do. They've got to at least take one moment in that film and just blow the doors off the audience's expectations, at any cost. They both love showing the audience something they could never possibly in a billion years have imagined themselves, and to learn anything from someone like that in this industry is amazing."

A sabre-toothed character Steve created for Die Antwoord's *Pitbull Terrier* music video. Photo courtesy of Steve Johnson.

"So, after working with both Greg and Rob, Rick figured from a distance that I'd learned the ropes from two of his previous protégés, where I had fucked up on their time and not his, so then

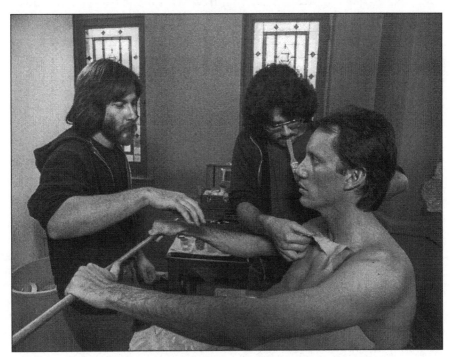

Steve works alongside Rick Baker on the set of *Videodrome* (1983).
Photo courtesy of Steve Johnson.

he pulled me over to work on *An American Werewolf in London*, and that's how we got started together," Johnson recalled.

Over the next few years, Johnson collaborated alongside his mentor on several notable films, including *Ghost Story* (1981), *Videodrome* (1983), *Greystoke: The Legend of Tarzan – Lord of the Apes* (1984), and the aforementioned *An American Werewolf in London* (1981), with the transformation scene not only earning Baker an Oscar, but also quickly becoming a pinnacle moment in special effects history.

"Rick's attention to perfection is legendary," said Johnson. "You could do an incredibly tight close-up on a background alien in one of Rick's movies, like *Men in Black*, and it'll look 20 billion times better than any other company's hero alien. Rick just doesn't differentiate. It's art to him, and Rick's not going to stop until every aspect of every single thing is perfect."

"Something I took away from working with Rick was the value of testing, because there's nothing worse in this industry than to show up as a highly specialized expert on a set and fuck something up. There is no worse feeling. The way Rick structured his company and taught me to work—and this was something I took into my own studio for decades—is to budget your work out, so that you've got enough time and resources to do all the testing you need."

"Whether it's Barry Convex exploding at the end of *Videodrome*, or it's just a simple makeup, you have to budget your time and your money so that you do it once, finish it, and learn from it—you then throw it away, start from the beginning, and do it all over again. That's something that's long gone in the industry these days, and that's why our work was so much better back then, because filmmakers and certainly the artists in my field took it a lot more seriously."

Throughout the time he spent working with Baker, Johnson honed his skills in the world of animatronics, which gave him more creative freedom, but also ended up pigeonholing him as an artist over time.

"When I started working with Rick, and even Rob to a degree, I was immediately exposed to high-end animatronics, and I really enjoyed that because it creatively allowed me the opportunity to move away from the human form. I wasn't stuck to where the actor's eyes or their nose and mouth were anymore. I could mechanically extend arms and heads, and you could even distort and alter entire characters in just one shot. I loved it."

Steve examines his "Onion Head" (or "Slimer," as he would come to be known) ghost from *Ghostbusters* (1984). Photo courtesy of Steve Johnson.

"But something surprising happened to me over the years, in that I actually became known far more for doing outrageously huge animatronic shit than I was known for doing prosthetic makeups. That's how this industry goes, though. If you go in for a meeting for a classic werewolf movie and you show them your portfolio, and all you have to show them is a classic vampire, a classic mummy, a classic Phantom, and a classic Quasimodo, all they'll say to you is, 'Well, you can't do the werewolf because we don't see one here,' and that always frustrated me."

That frustration was a big motivating factor behind Johnson's decision to venture out and find a way to make his own indelible mark on modern cinema. His first chance came via Richard Edlund, the multi-Oscar-winning visual effects pioneer who was also about to step out on his own after establishing himself as a visionary while working at Industrial Light & Magic (ILM) for over six years.

"*Ghostbusters* was my first job in this next phase of my career," Johnson explained, "and I had no idea what it would become. In fact, when I first read the script, I thought it was terrible. But the way it all happened was Richard Edlund had just set up the Boss Film Corporation to do *Ghostbusters*, where he wanted it to be an all-encompassing facility that would build miniatures, mechanical effects, pyrotechnical effects, optical effects, and creature effects. We had this sprawling industrial compound with three buildings and shooting stages—the whole works. We were just a bunch of kids at that time, so we didn't know. We were just having fun."

"But what was great about all of our projects at Boss Film was that Richard and all of the businesspeople were several blocks away, and we were all working somewhere else. I was mostly at the creature shop that I shared with Mark Stetson, and he did the models and mechanical stuff."

"We had a safety net there, which is why that work is so memorable, because if we needed to spend the money on something, we'd spend the money. Boss Film was literally a playground with a safety net. When I say a 'playground,' I mean the ghost shop was a playground. We were allowed to go wild and do what we wanted and they didn't bug us from the office building. They just let us do it, and once we'd proven ourselves on *Ghostbusters*, the same thing held true for every other project we did there. If I went to them and said, 'Hey, I want to stick eight thousand tiny feathers

Steve and his crew make adjustments to the "Library Ghost" for *Ghostbusters* (1984). Photo courtesy of Steve Johnson.

on this character. Do you think that's going to bust our budget?' They'd tell me, 'Just put a man on it and take care of it.' That was fantastic."

"Working with Richard was also an absolute godsend. He's a genius on several counts. He won an Oscar for coming up with motion control on *Star Wars*, which set a whole industry in motion. That right there makes him a genius to me, but the other thing is that Richard's a very wise businessman, which is another facet of his genius. He hires the right people and he doesn't ever breathe down their necks while they're on a project, and that freedom can really allow people to do their best work and grow creatively."

Johnson went on to work on several other notable projects for Boss Film in the mid-1980s, including *Fright Night* (1985), *Poltergeist II: The Other Side* (1986), and *Big Trouble in Little China* (1986).

"*Fright Night* was the second film I did at Boss Film, and because I had worked previously with two guys who were known for their werewolf transformations, I was excited at the opportunity to create a werewolf transformation of my own for *Fright Night*. I used the things I had learned from these great masters as a springboard, and tried to take it a little bit further from what I had already done myself as an artist. It was a pretty unique challenge, and it was pretty exciting to work on, too."

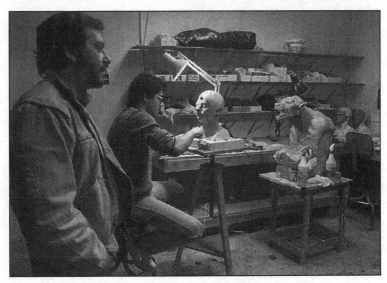

Steve works on a sculpting project during pre-production on *Fright Night* (1985). Photo courtesy of Steve Johnson.

When it came time to break down and tackle all the various creatures and vampire creations for *Fright Night* (1985), Johnson collaborated with special effects artist Randall William Cook in a joint effort, much like their approach to working on *Ghostbusters* (1984).

"In the beginning of Boss Film, Randy and I co-headed the creature department. Just like on *Ghostbusters*, where we split up the work—the characters and effects that we would each supervise—the same thing happened on *Fright Night*. Randy actually was in charge of all the Jerry Dandrige stuff, including the bat, and then I worked on all the Evil Ed effects."

"I'm pretty proud of the work we did on *Fright Night*, but you have to go back to the script, and you have to go back to director Tom Holland, because both of those elements are the cornerstones to a great film. It's also the casting and the performances, too, because if you don't care about the characters, you're not going to care about what's happening

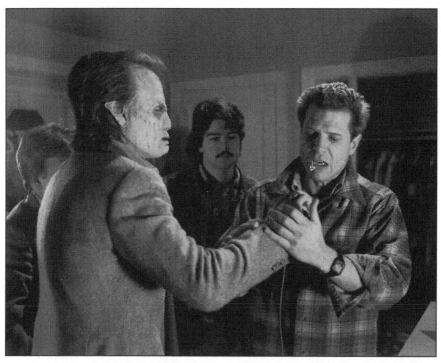

Steve watches Director Tom Holland block a scene with Chris Sarandon on *Fright Night* (1985). Photo courtesy of Steve Johnson.

with the effects. One of the main reasons the movie holds a place in so many people's hearts thirty years later is because you really did care about these characters."

One film on Johnson's résumé that he initially wasn't sure would become the highlight that it has over the last few decades is *Big Trouble in Little China* (1986), a project on which his own disconnect from the material made it hard to discern Director John Carpenter's exact vision for the film.

"I was excited initially to come onto *Big Trouble*, because John had worked with some of the most amazing effects artists up until that point; he had worked with Dick Smith, Rick Baker, Rob [Bottin], and some other amazing artists, too. Here's a guy who's responsible for creating a showcase for some of the most amazing, groundbreaking effects of all time, and now I get the opportunity to work with him. So I was like, *Great, I'm going to break new ground and kick some ass.*"

"I came in with all these outlandish ideas, and honestly, John just didn't want to hear it. I think he had recently been burned on some projects, so he just wanted the shoot to go quickly and smoothly, and didn't want any problems. He also wanted this cartoon vibe, which at that point, I didn't really understand. I was really young and I couldn't really interpret the written word to what the director's vision was going to be, so there was a disconnect there."

"There was kind of a battle between him and myself on *Big Trouble*, because I wanted to go a certain way, and he wanted to go another way. When I first watched that movie, I was like, *Oh my God, these effects are awful! I can't believe people can even make their way through this, because they look so awful.* But now, that work has become iconic over time and people still rave about it, so what do I know?"

Big Trouble in Little China (1986) became one of Johnson's final projects for Richard Edlund, and while his time spent at Boss Film was brief, the impact that his boss would continue to have on his career spanned decades.

"When we talk about the people who have influenced me over my career, I can never forget Richard, because he really taught me the most important thing of all about running a business, which is to hire the right people. If you've got to fire somebody, it's not their fault, it's your fault because you hired them."

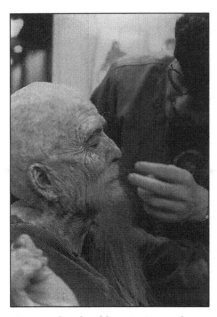

Steve applies the old-age Lo Pan makeup to actor James Hong on *Big Trouble in Little China* (1986). Photo courtesy of Steve Johnson

That lesson was something Johnson took with him once he ventured out and opened his own studio, Steve Johnson's XFX, in 1986. Taking the leap to being a shop owner wasn't necessarily something Johnson wanted to do at the time—it was more out of necessity after things went awry with Boss Film's involvement with *Predator* (1987) early in its storied production.

"I had given some of my best years to Bottin and Baker and now to Edlund, so I thought, *Why not go out and do this on my own, and get all the credit for myself?* But most importantly, I had to venture out on my own because I was fired from Boss Film. I had no other choice."

"They came to me on *Predator* with a design that was initially supplied by the production, who had done an almost impossible design to do. It had an extended head, extended arms, and extended legs, too. They wanted to shoot this character who would be blind, unable to take his own piss, or be able to walk or crawl in the jungles of Mexico."

"When I saw it, I instantly said to everyone, 'There's no plausible way this is going to work.' I'd already read the script and knew the only possible way it could work with that design is if we set up an overhead wire gantry system and flew the guy around like Superman. We'd just take some of his weight off that way, so he could try to move around and run. I tried to warn them, though, that doing things this way meant it was going to take half a day to shoot every single full-body shot, and all everyone said to me was, 'Fine. Make it work.'"

"So we went down there—and they were already weeks over schedule at this point—and guess what? It took half a day to set up every shot, and everybody was outraged that it took so long because they were weeks over schedule. The Director, John McTiernan, and the Producer, Joel Silver, called the studio and said, 'The creature doesn't work. Fuck it. We're sick of this hellhole anyway, so let's all go back to L.A. and figure it out.' That's when they took the job to Stan Winston."

"And while the character's gone on to become this iconic figure, it's nothing like what we had attempted. We were told that they would never film a guy with human proportions, because that was what I kept trying to suggest. But guess what happened? They ended up with a guy who had human proportions."

As an artist, though, Johnson chose to look forward rather than dwell on the past, and that's when he began his ascent as one of the industry's greatest innovators while establishing Steve Johnson's XFX as one of Hollywood's premier effects houses in the game. Johnson's first project post-Boss Film was New World Pictures' *Dead Heat* (1988), the low-budget comedy that featured Treat Williams and Joe Piscopo as undead cops.

The next film Steve tackled was *A Nightmare on Elm Street 4: The Dream Master* (1988), on which he created an ambitious sequence that involved captured human souls bursting out of Freddy Krueger's body, making for an incredible sight and also one of the series' most memorable effects moments.

"I had just seen *Nightmare 3* only two nights before I got the call to do *Part 4*. I remember talking to Linnea Quigley—who I was married to at the time—and I said to her, 'Oh my God, I want to work on a movie like that. The effects are so good. They fit the movie so well. It's so fantastically perfect and unique.' And then I got that call, and I was ecstatic."

"It just seemed so painfully obvious to me how to break all the shots down for that entire sequence, so it really wasn't a tough gig at all," Johnson explained. "There are probably about thirty different effects in it, but I knew exactly how every single one of those effects were going to work even before we made anything. It was storyboarded immaculately. We specifically built every board at the angle we were going to shoot it, knowing what lens we were going to shoot with, too. So, for us, it went like clockwork on the set, but it was also a really crazy environment to be in. They were shooting four simultaneous units where there were four Freddy Kruegers walking around. It was crazy."

"When I eventually saw the final sequence, everybody was going crazy, saying, 'My God, how'd you do it? This is so amazing.' I was absolutely horrified by it, though, as I usually am with most of my work. I just thought it was really obvious what we had done, and that the whole thing

Steve working on a demonic makeup for *Highway to Hell* (1991). Photo courtesy of Steve Johnson.

Various aliens created by Steve throughout his career, including the award-winning NTI (Non-Terrestrial Intelligence, featured in the center of the top row) from *The Abyss* (1989).

failed spectacularly. But as an artist, that's how you do your best work. You just have to constantly beat yourself up so you keep pushing yourself forward."

Over the next few years, Johnson continued to prove himself as one of the most talented artists of the 1980s and 1990s, with memorable work on films such as *Night of the Demons* (1988), *Highway to Hell* (1991), *Pet Sematary Two* (1992), *Innocent Blood* (1992), *Return of the Living Dead 3* (1993), *Species* (1995), and Clive Barker's *Lord of Illusions* (1995), as well as the award-winning Stephen King television miniseries adaptations *IT* (1990) and *The Stand* (1994). But it was his landmark work on James Cameron's *The Abyss* (1989) that would prove to be Steve's biggest challenge, and quite possibly his greatest triumph, as an artist.

"I was very excited to work with Cameron," Johnson expressed. "I will admit that I was more confused, though, as to why Stan Winston wasn't doing it, because Cameron had already worked with him on a couple of films. I later found out why. He forced me to drive down to the Fox lot, where he literally sat in his office as he had me read the script, because he wouldn't let it out of his office."

"So I read it and he said to me, 'Here's what I want you to do. I want you to make the most beautiful, ethereal image ever put on film. I want these creatures to be glass-clear. I want them to self-illuminate. I want them to light up and change colors like a goddamn sign in Las Vegas. And, I want to shoot them completely underwater.' So, anyone in their right mind would say, 'You're out of your mind. You're crazy.' And evidently he had called Stan up, given him the same spiel, and Stan virtually hung up on him, saying, 'There's no way. That's a crazy idea.'"

"But here I was, a kid, saying to myself, *Well, of course I'll go and work on a Cameron film.* And guess what? We made it happen. That's the magic of special effects. That movie was literally impossible to pull off, and there was no digital fallback solution at that point. Had I fucked up, the movie would have had to be rewritten. If we didn't show up with fifteen glowing, glass-clear aliens actually working underwater in San Pedro five months after I was hired, what could the producers have done? Write the aliens out of the script? They couldn't have made them digitally at that point. So, even though I had a lot of sleepless nights, and considered suicide almost every day on that project, it's still my favorite work because we did actually create something that was 99.9% impossible."

"And, to Jim's credit, he helped enormously on it," added Johnson. "He knew what he wanted. He tortured me, of course, throughout the entire build and certainly on set, but he made me do my best work, and I've got to hand it to him for that. I'll always respect him for that."

After contributing to notable films like *Blade II* (2002), *The Rundown* (2003), *The Cat in the Hat* (2003), *War of the Worlds* (2005), and *Spider-Man 2* (2004), Johnson found himself growing disheartened with the business side of the special effects industry, especially once technology began to take over and filmmakers, as well as studios, started relying more and more on digital imagery to bring their characters to life.

"When things started to go south, when digital technology took a huge chunk out of our business, the most frustrating part for me was not losing the bigger contracts. It was more about losing the respect, because even if we did manage an opportunity to pull off an absolutely brilliant practical effect, the audience just thought it was digital anyway. And to me, it was never about the money. It was more about the magic. It was about the adulation. It was about going into a theater and watching the audience gasp and knowing that my team and I had created magic."

Steve's crew testing one of the tentacles for "Doc Ock" during pre-production on *Spider-Man 2* (2004). Photo courtesy of Steve Johnson.

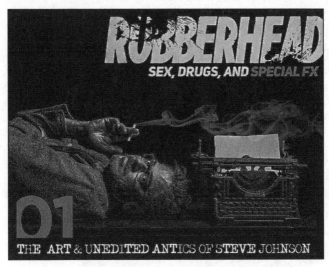

The cover art for Steve's first book, *Rubberhead: Sex, Drugs, and Special FX*. Image courtesy of Steve Johnson.

"To rise from a poor kid in Texas to all of this adulation, and making a million dollars for films where the money was just coming in and then vomiting right back out of the accounts, you think it's never going to end," Johnson admitted. "But then, to have it slow down and transform the way it has, I've been forced to become a better person because of all that. A lot of people have said that adversity will either kill you or make you be a better person, and it hasn't killed me yet, so I've learned encyclopedic knowledge about myself and the human condition of empathy for others just by watching what happened to our business."

While Johnson may have formally closed up his shop back in 2006, that doesn't mean he isn't keeping busy with various projects these days. He still consults as a designer whenever he's approached for a project he sees potential in, but for the most part, Johnson has been focused on putting the finishing touches on his series of memoirs titled *Rubberhead: Sex, Drugs, and Special FX*, which will shed a lot of insight into his creative processes, but will also hopefully act as a catalyst to inspire a new generation of artists and fans.

"The way I see it is that you've got to look at everything as a massive learning experience. Because anytime that anything I've ever considered to be bad has happened to me—like a car crash or a loved one dying—the only way to handle it is to make something good come out of it. That's why I've turned to writing, and I've become a much more private and gentle

Steve collaborating with artist H.R. Giger during pre-production on *Species II* (1998).
Photo courtesy of Steve Johnson.

person. I certainly see myself now as a much more spiritual person than I was back in the heyday. Had the business not changed, I would probably still be a millionaire, convertible-driving, coke-snorting brat. I just can't be that person anymore, because mainly, I can't afford it [laughs]."

13 David Martí

BORN IN BARCELONA, SPAIN, in the early 1970s, DDT Efectos Especiales [Special Effects] founder and Oscar-winner David Martí knows precisely why he first began falling in love with movies: it was all because of Steven Spielberg. And while he may have grown up (and still resides) nearly six thousand miles from Hollywood, Martí never let a little thing like geography get in his way of pursuing his dreams.

"Spielberg was definitely the catalyst for my career," Martí said. "When I was ten years old, that's when I discovered *Raiders of the Lost Ark* and *E.T.*, and I'm sure *Star Wars* was also a factor, too. But that's when I started drawing, and then I realized that I could do even more cool things if I started sculpting. I started sculpting a lot of creatures and monsters, but there was a disconnect because in the movies, monsters were always moving, and I wanted my monsters to move. That's how I started playing around with stop-motion."

"When I was working with stop-motion, I realized how hard it is to make movies. Even though it was hard, stop-motion was really cool to

Photo courtesy of David Martí.

229

me because it allowed me to do what I really wanted to do with monsters. I started to make these short films about Indiana Jones using my dad's Super 8 camera, where I would get together with my friends from school and pretend we were fighting and chasing away the bad guys. I was even dressing like Indiana Jones back then."

"After I started filming the Super 8 movies, I realized that using a little bit of blood would make everything look even better. That's when I realized that I needed special effects, but I didn't know anything about them, so I found magazines like *Fangoria* or *Cinefex*, and they blew me away. Obviously, I didn't understand a lot of what was going on just because I didn't know English then, so I was just looking at the pictures and trying to study them and see what was going on. That was the beginning of my interest in makeup and special effects proper."

"I really enjoyed the process of putting makeup on myself, too," added Martí, "especially when I would put something on myself and could go scare my friends or my neighbors with how I looked. To me, the reaction was everything."

While he was ecstatic to discover something that allowed him to express himself creatively and keep him connected to the world of film that

From left to right: Montse Ribé, Dick Smith, David Martí, and Rick Baker.
Photo courtesy of David Martí.

he loved so much, Martí knew early on that his path to becoming a professional makeup artist would not be an easy one.

"A lot of people didn't believe that I could do special effects because of how hard it is to do something like that in a country where there is no tradition of doing this kind of work, especially with fantasy or horror. But it's the strength of believing in something that much that leads you towards it, because I always say, 'You never get something you really want in this world without fighting for it.' A lot of times people ask me, 'How do I get where you are?' My only answer is that you have to work really, really, really hard. That's what me and my team at DDT have been doing since we started the company in 1991."

"I started studying effects in 1990, and I got in touch with Dick Smith through an advertisement in *Fangoria* magazine because I saw he was doing a class. I wrote him a letter and he responded with a fax, which was amazing technology at the time. I started to talk with him and he was super kind about everything. He asked me to send him pictures of what I had been doing until then so he knew if he was going to accept me as a student. Dick didn't want to start from scratch; he wanted somewhat advanced people so he could help them refine their techniques. I sent my pictures to him and he agreed to give me the course."

"But the thing was like a six-hundred-page book that was filled with information," Martí continued. "It wasn't easy for me because I didn't know much English then, and it was very technical and there were very little pictures. I read that thing with my dictionary right next to me and I took a lot of notes as I went through it. I tried to make some stuff, but there was no way to get materials here in Spain because this was before the Internet. I had to wait until my first trip to London to finally get a chance to buy foam latex. Everything was really difficult and slow because I was doing everything on my own."

"I did my own experiments with materials, and a lot of this stuff I learned to do by myself because there was no other option. We finally had the chance to do some monster makeups for kids' toys, and with those characters, we went around showing people our work. Little by little, we would get different stuff, but a lot of production companies would tell us if we have money, we're going to London, and if you don't have money, then we'll come to you. That was very hard, because we never had any money to really work. We did a lot of very low-budget stuff in the early years and

Montse Ribé and David working on an oversized head for a DDT client.
Photo courtesy of David Martí.

put in the money ourselves just so we could have something to show afterwards. We did that for five or six years, and we were doing all kinds of effects—it wasn't just traditional makeup. We could blow up a car or explode windows or make rain or wind, too. Little by little, we tried hard to get into specialized effects like puppets, animatronics, and makeup."

As DDT continued to make a name for itself in Spain, David found himself crossing paths with another up-and-coming talent by the name of Guillermo del Toro, who had come from the world of special effects in Mexico and successfully transitioned to being a notable filmmaker with his feature film directorial debut, *Cronos* (1993).

"In the mid-1990s, we had worked on a short film called *Aftermath*, which was this gross movie about necrophilia, but we got to create some amazing effects and it went on to play at the Sitges Film Festival. Guillermo was there with his first movie, *Cronos*, and he was in the room when *Aftermath* played. When *Aftermath* finished and the lights went on, he started screaming, 'Where's DDT? Where's DDT?' We had no idea what was going on. At that time, Guillermo was already kind of a famous guy, so it was a 'holy shit' moment for us that he was even looking to speak with us."

"We introduced ourselves and he was really nice to all of us. Guillermo told us that he had a movie that he wanted to shoot in Spain, and that he wanted to make all of the special effects with us. We were amazed and super happy to be in touch with him. He spent years talking about all of these different projects, but could never get a green light. Before we got to work together, Guillermo got to make *Mimic*, and that was the first time he experienced the Hollywood mechanism, which was a really nasty experience for him. But after *Mimic*, which was nine years after he first shook our hands at Sitges, he finally called us up and said, 'I'm finally getting to do the movie I want to shoot in Spain.' And that's how we got to work on *The Devil's Backbone*."

"In 2000, we shot *The Devil's Backbone*, which was a really cool experience, and we all liked working with Guillermo in the hard times and the good times. When we started working on it, Guillermo wasn't really known to many people here in Spain, but they were all familiar with the Producer, Pedro Almodóvar, who is probably the most famous director here. We've worked with Pedro on several movies since *The Devil's Backbone*, too, doing a lot of different stuff, and we were grateful Guillermo could connect us with Pedro. *The Devil's Backbone* was a great film, and it became a big thing in Spain because it opened doors for movies to start being made here. We were lucky to be in the right place at the right time, all because of Guillermo," David added.

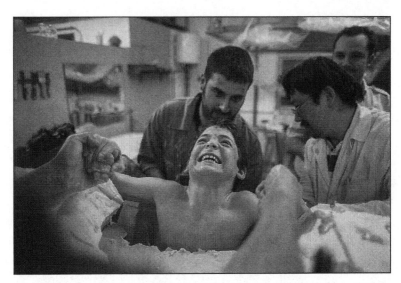

Junio Valverde undergoes the lifecasting process for *The Devil's Backbone* (2001).
Photo courtesy of David Martí.

Junio Valverde in the full Santi makeup on the set of *The Devil's Backbone* (2001).
Photo courtesy of David Martí.

While *The Devil's Backbone* (2001) certainly put Martí and his entire team at DDT on the map among genre fans, effects enthusiasts, and industry professionals, it was his next collaboration with del Toro that would make an even bigger impact.

"I would say that the movie where we really thought, '*Wow, this is the beginning of something,*' was *Hellboy*. When he [del Toro] started *Hellboy*, that was after *Blade* and *Blade II*, so Guillermo had much more creative power going into this one. *Hellboy* was something that he had wanted to do for such a long time. He could never get the budget for it, so when he finally got to make it, I was so happy for him. And I love Hellboy and was a fan of the comic books, too."

"Guillermo then started putting together his teams—he got [Rick Baker's] Cinovation [Studios] to do the Hellboy character, Mike Elizalde was doing a lot of the bad guys, and then DDT was asked to do some other stuff. That was like a dream for us, because we were surrounded by all of these amazing people who were all incredibly nice and we learned some tricks for sculpting from them, too. It was our first American movie, so we didn't know what to expect. Usually a Spanish movie will take a month and a half or two months to shoot, but for *Hellboy*, we were shooting for six months. That's how we realized you need a lot of time to shoot a movie like that, with all the action and adventure. It was very different from what we had been doing up until then."

"*Hellboy* also taught us a lot about how Guillermo works, especially at this level of filmmaking. For instance, one thing Guillermo really hates is to see lazy people, so if he comes by and sees that you are not busy enough, he will have you do something just to make sure you are keeping busy. Something that I will always remember from the *Hellboy* shoot is when the painters were on the set in Prague, and the whole team was sitting around and eating when Guillermo passed by them. He saw that they weren't working and said to them, 'Guys, I think that wall is the wrong color.' The painters were like, 'No, you said you wanted it brown, so we painted it brown.' Guillermo told them it had to be a green wall and they had to work quickly because they were shooting a scene with it tomorrow. So the painters rushed to get it done, and the next day Guillermo passed by them and said, 'Guys, why did you paint this green? This has to be brown, so you have to redo it right away,' [laughs]."

"Working with Guillermo is very different from a lot of the directors we know and work with, because he understands the process like no one else. Guillermo actually took the Dick Smith course, too, and his company worked on *Cronos*. I still remember this sign they had above their door at the workshop in Mexico that read, 'We are not good, but we are the only ones.' Guillermo knows a lot of things about makeup and can tell you, 'I want this in silicone,' or, 'I want this in foam latex.' Many directors don't know the difference, so it's always really great to work with somebody that understands the process."

Martí and DDT went on to lend their talents to another American studio project when they were hired to handle the second unit effects on *Doom*

Ladislav Beran as Kroenen in *Hellboy* (2004). Photo courtesy of David Martí.

(2005), the big-screen adaptation of the popular first-shooter video game starring Dwayne "The Rock" Johnson, Karl Urban, and Rosamund Pike.

"We were very lucky to be working with the second unit on *Doom* because there was a lot less pressure on us, and it was a more open environment to create in. Jon Farhat was the Second Unit Director, and I've worked with him two or three times, but *Doom* was our first project together. I remember that Stan Winston was also involved in *Doom*, and so was Bill Sturgeon [the Visual Effects Creature Coordinator]."

"Bill knows everything, and what's funny about that project was that we initially did a budget that, for us, was really high because we were thinking we would have to create all these creature copies. We were planning for the worst. But then Bill calls me up and says, 'Before you send the budget to the studio, let's take a look first.' So I sent him the budget, and he called me back and said, 'Let me give you some advice. Put down double the budget and you'll still be under the price of Stan's rate.' So *Doom* was the first time that someone told me to double my budget. That was crazy."

El Fauno mask from *Pan's Labyrinth* (2006), which shows signs of age after more than a decade. Photo courtesy of David Martí.

"*Doom* was really fun for us, but it was a lot of work," Martí admitted. "One of the worst days we had was when we were there for fourteen hours applying different makeups. The downside to *Doom* ended up being that whenever you did see some kind of creature or zombie, it was lit very darkly and it was always moving fast. A lot of the stuff we did, you never see because either it's too hard to see it or they shot it and didn't use it in the end. Some of that was frustrating, but we were still having fun doing a lot of makeups, and we got to work alongside some great guys from Stan's team."

Martí reteamed with del Toro shortly after *Doom* for *Pan's Labyrinth* (2006), Guillermo's heartbreaking fairy tale set amidst the Spanish Civil War. A film that would go on to win three Academy Awards, *Pan's Labyrinth* (2006) was the visionary director's chance to take the prototypical fairy tale entities—a faun, fairies, and an ogre—and give them his own patented, imaginative twist. For the project, del Toro relied on the talents of David and his team at DDT to handle his ambitious, now-iconic characters, including the Pale Man and El Fauno, as well as a troublesome toad living inside of a decrepit tree trunk.

Close-up of Doug Jones in El Fauno makeup for *Pan's Labyrinth* (2006).
Photo courtesy of David Martí.

"Guillermo started to talk about *Pan's Labyrinth* back when we were still working on *Hellboy*," recalled Martí. "He was talking about a fairy tale thing he wanted to do, and Pan [a.k.a. El Fauno] was actually [going to be] a goat guy with furry legs. After *Hellboy*, he kept talking about it and sending me parts of the script, which was pretty different from what you see in the movie now, because he didn't have enough time to really sit down and flesh out the story at that point. So the process for us on *Pan's* was that we started without actually knowing what anything was going to look like."

Doug Jones posing as El Fauno behind the scenes on *Pan's Labyrinth* (2006). Photo courtesy of David Martí.

"Then, in April 2005, when we officially started work on *Pan's*, we didn't have a look or a design or anything nailed down, so it was all still very open. I remember that the first drawings we did of Pan were of a little boy. We ended up changing it because Guillermo thought the little boy version of Pan wouldn't be powerful enough, so we changed it to Pan as he is in the film now. We also did a golden version of Pan, but it just didn't look right. Guillermo had mentioned that he was thinking that Pan should be this creature that is of the earth, so he should almost look like he's camouflaged in nature. We had Sergio Sandoval, an artist we worked with at the time, do Pan's legs, and we showed that drawing to Guillermo. He flipped out when he saw it."

Martí recalled the very first time del Toro laid eyes on Doug Jones as El Fauno, saying, "The first night we shot the makeup tests for Pan, they were shooting it from above on this hill, downwards into the labyrinth. We had to walk Doug up the hill while dressed as Pan, and as we're making our way through all the people, everyone got really quiet as Guillermo walked towards us."

"He just stopped, looked at Doug, and then gave him a really big hug, and everyone started to applaud. That kind of response from everyone on

Alternate design for the Pale Man for *Pan's Labyrinth* (2006). Photo courtesy of David Martí.

An alternate maquette of stage two of the Pale Man, which wasn't used for *Pan's Labyrinth* (2006). Photo courtesy of David Martí.

the crew was a first for me, and to this day, it's my very favorite creature we've ever done."

The concept behind the Pale Man's look was based on del Toro's idea of a very old man who used to be extremely overweight, but has become literally nothing more than skin and bones, with his epidermis hanging off his limbs like fleshy, sallow curtains. It was del Toro's idea to give the character a manta ray-like appearance, and the filmmaker asked Martí and his team to go with a look that removed most of the creature's facial features (save for the nostrils). Before the Pale Man's eyeball hands were conceived, though, del Toro had a different idea in mind—one that nearly derailed Martí and his team from working on the character altogether.

"Originally, Guillermo wanted the Pale Man to have these lips that would go so wide that the skull underneath the skin would then pop out," David said. "Then, a skeleton was supposed to crawl out, and Guillermo wanted him to go down on all fours and transform into something else, similar to the transformation scene from *An American Werewolf in London*. This was so he would be able to chase Ofelia, because otherwise he was a blind character, so that meant he couldn't traditionally find her."

When Martí initially rebuffed the idea and told del Toro that it wasn't something that could happen at their budgetary level, his response didn't exactly please the ambitious filmmaker, and the pair went several weeks without speaking. Realizing a few weeks later that they still needed to nail down the character, Martí visited del Toro's production office to have a meeting that would lead to the creation of the Pale Man's now-iconic eyeball hands.

As Martí acted out the role of the Pale Man for his longtime friend, using his hands to guide him as he pretended he was blind, del Toro realized that if they added eyes to the hands and mimicked the look of eyelashes with the Pale Man's fingertips, they could simplify the overall character design with just a few tweaks, making for a much easier concept to execute than a full-blown transformation sequence, thus solving a very big problem for everyone.

"Imagination isn't about having a lot of money," Martí insisted. "Imagination is about something magical. Sometimes, you have to go back and reconsider designs because of your budget, but that kind of

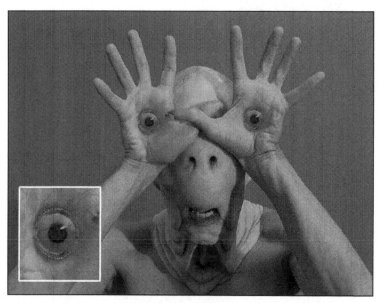

An eye test for the Pale Man during pre-production on *Pan's Labyrinth* (2006). Photo courtesy of David Martí.

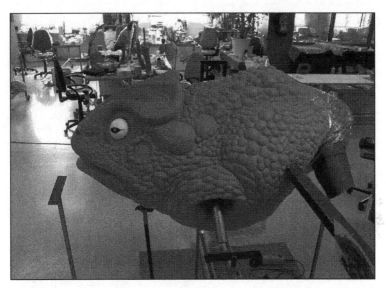

The giant toad sculpture created by DDT for *Pan's Labyrinth* (2006).
Photo courtesy of David Martí.

challenge gives artists the opportunity to push harder and come up with something new. Sometimes, what seems like a challenge ends up becoming a real opportunity."

As successful as the appearances of both Pan and the Pale Man ended up being, there was one creation from *Pan's Labyrinth* (2006) that proved to be the biggest challenge for del Toro and his crew: the toad who lives inside of the tree roots, whom Ofelia must conquer to retrieve a special key from his belly.

"The toad was always an issue because it was something that had a specific design, and the way Guillermo wanted to do it made it very difficult for that creature to move the way he wanted it to. My longtime partner, Montse Ribé, even got inside the suit herself, but it weighed almost as much as she did, making it nearly impossible to move, let alone jump in. He was never designed to jump, because that wasn't a function I had been informed of. When we got him to set and realized how limited his movements would be, we had to change the story to this frog being stuck inside this claustrophobic tunnel instead of how it was originally written, which was this elaborate and oversized set."

When David looks back on his experiences from *Pan's Labyrinth* (2006), there's an evident fondness in his voice for the work he created

David and Montse Ribé pose with their Oscars after winning an Academy Award for Best Makeup in 2007. Photo courtesy of David Martí.

on the project, especially since his and Ribé's extraordinary efforts were rewarded with an Oscar the following year. Martí, though, is still the first to admit that it all came at a price.

"*Pan's Labyrinth* was one of the hardest things we've ever had to do at DDT; in fact, we even ended the movie bankrupt and had two of our guys quit on us right after. It was like going through hell, with only a few moments of heaven to be found."

"All my best moments, really, came from being with Doug Jones in the makeup trailer. He was always singing and smiling and just doing everything he could to keep everyone in good spirits. When you get to work with someone like that, and also get to work with someone that has an imagination like Guillermo does, it all ends up being worth it in the end."

Even though *Pan's Labyrinth* (2006) put David and his partners at DDT through the wringer both financially and emotionally, del Toro promised to make good by his friend on his next directorial project, 2008's *Hellboy II: The Golden Army*.

"After *Pan's Labyrinth*, Guillermo said to me, 'I know you've been dealing with money trouble because of *Pan*, so I want to give back to you on the next movie, because you deserve that.' And I always appreciated that kind of loyalty in Guillermo. Many other directors wouldn't do that."

"At the time, we were actually working on the budget for *The Witches*, the [adaptation of the] Roald Dahl book, which Guillermo said was going to be next on his plate. Then, suddenly he called me up one day and said, 'Stop everything! We're making *Hellboy II* now.' That was a complete surprise. We had two or three meetings in London, because that's one of the locations where they were going to shoot [the other was Budapest]. I was with Mike Elizalde, Cliff Wallace, and Guillermo, and he had a bunch of designs that had to be redone. Together, we all went through the designs, and Mike and Cliff got to pick what they wanted to work on and then I got to pick what I wanted to create, too."

"Everybody went back home with a dozen monster designs, and we did our budget for the work I had chosen for us to do. For what Guillermo wanted to do in *Hellboy II*, there weren't enough people available in Spain to handle that workload, so I knew that I was going to have to get people in from France and London to help out. Beyond their rates being higher in those countries, I also had to pay for accommodations for everyone, too. I gave my first budget to Guillermo and he told me that I was insane and there was no way he could pay that. We worked together to try to change this and that, and we submitted a lower budget to him."

"Even after that, Guillermo told us that it had to be lower still, so we went back and forth for a couple of months, but I finally said to him, 'I can't spend any more time doing budgets that I know you are not going to pay.' He told me that there were probably people in London that could do it for a lower budget than what I was submitting, and he had to go ahead and use them. And to me, I'd prefer not to do something for Guillermo and keep being friends, because he's that important to me. I knew I just couldn't do what he needed me to do at that budget on *Hellboy II*, because we probably wouldn't have survived it. So I told Guillermo, 'It's good, we're still friends and that's the end of that.'"

Martí was okay with moving on from *Hellboy II: The Golden Army* (2008), even if he was disappointed he wasn't able to work with his long-time friend on his newest project—until, that is, del Toro once again surprised him with an unexpected phone call.

"One day, about three months later, Guillermo calls me up and tells me, 'David, I can't make this movie without you and Montse on it.' I asked

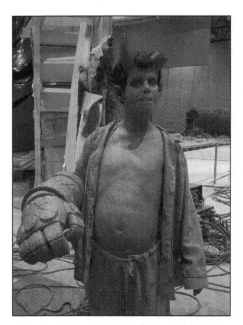

Montse Ribé as Young Hellboy on the set of *Hellboy II: The Golden Army* (2008). Photo courtesy of David Martí.

him what it was that he wanted us to do, and he told me that he had this one character in particular that was very special to him and I had to make it, no matter what."

"He told me about this flashback scene that he came up with at the beginning of the movie, showing Hellboy when he was ten years old with John Hurt. Guillermo wanted him back for another *Hellboy* movie, but he couldn't do it in present time. So Guillermo thought about opening everything with the father of Hellboy telling him the story of The Golden Army. I thought it sounded so cool, and we were more than happy to do it. We looked at the numbers Guillermo gave us and decided it was going to be tight, but it was a fair budget."

"We agreed to do Young Hellboy, but then Guillermo dropped another bombshell on us: he wanted Montse to play Young Hellboy. He didn't want to bring in an actor just for that one small scene, and he reassured me that she would be fine because Hellboy doesn't talk during the scene. It was all going to be flashbacks with music and no dialogue. Montse agreed to play the part, we started to work on everything, and it was even easier because we could do as many tests as we needed on her."

"When we were working on the makeup, Guillermo called me up again and said, 'Oh, there's something else I didn't tell you. I need you to do the wardrobe for Young Hellboy, too, so I need you guys to make him some pajamas.' I told him he was such a gypsy because something was always changing with him, but we'd do Hellboy's pajamas, too. In fact, my mother actually made the pajamas. When we did the two makeup tests, Guillermo didn't like either one of them, and honestly, we didn't, either. That character was really difficult because it was just a kid with a demon face that had to remind you of Ron Perlman, but you can't put Ron Perlman's face on the kid because it will look like a dwarf or a goblin."

"We left for Budapest, and we had one day to do the final makeup test. Guillermo came by and looked at the pieces and the prosthetics before they were applied, and I could tell he was not happy. He didn't say anything and then left. Then, we put on the makeup and went to set to see Guillermo, and he said exactly these words, 'Fuck, I re-

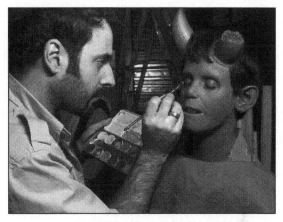

David touches up Montse Ribé as Young Hellboy between takes on *Hellboy II: The Golden Army* (2008). Photo courtesy of David Martí.

ally thought I was going to have to change Montse's hand, young Hellboy's hand, in CGI [computer-generated imagery], because what you showed me, I didn't like it at all. But now, I really love it.' We were so relieved."

A ghost baby gets caught up on the script for *Crimson Peak* (2015). Photo courtesy of David Martí.

"What's funny about that scene is that one week before we were leaving for Budapest, production finally sent over the script. I was reading through it and realized, *Oh, wow, there is dialogue here, and Young Hellboy is talking quite a bit.* Montse got nervous because all of the sudden she had to really be able to act. That was a really hard thing for Montse, but also fun at the same time because she got to work with John [Hurt]. Once we got to set, John didn't really know what was going on. That made her a little more comfortable," Martí added, "because here was this legend and they were both in the same boat together."

David and DDT have kept busy throughout the last several years both in the States and abroad. Easily one of their more noteworthy projects of late was del Toro's Gothic romance *Crimson Peak* (2015), on which Martí and his team helped bring Guillermo's haunting, spectral visions to life.

"*Crimson Peak* was an amazing time. We started off designing everything here in Barcelona, but then Guillermo told me that he wanted us to come to Toronto and work there exclusively on everything. He didn't want anybody to see what we were doing, and while I was a little afraid of leaving my city for a whole year, we thought it would be a new way of seeing how we could do our work. We went to Toronto and set up a workshop from scratch, which was very difficult. You would think in Toronto that you would find everything you need, but we didn't find everything, so a lot of stuff had to come from the States, and then we had to deal with customs. It all worked out eventually, though."

"I loved Guillermo's idea that these ghosts come from the mud and the mud of Crimson Peak is crimson, so the ghosts would be red. I just thought that sounded so cool. We wanted to make the ghosts look like very realistic mummified people, and he pushed us to go to the extreme with the design. Guillermo told us that he wanted to walk a very fine line between scary and almost comical with the design, so that's what we did."

Montse Ribé and David work on one of the ghostly residents of *Crimson Peak* (2015). Photo courtesy of David Martí.

"The whole process was really fun, because on all of the other movies that we had done with Guillermo, we sent the stuff through email and then we'd have a phone call about it. For *Crimson Peak*, we were able to sit down at a table with Guillermo and go through everything while we were brainstorming, so that was a great experience to have, too."

"One interesting thing that happened with the ghosts and their red coloring was that after we put the makeup on and then put the slime on to make them shiny, there was such a contrast on the monitor that they truly looked like some kind of visual composition. They looked like they weren't really there at all. Guillermo put a rough cut of the movie together to show it to some people, and the feedback was that the ghosts were all CGI, but there was no CGI even used at that point. I loved the design, but I think he [del Toro] ended up pushing them a little too far in the end."

For more than twenty-five years now, David and his team at DDT Efectos Especiales have blazed a trail in the realm of modern special effects unlike any of their peers. Throughout his career, Martí has been afforded the opportunity to collaborate with some of the most brilliant filmmakers of the last several decades, including the aforementioned Pedro Almodóvar

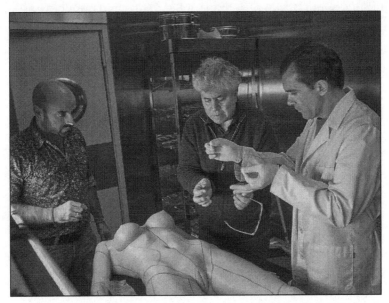

David on set with Pedro Almodóvar and Antonio Banderas during production on *The Skin I Live In* (2011). Photo courtesy of David Martí.

David poses on the set of *A Monster Calls* (2016). Photo courtesy of David Martí.

and Guillermo del Toro, as well as Jaume Balagueró, Stuart Gordon, Paco Plaza, J.A. Bayona, and Alejandro G. Iñárritu.

"It's pretty amazing that we are still here," said Martí. "We are still working and we're still doing crazy stuff, and the one thing that has been so surprising to me is that every year, we do something completely different that we have never done before. We're never bored because we're always dealing with new challenges, and that's important for any artist."

"Because I started from scratch, where I had to start my own business and I had to teach myself how to do everything, overcoming those odds is another reason why I'm still here. It was a difficult thing, being the first one here in Barcelona and not knowing a lot at the beginning, so I had no idea that we'd even make it half as long as we have. I feel very proud that a lot of our techniques are so unorthodox, too, because that means we can always bring a new perspective into any project. Plus, dealing with everything the way we did in the early days makes you grow up, and it makes you prepared for anything."

14 Phil Tippett

FOR OVER FORTY YEARS, Phil Tippett's name has been synonymous with cutting-edge visual effects and animation. Along with his many accolades, Tippett's body of work is demonstrative of his forward-thinking approach as both an artist and a technician. When you speak with him, Tippett will often refer to himself as a guy who either "got lucky" or happened to "be in the right place at the right time," but in reality, Tippett is a huge reason why modern filmmakers have been able to reap the benefits of advancing technologies for decades.

However, Tippett's fascination with the creative arts had much simpler beginnings than the innovative approaches he would later become known for, and it was another pioneer, Ray Harryhausen, who first inspired him to take his initial steps toward what would become a forty-plus-year journey as an artist.

"I saw *The 7th Voyage of Sinbad* when I was just seven years old, and that experience just stayed with me," Tippett recalled. "I didn't necessarily know how to do stop-motion; I just knew I wanted to do it. So, for me, it

Photo courtesy of Phil Tippett.

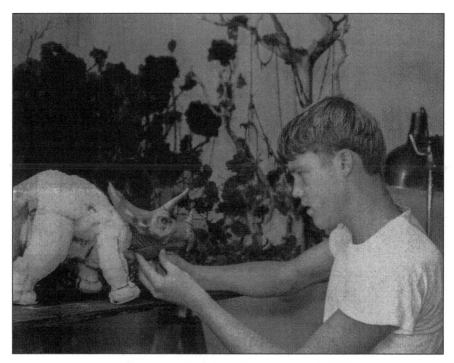

A young Phil sculpts a Triceratops. Photo courtesy of Phil Tippett.

was all trial by error. There were no places that you could go to that taught this stuff, and there weren't any books that I could find, either."

"I attempted to find people out there that could mentor me, and

A young Phil with Ray Bradbury. Photo courtesy of Phil Tippett.

somehow I got lucky and was able to meet a bunch of people over the years who all taught me numerous tricks and techniques. That's the only way I could figure out how to get started. Then, I mowed a lot of lawns, saved up some money for an 8mm camera, and just started pushing things around. I loved it."

During his teenage years, Tippett met two particularly influential gentlemen who not only fostered his love for stop-motion, but also made him realize that if you truly believe in something, you can't let the naysayers convince you otherwise.

"When I was fourteen or fifteen years old, I met this guy named Bill Stromberg, who was on a local television program in San Diego during the afternoon movies they'd show, and he had made a stop-motion movie. I was able to get in touch with him, and he was open to me helping him out and showing me the ropes."

"That led to me assisting Bill in making a 16mm version of Ray Bradbury's "A Sound of Thunder." When Ray came to visit a local college around that time, I wrote him a note and showed him some pictures of what we were working on, and that fostered a pretty long correspondence with Ray. He was really the only adult in my life that told me not to listen to the other adults who had been telling me the whole time, 'There's no way you'll be working in the movies because that option just isn't open to you.' He just kept saying to me, 'No. You have stick to your guns if this is what you really want to do.' So Ray was pretty crucial to me as an artist along the way."

After earning his degree in fine arts at the University of California, Irvine, Tippett wanted to work in stop-motion animation, but quickly

Phil at work on a Jolly Green Giant commercial at Cascade Pictures.
Photo courtesy of Phil Tippett.

learned that he would have to forge an alternative path in the industry before feature films came calling.

"At the time I began working professionally in stop-motion, there had only been Willis O'Brien and Ray who had really been able to make a career out of it, and O'Brien didn't actually work that much. Ray continued making a film every couple of years, so he was certainly more prolific. But that was about it. Except for those two guys, there wasn't much of a scene."

"The only real work we could get at the time was working on television commercials. I worked for a place called Cascade Pictures that had an insert stage—Stage 6—and that's where we did work with the Pillsbury Doughboy, the Jolly Green Giant, and all those types of animation jobs. That was a great learning experience for me because our boss was a guy named Phil Kellison, and he was very inclusive and would let us use the shop and the facilities to work on some of our own projects on the side."

"That's where I met Dennis Muren, Ken Ralston, and a bunch of the other guys that I would go on to work with a lot in my career. So that kept

Phil examines his holochess creations for *Star Wars: Episode IV – A New Hope* (1977). Photo courtesy of Phil Tippett.

me going for a while, but everything changed when George Lucas came onto the scene."

Tippett experienced a huge career shift in the late 1970s, as he was hired along with Jon Berg to create the stop-motion Dejarik holochess game that Chewbacca is fond of in Lucas' *Star Wars: Episode IV – A New Hope* (1977). Tippett was also heavily involved in the film's ambitious cantina set, sculpting and molding creatures for the iconic scene featuring dozens of space aliens, and he even performed as several members of the cantina band.

While he remembers the time he spent on *A New Hope* (1977) as being rather brief overall ("George was the kind of guy who, even if he had a set made that cost $1 million, would just get on and off of it as quickly as possible."), Tippett was indeed happy that Lucas was so thrilled with his work in making the holochess game on the *Millennium Falcon* a reality, and his efforts would continue to be rewarded on future *Star Wars* (1977) sequels.

Lucas' visual effects company, Industrial Light & Magic (ILM), approached Tippett and Berg to make the move from Los Angeles to the San Francisco Bay Area so they could work in their facilities to improve the stop-motion animation on *Star Wars: Episode V – The Empire Strikes*

Phil oversees the animation of an AT-AT walker on *Star Wars: Episode V – The Empire Strikes Back* (1980). Photo courtesy of Phil Tippett.

Phil manipulating Luke Skywalker riding his tauntaun for *Star Wars: Episode V – The Empire Strikes Back* (1980). Photo courtesy of Phil Tippett.

Back (1980). The risk of transplanting his whole life for ILM paid off, as Tippett ended up joining the team that would develop a landmark animation technique called "go-motion," which gave inanimate objects new life on the silver screen and forever changed the entire film industry.

"Being involved with go-motion was more a result of being in the right place at the right time. Stop-motion people had for years been trying to figure out ways of adding motion-blur to things, but it was too time consuming and cumbersome, and nothing ever looked very good anyhow, up until that point."

"When we got up to ILM and started to set up shop for *Empire*, it was very clear that one of the first things we had to do was experiment with combining motion-control technology that they used for the spaceships, and then find a way to apply it to stop-motion characters. It ended up being a very rudimentary array that we did, where it was just kind of latching together two types of technology and seeing what they could do."

Tippett's efforts were all worth it, though, as his contributions to the creation of go-motion helped lead many of us to believe that Luke Skywalker's tauntaun was a living, breathing creature in *The Empire Strikes*

Back (1980). The work of Tippett and the entire visual effects crew on the sequel garnered the film a Special Achievement Award at the 53rd Oscars, and the movie also took home a statuette for Best Sound Mixing.

After *The Empire Strikes Back* (1980), Tippett utilized the go-motion technique on the fantasy film *Dragonslayer* (1981), bringing to life director Matthew Robbins' ambitious vision of a realistic fire-breathing dragon by the name of Vermithrax. Tippett was in charge of Vermithrax's movements on land, and his friend Ken Ralston was tasked with handling the dragon's ability to fly convincingly throughout the film. Both Tippett and Ralston, as well as Dennis Muren and Brian Johnson, were nominated for an Oscar for their labors on *Dragonslayer*, but it was *Raiders of the Lost Ark* (1981), another ILM production that Tippett was involved with, that took home the gold that year.

When Tippett returned to "a galaxy far, far away" to work on *Star Wars: Episode VI – Return of the Jedi* (1983), Lucas put him in charge of the ILM creature shop, where he not only designed the iconic Jabba the Hutt, but was also tasked with creating several other characters at Jabba's palace, including the rancor that Luke battles in the pit. While it was a

Phil with his Oscar-nominated *Dragonslayer* (1981) creation.
Photo courtesy of Phil Tippett.

Left to right: Phil Tippett, Dennis Muren, Ken Ralston, and Richard Edlund pose with their Oscar statuettes after winning for their effects work on *The Return of the Jedi* (1983) at the 1984 Academy Awards. Photo courtesy of Phil Tippett.

whole new experience for him, Tippett proved that his skills as an artist were assuredly multifaceted, so much so that he found himself nominated for another Academy Award for his work on *Return of the Jedi* (1983), which he won for the very first time.

"I was, again, lucky to be in the right place at the right time," explained Tippett. "Being able to be a part of that award was pretty much a result of George deciding that I should get an Academy Award. Up until that time, only three people were officially given the award, and so he did a little politicking and worked with a producer that I knew who liked me. There is a whole process that is pretty involved to get to the point of getting nominated, so it meant a lot to me to be recognized for what I achieved on that film in particular."

Shortly after working on *Return of the Jedi* (1983), Tippett decided it was time to strike out on his own and founded Tippett Studio, providing him with the freedom to pursue his own personal projects.

"After *Return of the Jedi*, there wasn't a lot of work, so I decided to take a year off. I made this short film called *Prehistoric Beast* (1985), which was about dinosaurs, and everything with the company just kind of grew from there."

"*Prehistoric Beast* came across the radar of producer Steve Mark, of Phillips-Mark Productions in New York, and because he liked what I did in that, he had me work on an animated television special called *Dinosaur!* that Christopher Reeve narrated. Then it was just more and more work, eventually leading up to *RoboCop*."

Tippett's involvement in Paul Verhoeven's dystopian actioner came about because of the work he had done years prior on one of Joe Dante's early films, on which he had met another influential figure in his career, a producer by the name of Jon Davison.

"Jon was a big stop-motion fan who I had met back on *Piranha*," Tippett said. "The circumstances of us working together again in the future was another instance of me being in the right place at the right time, and connecting with the right people. We immediately clicked and always had a good working relationship, especially since we would go on to do *RoboCop 2* and *Starship Troopers* together."

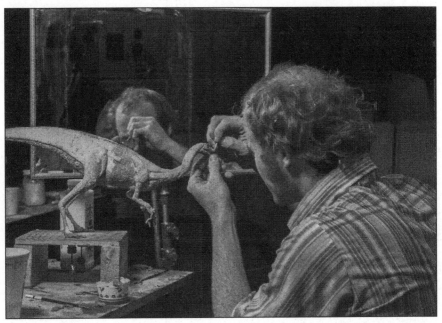

Phil prepares his titular creations for *Dinosaur!* (1985). Photo courtesy of Phil Tippett.

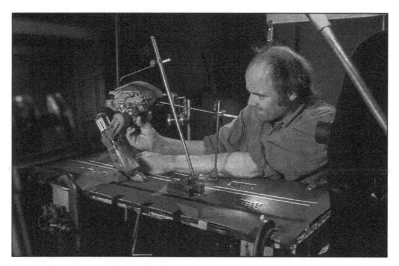

Phil manipulates an ED-209 (Enforcement Droid Series 209) for *RoboCop* (1987).
Photo courtesy of Phil Tippett.

"In 1985, Jon had this movie called *RoboCop* he was trying to put together that Orion [Pictures] was willing to fund, and I can recall that he spent a lot of time looking for a director. He practically pulled out the directory for directors, and he started with the As and worked his way down the alphabet, but nobody wanted to do it. He finally got down to the Vs and got in touch with Paul, and he didn't want to do it. I think his wife, Martine, talked him into it, and Paul eventually came on board, but he did initially turn Jon down."

Tippett was brought onto *RoboCop* (1987) to help animate the ED-209 robots, which were crucial elements of the movie that helped transport the look of Verhoeven's project into the future. The design work of the ED-209 was left in the hands of Craig Hayes, who worked in tandem with Tippett to ensure the robotic creations were up to the standards of the film's ambitious director.

"Every project is a challenge in one way or another," Tippett said. "It starts with interpreting the script and finding out what the director has in mind and what it is that they exactly want. Sometimes it's easy, sometimes it's more challenging. Each show has its own set of new things that you have to rethink, and this was no different."

"Even though in a lot of ways the work I did on *RoboCop* was very much using the same system that I had used many times before, that didn't mean I didn't have to change my approach to make sure I was meeting Paul's vision. All of the photographic approaches to the ED-209 had already been really well worked out, it was just a matter of doing it the way Paul wanted us to do it. As an artist, sometimes you have to learn to adapt."

Tippett's ability to adapt would be tested even more in just a few years when Steven Spielberg hired him to create the dinosaurs for his summer blockbuster *Jurassic Park* (1993), based on the successful work he had done on previous creature-centric efforts like *Dragonslayer* (1981), *Prehistoric Beast* (1985), and *Dinosaur!* (1985).

"Steven knew I was a guy who understood dinosaurs and dinosaur movements, so when we initially began discussions on *Jurassic Park*, we had planned to do it all conventionally with go-motion and high-speed miniature dinosaurs. Dennis [Muren] had been working with computer graphics for a number of years at ILM already, and he wanted to push the envelope and see if they could do it initially for the stampeding dinosaurs scene. He thought he could get away with computer graphics for the live master shots, and the more they got into it, the more the dinosaurs held up."

"Then, Steven and Kathy [Kennedy, the Producer] gave them money to do some tests, and once the tests were finished and looked great, Steven

Phil and Dennis Muren on the set of *The Empire Strikes Back* (1980). The two have remained longtime friends and colleagues for decades. Photo courtesy of Phil Tippett.

determined that's how he wanted to do the movie, and I knew I was in trouble."

But rather than being replaced on *Jurassic Park* (1993), Tippett remained a crucial part of the visual effects team, working with the newly developed digital Dinosaur Input Devices (DIDs): mechanisms that allowed stop-motion animators to put data into the computer. It was Muren who introduced Tippett to the world of computer-generated imagery, forever changing the direction of his colleague's career, and leading him to his second Academy Award for his extraordinary efforts on *Jurassic Park* (1993).

"There was no choice, in my opinion; I knew I was as extinct as those dinosaurs if I didn't embrace the technology. I had no real exposure to computer graphics, but over time, Dennis kept me in the loop regarding the kind of work he was doing and would occasionally bring me in to be another eye on projects he would be working on. I was aware of how the process was developing, but at the same time, I had no interest in the process in the beginning."

"Sitting at a desk and moving a mouse around all day long didn't hold my interest, but being able to come in at an advisory capacity, and working with all kinds of new approaches, was career-changing. Plus, my area of expertise was that I was very conscious of how live-action animals, dinosaurs, or whatever would move around in an environment, and at this time, a lot of the animators were from a more traditional animation background, so I had the edge in that regard," Phil added.

Phil with a Bug appendage on the set of *Starship Troopers* (1997). Photo courtesy of Phil Tippett.

A few years later, Tippett was contacted by Davison for the aforementioned adaptation of Robert A. Heinlein's novel *Starship Troopers* (1959), which reteamed them with Verhoeven to bring the classic sci-fi novel to the big screen. Even though *Starship Troopers* (1997) wasn't as high-profile as other blockbusters that Tippett had worked on, he faced insurmountable challenges to create hundreds of swarms of the film's hostile alien adversaries known as the Bugs.

"Jon Davison and Ed Neumeier, who wrote *RoboCop*, were working on a lower-budget, *Pork Chop Hill*-like movie, only with giant bugs. Joe Dante was to direct, too. So when they went to Sony looking for the money, Sony told them, 'Well, we have this property called *Starship Troopers* and we'll give you the money if you make a *Starship Troopers* movie instead of what you're working on.'"

"I don't exactly recall what happened with Joe, but Paul was brought in to direct *Starship Troopers* because we had all worked well together on *RoboCop*. The sheer amount of aliens we had to create was unlike anything I had done up until that point. Of course, the movie totally tanked when it was released, and it took a while to gain some kind of following, but fans always ask me about it. Nobody quite understood what Paul was doing at the time, but I recognized that what he was doing was genius."

After receiving yet another Oscar nomination for his contributions to *Starship Troopers* (1997), Tippett lent his talents to various projects at the turn of the century, including *My Favorite Martian* (1999), *The Haunting* (1999), *Virus* (1999), *Evolution* (2001), *The Spiderwick Chronicles* (2008), *Cloverfield* (2008), and the *Twilight* (2008) films. While he was clearly an artist working at the top of his game, Tippett was ready to challenge himself in a wholly different way.

"I was already interested in filmmaking and spent the better part of ten or twelve years playing around, making short films," Tippett said. "Over the years, I had worked with other writers—even Ed [Neumeier]—and I tried to develop some ideas, and Jon and I even tried a couple of times, too. At one point, writer Michael Chabon and I wanted to make a horror film, but none of that stuff ever happened. So, eventually Jon came up with the idea to go to Columbia [Pictures] and pitch a direct-to-DVD sequel [*Starship Troopers 2: Hero of the Federation* (2004)] to *Starship Troopers* that I would direct myself."

"Being able to work with Jon and Ed again on *Starship Troopers 2*, and having them on the set and working with me throughout pre-production, production, and post-production, was invaluable. I have also learned a lot from working with some really terrific directors throughout my career, and at the end of the day, that's the best kind of film school you could possibly have."

Phil looking over his notes while on location for *Starship Troopers 2: Hero of the Federation* (2004). Photo courtesy of Phil Tippett.

"The one thing I have found is that it is very difficult to creatively have a vision and follow through on it when you're working within the confines of the studio system. That inspired me to work on the projects that excite me, but to do them on an independent level. This allows me to further my path in film with my own personal projects where I don't have to account for everything to a bunch of executives. The only person I have to answer to is myself, and whoever I'm working with, of course."

Recently, Tippett continued to blaze his own fiercely independent trail with his stop-motion animated film series, *MAD GOD* (2014), which resurrected a long-dormant passion project due to a successful fan-driven Kickstarter campaign. Shortly after the film series was released, Tippett found himself working with Michael Levine (from the mobile game developer and publisher HappyGiant) on *HoloGrid: Monster Battle* (2016), an immersive digital gaming experience that features a cutting-edge approach to augmented reality technology, all with a traditional board game twist.

At this point in his career, Tippett has proved time and time again that he's an immensely talented innovator, and the fact that he's spent much of that time continuing to carry the legacy of his heroes that first

Phil working on the rancor monster for *Return of the Jedi* (1983).
Photo courtesy of Phil Tippett.

inspired him to become a stop-motion animator is demonstrative of just how dedicated Tippett has remained to his roots.

"I will always love stop-motion, regardless of where technology goes. Looking back, I can't characterize my career in any other way than being lucky. If you've lived as long as I have, you realize that things change. You have to be willing to adapt to change. The switch from stop-motion to go-motion required a lot of rethinking, and then trying to understand the computer graphics process required jumping though a bunch of hoops that I never could have imagined. Those kinds of challenges are actually exciting, even though when you're in the moment, they are terrifying."

"I am more interested in the creative aspect of things, so that's what I spend my time on these days. If there's one thing I took away from all my experiences, it came from working with Paul [Verhoeven]. Paul was very good at fighting for exactly what he wanted, and that's my thing now. I carry those lessons from Paul with me, because I always want to fight for those things that I believe in. That's always been important to me as an artist, regardless of the medium."

15 Tom Woodruff, Jr.

GROWING UP IN WILLIAMSPORT, Pennsylvania, the world of Hollywood seemed like a distant dream to Tom Woodruff, Jr., but what began as a hobby quickly evolved into something much more as he became fascinated by how movie monsters were made.

"None of this was planned," explained Woodruff. "When I got started in all of this, it wasn't anything like it is today. It was really kind of an offbeat idea, and even as a kid, I only had a couple of friends that used to

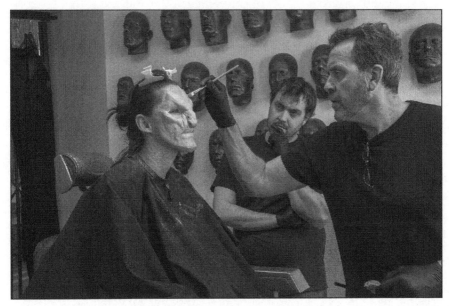

Photo courtesy of Tom Woodruff, Jr.

like watching these movies, too. There was a monster magazine available at that time, *Famous Monsters of Filmland*, but it was the only thing you could find. For all of us, it was something that was cool, but for me, it struck a chord creatively because I wanted to figure out how to duplicate those things I'd seen in different movies."

"I remember this journey of trying to find how to get my hands on makeup supplies and makeup materials, and it was really difficult because it was a time when it was virtually unknown outside of the industry. I was also living in a very small town back east, and so makeup effects were basically unheard of. When I finally found a local pharmacy that said in the Yellow Pages that they had theatrical makeup, I thought, *This is it.* I thought I hit a gold mine."

"My mom gave me a ride over, and because I was a kid, I had this fantasy that I would walk in and there would just be racks and racks of foam appliances and materials that I had read about in *Famous Monsters of Filmland*. When I got there, it turned out that all they had was a little glass case with a couple of sticks and greasepaint for sale. It didn't deter me. I bought a couple of old-fashioned sticks, greasepaint, and some spray paint and went home with some spirit gum, too."

"When I went home, I tried to figure out how to duplicate a Wolf Man makeup on myself. Lots of times, because it was me trying to work with a mirror on myself, it was less than satisfying. Sometimes I would even do makeups on my own hand, because it was something that I could see very easily and play around with, and that helped."

As he continued to pursue his interest in makeup effects, Woodruff, Jr.'s parents were generally supportive of his interest in the creative arts, but it was more his own belief in wanting to do effects professionally that kept him going throughout his childhood.

"I had a feeling when I was ten years old that this was something I just had to do. I didn't think of it in terms of a profession or in terms of making money, because at that age, kids just have this kind of acceptance that there is always food on the table and there's always a roof over your head. You don't think about how you need to approach life as an adult and be responsible for yourself. I did think of it as something I wanted. I wanted to be those guys working in the movies. I wanted to be the guy putting makeup on actors, and I wanted to be the guy creating monsters and working on monster movies."

A demonic co-star created by ADI [Amalgamated Dynamics, Inc.] for *Bedazzled* (2000).
Photo courtesy of Tom Woodruff, Jr.

"I always thought my parents were supportive, but they were supportive in a much less involved way than parents are today. For me, it was a much more pure method of me finding out what I really enjoyed, what things I had a knack for, and what things I had an interest in learning more about. They never dissuaded me, nor did they artificially prop me up, either. It was just that they had accepted that I was at a point of my life where I was learning different things and trying to find my way, and I had a career goal. It was their way of giving me some time and some space to figure out what I would want to do or what I wanted to try to do, but I already knew monsters were 'it' for me."

On his quest to gain as much makeup effects knowledge as he could, Tom reached out to one of the great pioneers in the industry, John Chambers, for guidance and feedback on his work.

"Through various means, I was able to contact John Chambers, who was the makeup artist behind the original *Planet of the Apes* movies. When I was in college, a friend of mine said, 'We should go out to California and look for a summer job.' I thought, *Wait, what? Go out there and do what?* I had never even heard of doing something like that, so going out to California was our adventure during the summer of 1978."

Tom on the set of *The Cat in the Hat* (2003). Photo courtesy of Tom Woodruff, Jr.

"When we came out here, I met John Chambers in person and he sent me around to meet a bunch of these makeup artists that I had read about so I could speak with them and get to see their labs. It was a really amazing time to get out of my small town back home and step into these environments that I always thought about, always pictured, and always imagined. It was really a big thing in my life, and the fact that John Chambers was so open, and immersed me in all of this in a very comfortable way, was something I'll never forget. After that summer, I went back to school and finished out my college days on the East Coast."

"The next time I came out here was right after I graduated in 1980. I came out and loaded all my stuff in the car and drove out here by myself. It was really tough because it was in the time of a really big writers' strike and the whole town was shut down. I remember John Chambers saying to me, 'You know, there are makeup artists that have worked out here for twenty years that are losing their homes because they don't have work right now.' So that really made me think. It was tough. People who have been struggling for work do not want to see somebody new in town that's looking for work, so I think I lasted for a couple of weeks, and then I headed back east."

Once things began to get back to normal in Hollywood, Tom decided it was finally time to make an official move across the country, and John Chambers was once again instrumental in helping him get established on the West Coast.

"After I got married, I finally made the move out here in 1982. When my wife and I moved out here, we found an apartment and again, John Chambers was integral in that, because of being from out of state, we had a hard time finding someone who would lease to us. They didn't know if we'd be able to find work or not, so John talked to somebody he knew and told the landlord that he was my uncle. He put himself out there for me in a way he didn't need to, but I was grateful that he did."

"Thankfully, I got a job right away, and my wife found a job right away, too. I was selling cameras in a store in North Hollywood. I had a day off during the week, and on those days, I would call John and spend some time with him, or he would set me up to go see some other people. That's how I got to meet Tom Burman, [Stan] Winston, and eventually Allan Apone, who owns Makeup & Effects Laboratories. I would go around to all these places, and I had this meager portfolio of my work to show

Tom sculpting in the studio at ADI. Photo courtesy of Tom Woodruff, Jr.

them, but that was it. I had to show them that I had some ambition and I was willing to try new things and would be willing to put in the work to become a better artist."

"I finally got a call from Makeup & Effects Lab. They were crewing up for a movie called *Metalstorm: The Destruction of Jared-Syn*, which was a 3D science fiction movie. To me, it didn't matter what the movie was, I just wanted to go to work. I put in my two-week notice at the camera store and I was gone. So, in November 1982, that's when I finally became a legitimate, working, paid contributor to the makeup industry."

"It was such an unbelievable feeling for me to walk into a shop," Tom continued, "and that's what I was going to be doing every day for the next few months. The thing that I always thought was so great about Makeup & Effects Labs was that it was a time when I got to go in there as basically an unknown, but I was turned on to things and shown things and taught things. We got a chance to do everything, and I quickly realized that I had talent for it all."

"For that first show, I learned how to sculpt creatures. I sculpted some appliance makeups, too. I did my own mold, I ran my own foam rubber, I did all my own painting, and then I went on the set and applied them to the actors. It was incredible to have so many opportunities in one film, and to learn so much in just four or five months. It was a great time."

Following *Metalstorm* (1983), Woodruff, Jr. didn't have to wait too long for the opportunity to work for another giant in the world of modern special effects, Tom Burman.

"After *Metalstorm*, it just felt like the show was over so suddenly, and you're starting back at square one in terms of trying to line up work and keep things going as an artist. Luckily, it wasn't long until I got onto my next show. Tom Burman, who I had met through John Chambers, brought me onto his crew for *Star Trek III* [*The Search for Spock*]. It was one of those mind-blowing things for me, because Tom Burman was such an important part of the original *Planet of the Apes* makeup, along with John, and now here I am working with him in his shop."

"It just felt like there was some kind of predetermined path that I was following, and it all felt so right. I learned a lot on *Star Trek III*, too—I was sculpting and making molds, and I was learning rubber and casting and painting, too. It was all very fulfilling. Before that was over, we started working on [*The Adventures of*] *Buckaroo Banzai* [*Across the 8th Dimension*], so to be a part of the *Star Trek* franchise and this great cult film so early on in my career was really cool."

As he continued to establish himself in Hollywood, Woodruff, Jr. started to notice a shift in the industry as filmmakers began embracing the possibilities that special effects afforded them on their ambitious cinematic endeavors. While it was a time of great creativity in his chosen profession, many artists found themselves pigeonholed by their artistic specialties rather than being allowed to flourish as general artists, which had been the industry standard for so long.

"The timing was so different back then," explained Tom. "We were all doing everything in terms of the different specialties within the world of special effects, so there were always general artists who could jump in at any given moment to help out on anything. But as makeup effects started to grow, I noticed this shift happening to this more segregated artistic approach, where people's strengths were the only kinds of work they were given to do. What was starting to fall away were the general artists, and it's incredibly important to have those kinds of people working with you, because they can bring so much to the table. That's why I was always happy to jump into anything and everything—I wanted to know how to do it all."

Shortly after contributing to several projects for Tom Burman, Woodruff, Jr. found himself working for another legend that John Chambers had introduced him to, Stan Winston, who was gearing up for an ambitious science fiction film by James Cameron that promised to push the boundaries of special effects in unprecedented ways.

"For *The Terminator*, it was once again a case of being in the right place at the right time. Stan had a pretty well-established career by then, and had even received a few award nominations. He had a name, but I do think it was *The Terminator* when people sat up and took notice of what Stan could really do. When he started to build his crew for it, we were all new to him. We were all young kids and he was a very energetic, engaging, and creative person to work for, especially during that time in my career."

"Jim Cameron was also certainly an unknown force at that time. He had been around working on different things, but no one knew him as the director we know him as today. So it was exciting to be part of that open playing field, with all this rising talent coming together, and to be instrumentally involved in bringing in ideas and techniques that no one had ever dared to do before. Also, I want to mention the script for *The Terminator*, because I can still remember the first time I read it and how

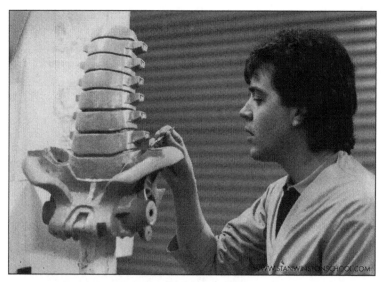

Tom does some endoskeleton sculpting for *The Terminator* (1984).
Photo courtesy of the Stan Winston School of Character Arts.

I just couldn't get over how great it was. I knew it was going to be a great movie. I knew it was going to be a good story, visually. But, of course, I had no idea what it was going to become."

"When we started *Terminator*, we had one little shop, and then, all of a sudden, we had to rent another small unit in the same complex, and then we had to rent a third one. It just kept growing and growing. When you're in the middle of something like that, you don't really have a feeling for how vast it is until it's over and you can give it all a little perspective. You just concentrate on everything that's surrounding you and just keep pushing forward."

"*The Terminator* was certainly the biggest show I had been a part of up until that point, and the work we were doing was expanding the world of special effects. Suddenly, anything was possible, and it was really an exciting time to be a part of this industry. There's almost an energy that happens when you're on a set like that, where everything is so innovative that it just takes over, and it's a very positive vibe."

"Obviously, this wasn't going to be a movie where we were going to be able to put a guy in a robot suit and just let him walk around," explained Tom. "That was the approach that everyone had been using up until that point, but I don't think there's any way that [the Terminator] would have been as effective as it was had the endoskeleton not been created and James had gone a different direction with the look of the Terminator."

"Something else I always thought was very smart of James was to not reveal the secret about Arnold until we're deep into the movie; it's such a great, '*What the hell **is** this guy?*' moment that does an excellent job of bringing the audience right into Sarah [Connor] and [Kyle] Reese's nightmare as they try to outrun this thing. That was really smart thinking on his part."

"What also sells the effects even more is how the design looks like it really could be existing inside of Arnold's body, because of the way he was built and how we did all the appliance pieces for him. James, Stan, Arnold, and every single person who worked on *The Terminator* found a way to make everyone believe that Arnold really was this unstoppable mechanical monster, and very few sci-fi films of that era were able to leave such a lasting impact. It was hard to not recognize that James was a really forward-thinking filmmaker and this was a movie that was going to get a lot of attention."

Arnold Schwarzenegger and Tom working on Arnold's puppet self on the set of *The Terminator* (1984). Photo courtesy of the Stan Winston School of Character Arts.

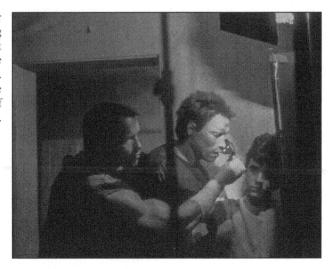

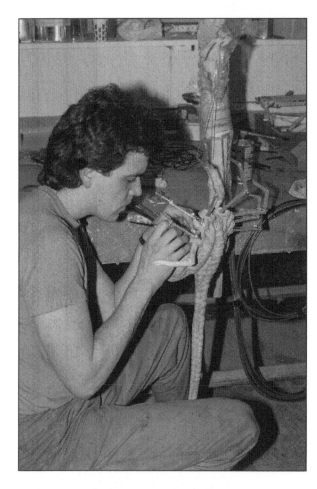

Tom working on a Facehugger for *Aliens* (1986). Photo courtesy of Tom Woodruff, Jr.

Tom once again found himself on the set of a James Cameron film a few years later when the visionary director hired Stan Winston and his talented crew to tackle the gargantuan effects needed for his lofty sequel *Aliens* (1986).

"There was a good amount of time for us between working on *The Terminator* and *Aliens* for Jim—we had a few more films, like *The Vindicator* and *Invaders [from Mars]*, that we worked on first. But I remember when *Aliens* came in, we only had a couple of months to work on it, so we were definitely feeling the pinch."

"I also remember that we were griping and joking with Stan because at the same time we were doing *Aliens*, Rick [Baker] was over working on *Harry and the Hendersons*, and they gave him something like nine months for that show, where we had only something like six months for *Aliens*. Of course, we got it all done, and sometimes I think it's better when your schedule pushes you like that. I thrive on that kind of energy because it forces you to keep moving and working. There's no time to second-guess anything, and that's something I enjoy when I'm on a deadline."

Stan Winston prepares actor Lance Henriksen for Bishop's dismemberment scene in *Aliens* (1986). Tom is kneeling, bottom left. Photo courtesy of the Stan Winston School of Character Arts.

"And the thing is that, whether you're working on *Aliens* or any other show, there's never enough time. You could have six weeks, six months, or a year, and it's never going to be enough time to get everything exactly perfect. That's when you have to get creative."

Soon after completing *Aliens* (1986), Tom contributed to another dream project, Fred Dekker's *The Monster Squad* (1987), which gave the entire crew the opportunity to pay homage to the Universal Monsters so many of them grew up loving and wanting to create in the first place.

"It's hard to even describe what it was like to be a part of *Monster Squad*," Tom admitted. "We had just come off of *Terminator* and *Aliens*, and I remember thinking to myself, *Man, how is it that this job just keeps getting better and better?* It was amazing. And even when we found out that Universal would not be granting the license to duplicate their characters, it didn't kill our enthusiasm at all. In fact, it was very exciting to think about the prospects of doing something new on all these classic movie monsters."

"Stan broke the show down, and he assigned out the characters. I don't remember at that time if any of us lobbied for a particular character, but I do know I was thrilled when he said I could do the Frankenstein monster. For me, though, an even bigger thing was to get Stan's

Stan Winston helps Tom (as the Gillman) get ready to shoot a scene for *The Monster Squad* (1987). Photo courtesy of the Stan Winston School of Character Arts.

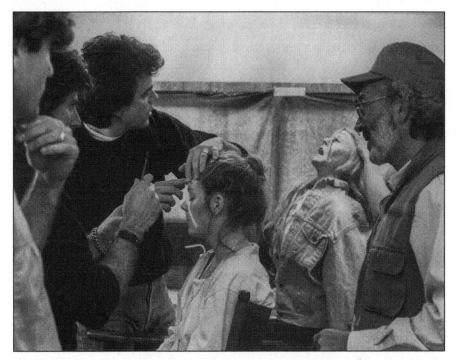

Tom works on Kerry Remsen for *Pumpkinhead* (1988) while Director Stan Winston looks on. Photo courtesy of Tom Woodruff, Jr.

support for me playing [Gillman, based on] The Creature from *Creature from the Black Lagoon*. I always thought that making monsters was amazing, but being able to make them physically come alive and play them myself was even better. There was no end to the amazing things in my life. I was constantly getting to live out my dreams that I had since I was just a kid."

"*Monster Squad* was nice because Stan was totally in the role of director over us. He actually turned the design of the creatures over to us. There were four of us—Shane [Mahan], John [Rosengrant], Alec [Gillis], and myself. We started doing sketches and we had these design meetings, and when we got something to a certain level, we would show Stan and he would approve it. It was a great testament to Stan and his ego, because he really let us be the ones driving how these creatures would eventually turn out."

"Even though I was playing the [Gillman], it was nice to be able to go on the set and help apply the Frankenstein's monster makeup to Tom [Noonan], too. He was a great guy. Stan and a makeup artist named

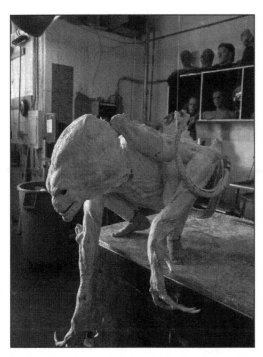

Tom performing a suit test as the titular monster for Stan Winston's *Pumpkinhead* (1988). Photo courtesy of the Stan Winston School of Character Arts.

Zoltan Elek did the application to Noonan's face, and I was able to do his hands."

Tom continued working at Stan's shop over the next few years, helping bring to life various creatures and characters on *Alien Nation* (1988), *Leviathan* (1989), and *Pumpkinhead* (1988), the lattermost being directed by Winston, with Woodruff, Jr. once again getting the opportunity to have some fun while playing the titular monster for his boss. Shortly after those projects, the timing seemed right for Tom and longtime collaborator Alec Gillis to step out on their own.

"There were two things that developed," Tom said, "and it just seemed like the timing was right. As we were wrapping up *Leviathan*, Stan had lined up his next movie that he was going to be directing, *A Gnome Named Gnorm*. Shortly before that, Alec and I had done a short film of an idea we wanted to do, which was similar to the *Tales from the Crypt* anthology stories. We wanted to have these three weird stories introduced by this demonic character who works in Hell. We shot that and we were sending it around, and as soon as we got back from *Leviathan*, there was some interest in this thing from Producer Max Rosenberg, who ironically was the Producer of the original *Tales from the Crypt* movies."

"So, we just thought at that time, *'Okay, Stan is at a point now where he's firmly going to be directing things, and he doesn't really need us because it's not going to be a huge show.'* He had said after *Pumpkinhead* that he was going to start focusing more on directing and not taking on all of the shows like we had been doing for the last five years. The thing is, Stan would never dismiss us. Never. But we had this opportunity and we thought, *'We should go for this, and at the same time, we can also help light-*

en Stan's load.' That way, we weren't jumping ship to do our own thing. We were jumping ship to help Stan, and he gave us his blessings—we left on very good terms with him."

"Obviously, the movie never got made, but there we were, out on our own, and that was kind of a shock because for the first time it was up to us. Alec and I were both wholly responsible. It was like when I first moved out to California and was responsible to find my own work. It wasn't like sitting and working with Stan and having work delivered to you on a constant, daily basis."

"We got to do makeup on Mary Woronov's character for the movie *Warlock,* and we did a couple episodes of a TV show called *Monsters.* We were barely getting by, honestly. But then we were contacted by Gale Anne Hurd, and she said she had gone to Stan with this low-budget project and Stan had told her, 'Well, I'm really kind of tied up with my own thing right now, but go talk to Tom and Alec.' That's how we got involved with *Tremors.* It was a great project, but it was also the show that jump-started ADI [Amalgamated Dynamics, Inc.], and got us off and running as our own company."

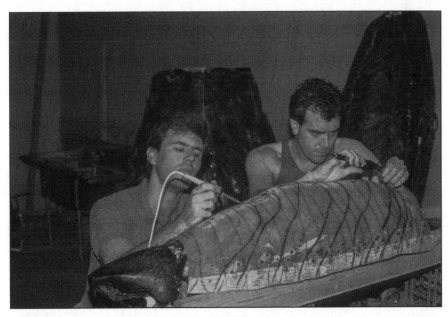

Tom Woodruff, Jr. and Alec Gillis hard at work during pre-production on *Tremors* (1990). Photo courtesy of Tom Woodruff, Jr.

While Ron Underwood's *Tremors* (1990) was just as ambitious as many of the other big creature features Tom had worked on previously, the horror comedy came with a much smaller budget, which meant that he and his business partner, Alec, were going to have to get really creative with the Graboid creatures lurking beneath the soil of Perfection, Nevada.

"*Tremors* was a very low-budget movie, and we had to find a way to just muscle things around from inside these pits that were dug in the desert for us with big, long aluminum poles and cables. Somehow, it all worked. It certainly worked for the level of the movie, and what was interesting about it was when we got the script, I could just tell that *Tremors* was going to be a fun movie because it had that fun approach to the monsters."

"Also, when I saw the script, I immediately recognized one of the names, S.S. Wilson. That's when I remembered he had written a book about stop-motion animation, and just for the hell of it, I picked up the phone book and looked at his name, and here he was, living in Reseda, California. I called him up and I said, 'Well, I just got this great script, and I hope I get the job because I'd really love to work with you. Oh, and do you have any more of those *Puppets & People* books by any chance?' He laughed and said, 'Funny enough, I've got a couple left in the garage. I'll bring you one.' S.S. and I had a shared enthusiasm about stop-motion creatures, and Director Ron Underwood and Producer Brent Maddock brought so much to the movie, too, so *Tremors* really felt like a big family-made movie. Everybody seemed to work so well together, and we all appreciated each other's enthusiasm."

Although the original *Tremors* (1990) was not an initial financial success for Universal, the studio moved ahead with several sequels over the years, with Woodruff, Jr. and Gillis handling the practical effects on most of them.

"I was bummed that *Tremors* didn't do well when it was first released, but I guess I should have realized that [would happen] because it was such a unique take on monsters at that time. If you have a film that crosses genres the way this did, it's tough to sell. I remember that Universal was in this weird position of knowing that everybody out there wanted a sequel, but they couldn't put in the money to do one theatrically. They were smart, though, and realized there was still a way to make a sequel that was going to be profitable enough to make it worthwhile, so they embraced the idea of doing direct-to-video sequels, most of which we were involved on."

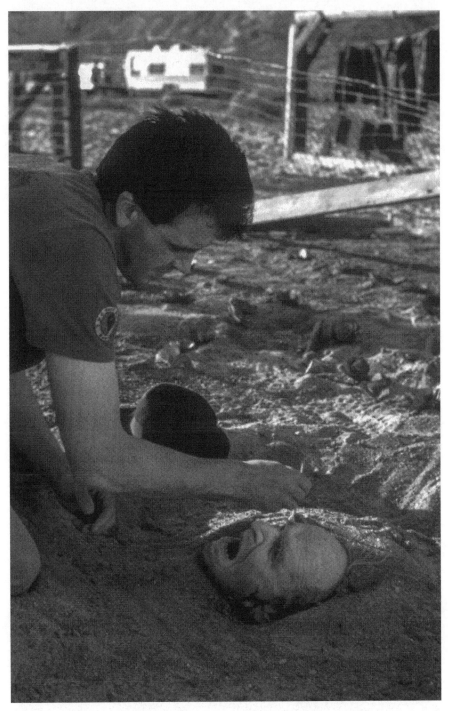

Tom prepares a Graboid victim on the set of *Tremors* (1990).
Photo courtesy of TomWoodruff, Jr.

"We worked on the first three *Tremors,* but by number three, that family feel of the production company was gone. The meetings we had on that *Tremors* [*Tremors 3: Back to Perfection* (2001)] were a struggle, and it was so low-budget, too. New producers were involved and everything felt very different. That's when we knew we were done working on them."

In the early 1990s, both Tom and Alec had an opportunity to return to the Xenomorph universe with David Fincher's *Alien 3* (1992). ADI was in charge of bringing the titular villain to life for the sequel, and Tom was given the opportunity to do more creature performance work at Fincher's request. While *Alien 3* (1992) did fairly well financially, it received very mixed reactions from critics and fans upon its release.

"Both Alec and I came into *Alien 3* excited to be back working with these creatures," said Tom, "and we were also excited because of David Fincher and everything he brought to it. Looking back now, I guess a lot of people didn't get what he was trying to do. People were blind to what *Alien 3* was all about, because they had just come off of this big action-packed movie with tons of Xenomorphs, and the notion in Hollywood is that you have to go bigger and bolder when you're doing a sequel. *Alien 3*

Tom gets into the Xenomorph suit on *Alien 3* (1992). Photo courtesy of Tom Woodruff, Jr.

Tom and the crew transporting the Meryl Streep effect on *Death Becomes Her* (1992).
Photo courtesy of Tom Woodruff, Jr.

wasn't that at all. I loved that David decided for *Alien 3* to go back to doing just one creature, but I don't think audiences back then were expecting that."

"Over time, though, it seems fans have come to appreciate the intimacy of the story, and I loved being a part of that on both sides: the effects and [playing the] creature. People come up to me at a lot of these conventions that I do and they say to me, 'I hated *Alien 3* when it first came out, but now, it's one of my favorites.' Time can always help you find a fresh perspective," Tom added.

"*Aliens 3* was probably the last movie that I did any real sculpting on, though. By the time we did *Death Becomes Her* [which also came out in 1992], we had to start bringing in specialists because there just wasn't the time for me to run the company, make sure things were being done, and be able to sit down and do any of the artistic work, too. That was tough, because that was always so much fun for me. I'm lucky if I touch any clay once every three or four weeks when I work on projects. I still do small projects of my own at home because I enjoy doing them, but it's a whole different thing to be able to do it today while I'm at the shop."

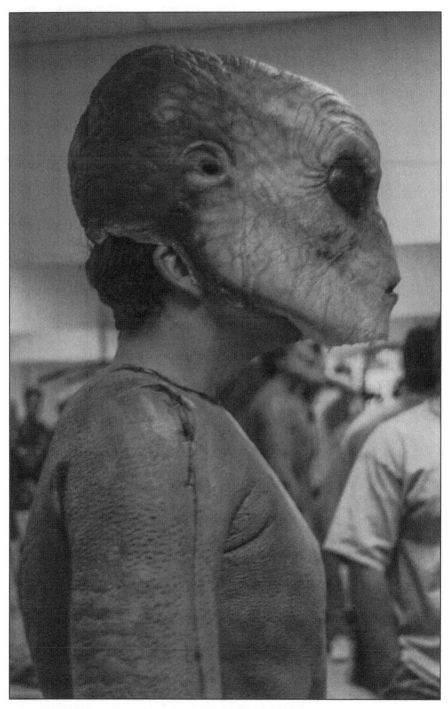

A close-up of Tom testing an alien suit for *The X-Files* (1998) movie.
Photo courtesy of Tom Woodruff, Jr.

Another 1990s science fiction project for ADI that has gone on to become a modern cult classic is Paul Verhoeven's *Starship Troopers* (1997), which pitted soldiers against "Arachnids," an insectoid species of aliens hell-bent on exterminating the human race. While ADI was tasked with the practical effects on *Starship Troopers* (1997), Woodruff, Jr. saw the unlimited potential visual effects brought to the table to take Verhoeven's bold vision to another level.

"I always felt that *Starship Troopers* was successful the way *Jurassic Park* was successful, in combining the world of digital creatures and practical creatures by taking full advantage of both approaches," said Tom. "When I first started out in this business, I had a list of heroes I wanted to meet and work with. Phil Tippett was one of those guys. Here's a guy that was probably every bit the animator that Ray Harryhausen was, and because of *Jurassic Park* and where that pushed [things], he was the guy that made the jump from traditional hands-on creature animation to digital animation. He was always the best at it and always knew how to make things right, how to make them look good, and how much time it really took to do it the right way."

"When *Starship Troopers* came along, we were more than ready. We immediately saw it as an opportunity to do a big creature movie that, had there been no digital [effects], could not have been made. It would have been impossible to tell the story with the scope that the filmmakers chose to use without digital effects, and Paul had such a specific vision that it made everyone's job so much easier on that show."

"*Starship Troopers* also gave us the opportunity to do the level and scope of work that we wanted to do, like what we had done earlier in our careers. Things have gone downhill in terms of how involved we are in movies with a few occasional upbeats along the way, but that scope of work just isn't happening anymore, at least in the practical effects world. It was a rare opportunity, and we loved it."

ADI returned to the world of science fiction later that year with *Alien Resurrection* (1997), and the team was also involved with the big screen debut of *The X-Files* television series (1993), which was released in theaters in 1998 and gave Tom another opportunity to step inside a monster suit.

"*X-Files* was an interesting show for us. On one hand, I got to play the alien in the movie that they thawed out of the ice containers. That was

Tom in the full alien suit during production on *The X-Files* (1998) movie.
Photo courtesy of Tom Woodruff, Jr.

great, and any time I can be in a monster suit, I'm always happy. But on the other hand, the production process itself wasn't always a lot of fun for us."

"It started off great, though. We got to meet [*The X-Files* (1993) creator] Chris Carter, who was a really nice guy, but I had never watched *The X-Files* series, just because I didn't feel I ever had the time to get hooked on a TV series. So, I didn't know the world that well. The big thing that we didn't know going into this was that these guys came from the TV world of *The X-Files*, where the producer is in charge, and we had come from the world of film where directors are always in charge. We always worked with the producers and with the production crew, but at the end of the day, we still always took on the director's point of view."

"For us, film is the director's medium and we always wanted to be attentive to the director at the expense of anything else," Tom continued. "On *The X-Files* movie, we had it backwards. We would work with [Director] Rob [Bowman] and he would say, 'Oh, I want to see this and I want to see that,' and we would put those things into it. The producers would then give us some notes and we would do what the producers were asking, but if there were any differences, we would always defer to the director. So there were a couple of times where we just didn't understand why the producers were so unhappy with things that came to set, and in one case, we even let the size of the embryo inside of a frozen caveman become an issue."

"It all came down to them feeling like we weren't honoring the construct of the way television was, which was the producer's medium. We were still working within the production medium, so there was a little bit of a glitch for us when it came to getting things off and running on that show, but once it was underway, it all went fine and we were happy with the results. And I think the film came out incredibly well, too," Tom added.

Just a few years later, ADI had the opportunity to re-team with visionary filmmaker Paul Verhoeven for *Hollow Man* (2000), his modernized take on H.G. Wells' *The Invisible Man* (1897) that did a brilliant job of marrying practical and visual effects, much like Verhoeven's previous film, *Starship Troopers* (1997).

According to Tom, "*Hollow Man* was another great example of a movie where the digital effects were working hand in hand with practical effects, and they complimented each other perfectly. For example, after Kevin [Bacon] is turned invisible, his team makes this rubber mask to put over his 'face,' and that gave us so much to work with in terms of the ex-

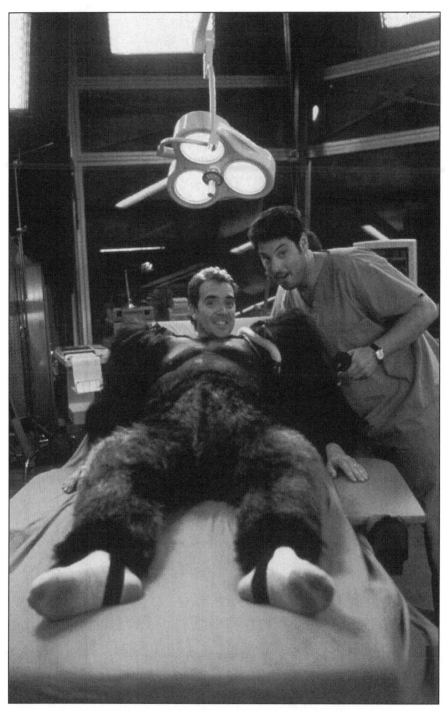

Tom poses with actor Greg Grunberg on the set of *Hollow Man* (2000).
Photo courtesy of Tom Woodruff, Jr.

pressions, particularly this one mask we sculpted with this creepy expression to it. That look had this bizarre quality, and to me, what really sold *Hollow Man* as a concept and made it cool was when he would take the glasses off or open his mouth, and you could see hollow rubber skin all the way to the back of his head. That just made it so compelling and realistic."

"Being a practical effects guy, I know there's this mentality out there that when it comes to practical and digital, one of those ways is better than the other. To me, it's not about one or the other. The truth is, there is no way to really quantify what technique is better for all cases anymore. When you're building a house, what is more important, a hammer or a saw? It all depends on what you're trying to achieve. That's where people get lost and swept up in the frenzy of an Internet discussion or an online battle. Both can be equally effective in different circumstances."

While they have always embraced the possibilities of digital effects when trying to bring creatures and monsters to life, Woodruff, Jr. and Gillis learned a painful lesson while contributing to the 2011 prequel to John Carpenter's *The Thing* (1982), itself a landmark film in the world of special effects.

Tom poses as Isabelle the gorilla for *Hollow Man* (2000).
Photo courtesy of Tom Woodruff, Jr.

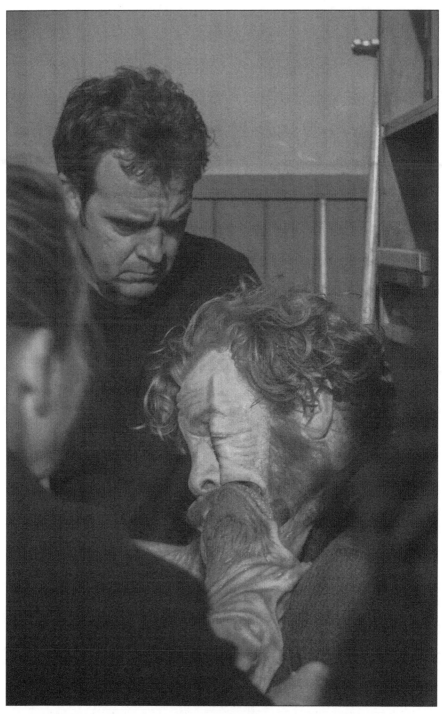

Tom working on the set of *The Thing* (2011). Photo courtesy of Tom Woodruff, Jr.

"When you talk about the original *The Thing*," Tom said, "the creature effects were one of the most important aspects that became a driving force to complement the human performances. So, for this version, that's the way it was presented when it was brought to us. The producers said, 'We came here because we want this to be very much like the first movie, except let's do the digital stuff to assist what you're doing practically with the effects.'"

"The idea was that we were all going to be working together and the digital effects were going to support the practical effects, but the practical effects were going to drive the way the creature was being done on screen. But, by the end, everything that we had done—and I mean **everything** that we had done—was covered with this layer of altered digital effects. I don't know if 'frustrated' would even begin to describe how we felt."

"But we were also frustrated on a basic level because a lot of creative work that went into what we did on *The Thing* [2011] was completely lost because digital effects were misused. It also seemed like it was this deep, dark secret that was never revealed to us until we literally were driving in the parking lot to go to the screening of the movie three days before it hit theaters."

"That was like a kick to the stomach, and we were left wondering if our work was so bad that they had to replace everything. We realized after seeing the movie that it wasn't that at all. It ended up being that somewhere along the line, the choice was made to create, or recreate, everything as a digital effect. I think that decision drove the core audience away, and I'm sure the studio was hoping that it just wouldn't matter. People would go see it because it said '*The Thing*' in the title, and it didn't matter how the effects were done."

"Alec had this idea, and he said to me, 'Look, we've got all these behind-the-scenes and on-set videos that we shot ourselves that show the kind of work we really did on *The Thing* [2011]. Let's put it up on YouTube.' That's when we created the studioADI channel. It started off with us trying to reach out to the fans of *The Thing* [1982] that didn't know where to go with their frustration as to what happened with the effects on the new film. It wasn't so much about proving it wasn't our fault, but it was about us saying, 'Look how it could have been and how we wanted it to be.' We wanted to show that practical effects were still relevant, even today," Tom added.

Tom looking over an effect for *Fire City: End of Days* (2015).
Photo courtesy of Tom Woodruff, Jr.

Shortly after *The Thing* (2011), both Woodruff, Jr. and Gillis decided it was time to explore their creativity in other avenues while still keeping true to their love of practical effects and monsters.

"*Fire City: End of Days* came about because the writers and producers approached us to see if we'd be interested in helping them out. They said they had very little money in their budget, but they wanted to create this creature for what was basically a teaser highlighting what they wanted to do for this whole series of films they had planned. They gave me the script for the first one, and it was page after page of monsters and creatures and demons. I immediately recognized that they had to find a way to do this, but in a pared-down way, so it feels big and gets people excited, but also doesn't cost millions of dollars, either."

"I remember thinking to myself after I read the script, *Man, it would be great if this becomes a movie in three or four years, and it would be wonderful to be connected with it from the very beginning.* So we built the creature you see in the short, and I got to play the monster, too. The next step was to do a simplified version of the movie through crowdfunding that was going to basically show what the world of *Fire City* was like. They came up with this idea for a prequel, and I knew it was something I really wanted to direct. We had some long talks and these guys decided that they would first do a short film as a test called *Fire City: The King of Miseries.*"

"To their credit, they put up the money to have this thing made, we shot this short, and they were sold. They were very happy, and that's when we officially went forward with the crowdfunding so we could raise the money, and we were able to create the feature film, *Fire City: End of Days.* When it comes to what originally got me interested in film in general, it's always been characters and their relationships. And to me, there's this whole relationship between the main demon character and this little girl in *Fire City* that I absolutely love. That alone was enough for me to want to direct the project—it had nothing to do with the creatures."

Over the thirty-plus years he's been professionally working in Hollywood, Woodruff, Jr. has been able to live out many of his dreams, whether it's making creatures and memorable effect gags, getting to perform in a creature suit, or even directing. He's collaborated with iconic artists and filmmakers throughout his career, and the company he founded with Gillis in the late 1980s continues to stay busy on film and television projects

Tom Woodruff, Jr. and Alec Gillis working together on the set of *Michael* (1996).
Photo courtesy of Tom Woodruff, Jr.

to this very day. Tom credits a lot of the successes he's shared with Gillis to the strong partnership they forged back when they first started working together under Stan Winston.

"Although we're very different people, Alec and I have similar backgrounds. He grew up as a kid working out of his garage in Arizona doing masks, makeup, and stop-motion, and when I was a kid, I was growing up in Pennsylvania working out of my parents' basement doing the exact same things. We were born of the same stock, but when we got together at Stan's, it seemed like we had the same sensibilities in terms of not just monster-making, but also in how the monsters would end up moving and performing on set."

"When we got interested in doing our own short films, we both wanted to be directors and we figured that if we just hooked our wagons together, it would be great to have the support of somebody that isn't just there to say 'yes' to everything you say, but can offer a different point of view in a very respectful way. One of Alec's gifts, besides being artistic, is that he's a great communicator. He has a great way of balancing out the good and the bad of how you choose to look at everything. There have been so many times over the last thirty years where one of us will get off the phone after having a bad experience with a producer or just general problems, and then we can just talk about it and work it out ourselves. To have another voice to help keep things in perspective so that you can still move forward, do a good job, and make great monsters, is the absolute best resource you could possibly have."

"I'm not sure if I have any definitive answers as to why I've been as fortunate as I have been throughout my career, but a lot of it comes down to something [artist] Don Post once said to me. He told me, 'It's great that you young guys come out here and you want to make monsters, but you always have to remember, things always change, so you have to be prepared and be just as willing to change, too.'

"It was great advice," Tom said, "but I just don't think we'll ever see an end to monsters. There isn't really money in doing special effects anymore, so we keep working despite it. You just have to realize that you have to roll with it."

"Something that stayed with me from that very first time I came out here, was that I found out that something like a writers' strike can completely crush a person's lifestyle, even if you're not a writer. I never

Eternal Monster Kid, Tom Woodruff, Jr. Photo courtesy of Tom Woodruff, Jr.

became part of that lifestyle. I was always smart. It was always about keeping things working at home, keeping the shop in place, keeping the shop open, and not being so cavalier about the work you are doing. I've been fortunate because I've gone through a good portion of my career now just trying to make sure I'm still that kid who fell in love with all this stuff in the first place. I make the decisions based on that kid's excitement and that kid's love of the world of monsters."

16 **Gabe Bartalos**

FOR NEARLY THIRTY-FIVE YEARS, artist/director/writer/producer Gabe Bartalos has been leaving his imprint on the filmmaking world at large in very unique ways. Not only did he help bring to life the now-iconic Leprechaun character that has terrorized horror fans for decades, but he has also been a frequent collaborator with boundary-pushing filmmakers like Frank Henenlotter and Stuart Gordon, and he recently worked with

Photo courtesy of Gabe Bartalos.

visionary artists David Byrne and St. Vincent. For Bartalos, this wild ride of a career was born out of his love of Japanese monster movies that began at a very early age.

"When I was a kid, I can remember taking out my dad's Super 8 camera and making horror films," Bartalos said. "It's interesting, because back then the biggest influences I had were the Japanese monster movies I'd watch on television. Then, I saw some of the Universal Monsters movies, and then *Planet of the Apes* came along, too. Looking back, I was probably at the perfect age during that Golden Age of Horror and Splatter in the late '70s and early '80s, when there was an explosion of films celebrating makeup effects with Dick Smith and Rick Baker at the forefront."

"As I was making these homemade movies, I realized that someone had to do the effects if a head was being chopped off or someone was getting cut, so I was doing that, too. It was through that process where I began to realize that for as much I loved cinema, I also loved art. And it was during that period when there was a new awareness, through publications like *Famous Monsters* [*of Filmland*] and *Fangoria*, that this is a real profession. That's how I learned about Tom Savini and Rick [Baker], and Tom was this important force in the business because he was so charismatic and a big

Gabe working on a head sculpture for *Jack & Diane* (2012). Photo courtesy of Gabe Bartalos.

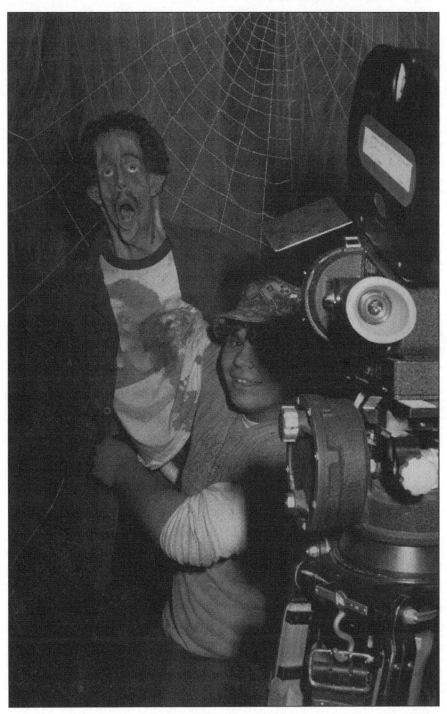

Gabe poses with a shriveled body on the set of *Spookies* (1986).
Photo courtesy of Gabe Bartalos.

character who was always ready to talk. I've been fortunate to know Tom, and getting to work with him was amazing because he was a really good person to help lead the charge of this new art form of special effects."

"Because I grew up in New York, I had access to Dick Smith and was able to visit him from time to time. He was very open with his technical advice and that was exciting. Then, I met makeup effects artist Arnold Gargiulo and I worked at his studio, first as part of an internship. I got to go on sets at a very young age under Arnold, too. As I was learning about the business, it was a much different landscape than it is now, as there was a real destitute of information back then. It was very hard to get information on anything, but I quickly understood from Dick Smith to take pictures of everything I was working on and use that as my way of building a portfolio."

One of the films that helped establish Bartalos' career as a professional artist was *Spookies* (1986), a low-budget cult classic burdened with complex production issues (it is still debatable whether or not the film even received a proper release in the mid-1980s). For Gabe, though, it was a chance to prove himself at the young age of seventeen.

"I came on *Spookies* with Arnold, but he had some creative differences with the production and left the project," explained Bartalos. "We were already into filming at that point and the producers said they would be happy if I just took everything over, and with Arnold's blessing, I did just that. That was the first project where my work that was being built would be on the screen, so that was exciting. The history of *Spookies* is a little sad, though, and I think the foundation of the film, why it still works, probably comes from the original directors, Tom Doran and Brendan Faulkner. If they would have finished the film the way they had wanted to, especially now, looking back at the films coming out at that period, they would have had a pretty good film, maybe above average because of the monster count."

"During post[-production], they got into difficulties with the British financier, who panicked, withdrew them from the project, and brought in a new director [Eugenie Joseph] from the adult entertainment world. The film was never the same. I remember when it came to the Muck Men, these big creatures I had created, the new team added this flatulence to them, which I always thought was a little weird. They thought it was hilarious, and there it is in the final version of *Spookies*. They came back

Beyond creating the Muck Men, Gabe also had the opportunity to play one for *Spookies* (1986). Photo courtesy of Gabe Bartalos.

and shot all this extra stuff with the wizard and this girl running around, which didn't make much sense, and they brought in other effects people, too, just to fill it all in. In the end, it just seems like one big confusing movie to those of us that were there."

"Despite all of that, I still got to create the Muck Men, and there's a mummy with a Ouija board that I also got to do, which was very exciting to me as a teenager. I got to do the shriveling head of actor Peter Iasillo [Jr.], too, which was my homage to what Chris Walas did in *Raiders of the Lost Ark*. His shriveling head just blew me away, and then here I was calling him up at seventeen, and for two hours he described the entire process—how to do it, what I was going to run up against, everything. So being a part of *Spookies* was a very special time for me in my career for a lot of reasons, even if the film itself turned out to be inconsistent in tone."

While he had already enjoyed a fair amount of success on the East Coast as an up-and-coming effects artist, Bartalos began to realize that if he wanted to continue following his dream of creating the kinds of monsters he grew up loving, he was going to have to take the leap and move to Los Angeles.

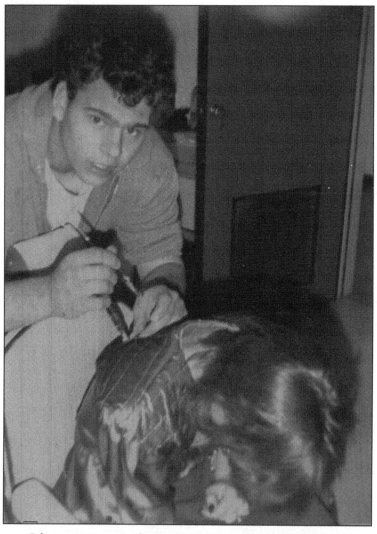

Gabe preps actress Carolyn Purdy-Gordon on the set of *Dolls* (1987).
Photo courtesy of Gabe Bartalos.

"One thing I started to realize was that a lot of makeup artists in New York, when they were not doing special effects makeups, they would be doing straight makeup instead. That was their foundation to survive, but I wanted to do special effects makeup every day, and I understood that in order to do that, most of that work was consistently happening in Los Angeles. And so, at nineteen, I decided it was time to move out here."

Gabe found his cross-country transition an easy one to make, as he quickly landed work and has stayed busy in the world of special effects ever since.

"As soon as I came to L.A., I got an interview at John [Carl] Buechler's studio, MMI [Magical Media Industries], and he hired me that day. John quickly recognized that I had already been running crews and was great at organizing projects, so he made me the makeup supervisor on *Dolls*, which was a Stuart Gordon film."

"It was funny, but actually we prepped *From Beyond* first, and it had a huge workload with various studios working on it. During that process, *Dolls* got pushed to shoot first, so we had to change gears to give *Dolls* our full attention. *Dolls* is a really interesting film to me because it firmly has its foot in two different worlds, where part of it is a kids' fairy tale and the other part is a dark genre film, and both succeed. The film is actually a really good example of Stuart, because he has many sides to him. It was fun to watch Stuart at work because this was coming off the success of *Re-Animator*, and we had a great time."

"Then I was quickly off to Italy, working on a parallel film called *Crawlspace* with Klaus Kinski, so that was really a fun way to start off a career in L.A., with Stuart Gordon and Klaus Kinski. While working, I was always very focused on trying to find an expression for my imagination, so I was constantly sculpting and designing. There was so much to learn in proper mold techniques, proper fiberglass techniques, and proper foam running that at every shop I worked at, I was given all these great learning opportunities. I still really appreciate that to this day."

"After working on those films at John's, I started working for a company called Reel Effects," Gabe continued. "They specialized in creating physical effects like explosions, rain, and wind effects. But there was a period when they were taking on makeup effects just to see if more was better, and we did *Friday the 13th Part VI* [*Jason Lives*], which was significant for me. The original *Friday the 13th* was the first splatter film I saw

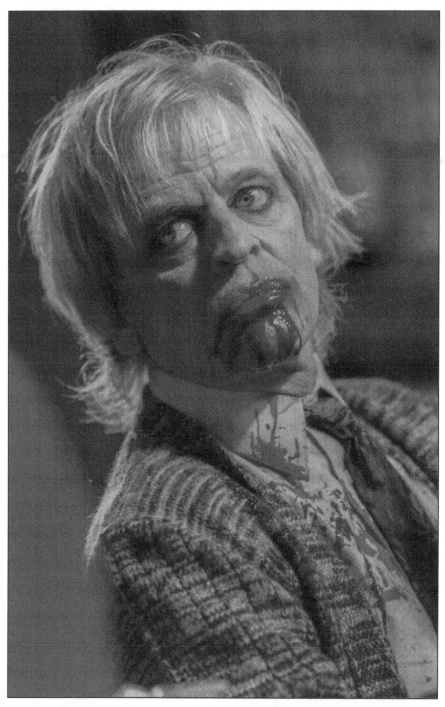

Klaus Kinski between shots on *Crawlspace* (1986). Photo courtesy of Gabe Bartalos.

Gabe poses with Jason's iconic hockey masks that he created for *Friday the 13th Part VI* (1986). Photo courtesy of Gabe Bartalos.

that had no apologies, and Tom [Savini]'s work is amazing in it. To get to work on one of the sequels years later? I was all over it."

"I got to make the Jason masks," Gabe reflected, "I think we made thirteen, because at that point ripping off the masks from the set was a big thing because the franchise was in full swing, and producers knew that people were going to steal them—how weird. I also got to work on the scene where Jason cuts off the guy's arm with the machete, and we had to design a really interesting mold that would come apart. There were fun little technical challenges among all of the bloodshed, including the sheriff's death, where Jason breaks him in half. We had just done a body breaking in half for a film called *The Outing* [a.k.a. *The Lamp*], so we used that same rig when the sheriff got cracked, and it worked great."

"But every trip was an adventure, and while I was working on *The Lamp*, Savini called me up and said, 'Oh you're in Texas? We're doing [*The Texas*] *Chainsaw* [*Massacre*] 2, come on over and help out.' So I went over to Austin for that. My career at that point was a lot of fun because these were the people I had read about and respected, and now I was getting to

Tom Savini (front row, second from the right) and his crew from *The Texas Chainsaw Massacre 2* (1986), which included Gabe (front row, far left). Photo courtesy of Gabe Bartalos.

work for them. I began a relationship with Frank Henenlotter around that time while I was on the film *Brain Damage*," Bartalos added, "and we've worked together many times since then."

Throughout his career, Henenlotter has always been a director looking to push horror into some rather bold territory, and for over twenty years, Bartalos has helped him do just that, creating the special effects for the aforementioned *Brain Damage* (1988), *Frankenhooker* (1990), *Basket Case 2* (1990), *Basket Case 3* (1991), and *Bad Biology* (2008).

"Frank is just great, and his sense of humor is outrageous," said Bartalos. "On *Brain Damage*, what was so cool is that the three heavy effects in that film—Aylmer the parasite, the gore effects, and the withering effects of the old couple—those alone would be a dream on any one film, but the fact that all three of those were in one film was so much fun. That film is one of my favorites of Frank's, and it was great because that's where we got to know each other. There's nothing more personal than shooting a film and being in the trenches."

"Frank is also a real taskmaster, but it's in the quest of this ultimate vision, and he's amazing because he knows exactly where he's going. Com-

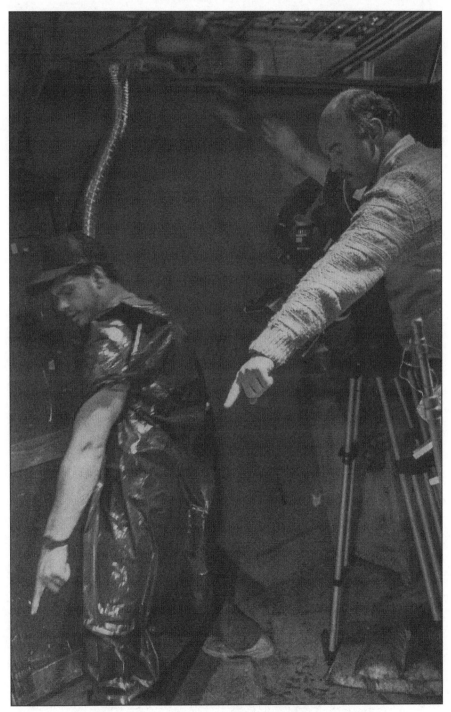

Frank Henenlotter and Gabe on the set of *Brain Damage* (1988).
Photo courtesy of Gabe Bartalos.

ing from the low-budget world with *Basket Case, Brain Damage*, and [so] on, he's learned how to make sure every cent goes on the screen. We hit it off and we had fun, so when he got the deal for *Frankenhooker* and *Basket Case 2*, he asked me back. Looking back, it was at a great time, because my imagination was just exploding at that point, and he must have sensed something way in advance with the amount of freedom he gave me."

"He was probably like, 'Well, let's exploit Gabe; he's crazy, his energy is boundless, and he will always give me a bunch of monsters.' He was really smart in tapping into what I had to offer, because it just makes him and the film look good, and someone who is excited about the work is the best employee. My imagination and taste tend to go towards the surreal anyway, so it was a very easy fit to collaborate with Frank."

"I also think being very young, to have a director recognize your talent is completely liberating, and it is a huge confidence builder. Looking back at that time, it was an incredibly healthy atmosphere to be working in, and I was lucky that it was with someone like Frank, who had enough confidence in himself to allow everyone else the chance to rise to the occasion."

Gabe sculpting the gargoyle for *Basket Case 2* (1990). Photo courtesy of Gabe Bartalos.

Gabe painting several copies of Elmer for *Brain Damage* (1988).
Photo courtesy of Gabe Bartalos.

Around the same time he began his longtime working relationship with Henenlotter, Bartalos was called to join Bart J. Mixon's crew to work on Tommy Lee Wallace's *Fright Night Part 2* (1988).

"Bart had been working at a studio within Fantasy II [Film] Effects, which had been known more for visual effects at that time, but they began to find themselves working a lot with miniatures and makeup effects, so they wanted to just do it all under one roof. *Fright Night 2* was fun because everyone got different effects to do. I got the scene where the vampires go bowling with the guy's head, and I got to make the head."

"Bart was a great guy to work for," Bartalos added. "He let everyone run with their own effect, so at the end of the day you could say, 'I did this,' or 'I did that,' and it made you feel like you had ownership of the work, which was nice. It doesn't always happen that way."

In the late 1980s, Bartalos was given the opportunity to work alongside one of his heroes when none other than Rick Baker brought him on board to contribute to *Gorillas in the Mist* (1988).

"*Gorillas* being the first project with Rick was so cool because in the years of reading about him, I learned that his biggest professional pursuit was to build the ultimate gorilla suit. And now, he was going to have the

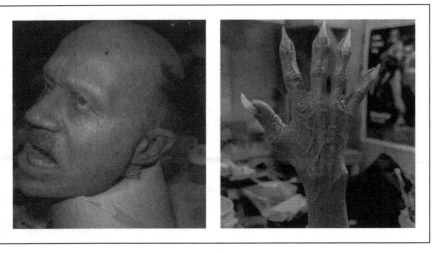

For *Fright Night Part 2* (1988), Gabe sculpted the bowling ball head and worked on a monstrous hand as well. Photos courtesy of Gabe Bartalos.

budget and he was very aware of the challenges ahead of us. He said, 'You know, this isn't a fantasy ape and this isn't a gorilla on its own. Our stuff has to be able to cut in with the real stuff.' And when you think about that, it becomes a really challenging prospect."

"Rick was pushing everything that he had learned to another level on *Gorillas*. It was a great time because he got the pre-production period that he wanted to get the job [done] right. It was a very small crew, especially compared to where Rick would go in the following years, but for this film, there were only eleven of us. Rick built a prototype suit on himself first, and the idea was that any complaint or problem that would come up, Rick would know about it first and would completely understand how to fix it."

"So the suit was put together almost to completion on Rick, and then we began on John Alexander, who played Digit. I started in the mold department and when the molding and fabrication were done, I got pushed to the paint department as the crew got smaller and smaller. When there were only a few of us left, I was moved to the hair department, and it was really nice to watch all these components come together all the way to the end. Still, to this day, the work we did on *Gorillas in the Mist* is some of the best work that I've seen, and Rick's Digit became the benchmark for gorillas in film."

Gabe would join Rick on another ambitious project shortly after wrapping on *Gorillas in the Mist* (1988): Joe Dante's ambitious sequel, *Gremlins 2: The New Batch* (1990). To take on the formidable amount of special effects the production would require, Baker insisted on a key stipulation before coming on board the project.

"Rick turned down *Gremlins 2* so many times because the studio initially wanted to follow in the path of the first *Gremlins* and go the same route with the Mogwais and the Gremlins. Rick told them he would only do it if he could make them into individualized characters, and when they agreed, that's what finally sold Rick on it. There was a really fun period where, for six weeks, we were just designing all different types of Gremlins. Some were just a free-for-all of different styles, and there were others that Rick was specific about. Rick gave me the Vegetable Gremlin because it was just my kind of crazy. Again, it was nice to have that one character you know is your own up there on the big screen."

"*Gremlins 2* took a massive turn once the characters were picked and we had to make all the versions. As Rick does on every job, there is a hero, there's a backup, there's a stunt double, there's one to fly through the air, and there's a hand puppet version of every type of creature. Suddenly it was like, *Holy smokes, we're going to do eleven versions of twenty-eight characters?* It was a massive amount of work. It became a bit of a factory line then, where instead of characters, there were tables of ears, there were tables of teeth, and all the other parts, too."

"Rick, to his credit, built everything on *Gremlins 2*, which was a huge project, with the same quality and care that he would use if he were doing a smaller show, where he could

A look at the immense amount of practical effects that went into bringing *Gremlins 2: The New Batch* (1990) to life. Photo courtesy of Bart Mixon.

handle [things] personally for the entire show. It was very impressive to watch and to be a part of. There were so many cool sculptures being generated, and then there was some standout mechanical work happening on the Spider Gremlin and the Brain Gremlin, too."

"I think why Rick Baker is so admired by many, and what really impressed me, is that when he is hands-on, he is one of the best designers and craftsmen out there. Then, when he has a project like *Gremlins 2*, where it was impossible for him to do it by himself, he hired a good team and insulated us from the drama that every production has, and let us focus on our art. Rick made me feel proud to be a member of his crew."

"What is really cool about Rick is that sometimes you get close to your heroes and it's not so great. When I got to work for Rick after looking up to him for all those years, he was a gentleman, he was funny and caring, and he was more than I could have ever imagined. Rick actually took the idea of hero worship and made it even better."

As Gabe continued to establish himself as a special effects technician, he realized it was finally time to put his official stamp on the industry and opened Atlantic West Effects, which is still running to this day.

A variety of sculptures and makeups that Gabe created for *Basket Case 2* (1990).
Photos courtesy of Gabe Bartalos.

"Starting my own company was a pretty organic process," Bartalos explained. "I continued to take on small jobs while working for Rick, like a friend's play or a photo shoot, and so I turned my apartment's dining room area into a little studio, where one side was sculpting and the other was mold-making. I was working on a film called *Wild About Harry*, a werewolf film for HBO, and my friend Dave Kindlon and I decided that we should go get a space because we were tired of trashing our apartments. We found a raw space in Sylmar, and right around that time, *Basket Case 2* happened. That deputized the space with a real job."

"It wasn't like I hung my name on the door, cracked my knuckles, and said, 'Okay, now I have to go find work.' I basically hit a point where I said to myself, *I can't run all this through my personal accounts anymore, and now I need to hire people to help with everything because I can't keep up on my own.* As more demands of work came, it made sense to become incorporated as Atlantic West Effects."

"We were fortunate to get a big rush of work early on, like *Leprechaun* and this film I did for [Roger] Corman called *Dead Space*, and then I worked with [*Jason Lives* Director] Tom [McLoughlin] again on *Sometimes They Come Back*, which was a TV movie. It was nice of him to call me back on that. [Robert] Rusler was just great to work with as he went through the head cast process, and we designed this elaborate makeup for his character. What's interesting about *Sometimes* is that Tom had us build 100% graphic stuff, but because this was a TV movie, he knew he was just going to show it in bits, and if those bits weren't fully realized, it might not have had the impact that he knew he wanted."

"That was interesting, because as time goes by, you realize how different directors handle your work. This was a good lesson for me. If we didn't build it full-on, it wouldn't have sustained just a few frames. He was also working for television, so he knew what he needed to get through the shoot because he knows the medium very well."

Considering Bartalos was always fond of breathing life into vivid cinematic characters that he could take some ownership of, in the early 1990s, he was given a huge opportunity to create one of the most iconic modern movie monsters to ever grace the silver screen: the titular baddie from *Leprechaun* (1993), portrayed by Warwick Davis. In fact, Bartalos had the rare chance to continue overseeing the handling of Davis' killer character, as he worked on all of the subsequent *Leprechaun* (1993) se-

Actor Robert Rusler in his demonic makeup for *Sometimes They Come Back* (1991).
Photo courtesy of Gabe Bartalos.

quels (although he had nothing to do with the 2014 remake *Leprechaun: Origins*).

"What my vision of a leprechaun had been reduced to at the point I was hired for *Leprechaun* were these ridiculous images from traditional fairy tales and a cereal box," Gabe said. "None of those images were all that interesting to me, so the direction I took the character was almost like my way of saying, 'F you.' You have to embrace the absurdness of the concept and then just jackhammer it into a very bold conceptual area. The punch line to all of this was that they had Warwick, who is an amazing actor and treated the role with an incredible sense of seriousness. That, to me, was the cherry on top."

Warwick Davis in makeup during production on *Leprechaun* (1993). Photo courtesy of Gabe Bartalos.

"I remember listening to the producers early on discussing what they thought they wanted. They had done two sketches, and one of them had a clover hanging off a derby hat he was wearing. I didn't want to go in that direction at all, because if that's your monster, which is going to forever brand this character, you have to make that interesting. I realized the producers weren't going to see it that way, so I quietly pushed their artwork aside as I started to design him."

"I did a full miniature body sculpture right down to the little Irish straps in his shoes. I thought, *If this is a real creature, it has to swing the pendulum in a very tough direction.* I sculpted the Leprechaun with an ultra-aggressive sculpted brow and chipped tooth just to give him that edge. In *Leprechaun*, there are actually three different stages of makeup. If you look at the first images of the Leprechaun in the movie and again at the end, you can clearly see it. But because we cross-pollinated the pieces with three different stages, he looks like he has almost six to eight guises in the film. By the end, his final look is what they kept for the rest of the films."

"The professionalism of Warwick added so much more to the character beyond just the makeup," Bartalos added, "and it was cool how *Leprechaun* became this Holy Grail for the studio, because they wanted a monster franchise and they got it. I don't think they would have had it not been for Warwick."

A close-up look at the "Mittenspider" head Gabe designed for *Leprechaun 4: In Space* (1997). Photo courtesy of Gabe Bartalos.

As he continued to work throughout the 1990s and 2000s as an effects artist and a leader in his industry, Bartalos realized he had other creative itches that needed to be scratched.

"Because this all started with me making films, that feeling just never went away. As a makeup artist, there is nothing worse than turning a prosthetic character over to wardrobe, and ten minutes later they come out with a bad Carol Burnett scissored-up outfit. That can be so frustrating. You begin to understand that you can't control a lot of aspects in a film when you come on as a hired gun makeup effects artist. You're just not in a position to challenge that world. It made me realize that I wanted to go back to the world of filmmaking so I could explore that feeling again and have a chance to realize more things the way I first envisioned them."

"That's what *Skinned Deep* [Gabe's 2004 directorial debut] became. I thought, *Let's not just sculpt the characters, let's sculpt the entire world. Let's build the sets, let's make our own reality and create a dream and then film the dream.* Putting together your own film that you're writing and directing allows as much of your imagination to get in that you want to try and get on the screen. That's what I find really fun about the process. The fact that these are homegrown projects that are lucky to find a release means there isn't a responsibility to a studio yet, so I can be as absurd and playful as I want. When they do land in a good place, that's great. It allows me to really clean out my head and get it all out there on the screen."

"It also puts a different light on your responsibility as the makeup effects artist after you've directed, because you really can respect the fact that the director is managing an entire film, and here you are just worried about your precious little effects."

A few years ago, Gabe had the chance to work with another purveyor of the strange and surreal, musician David Byrne, who hired Bartalos to help create the image manipulation for the cover of his album with St. Vincent (a.k.a. Annie Clark), *Love This Giant* (2012).

Gabe being stalked on the set of *Skinned Deep* (2004). Photo courtesy of Gabe Bartalos.

Gabe applies prosthetics to David Byrne. Photo courtesy of Gabe Bartalos.

"David totally embraces the underbelly of intellectualism through art. At my first meeting, it was such a subtle modification that he was looking for on him and singer Annie Clark that, while I really didn't want to talk myself out of a job, I told him that it sounded like what he needed was just a digital tweak. David said, 'No, I want to go through a face cast, I want to see the sculpture, and I want to wear a thing.' He wanted to celebrate the art of prosthetic application, and the fact that it was so subtle is what really got it exciting for me as a challenge. It's much harder to hide a subtle nuance."

"When the makeup was done, we had a photo shoot with large monitors. As they were taking the first shots, I heard this hilarious laughing that came out of the room where David was, and Annie, who was sitting next to me, said, 'Oh, I think David is happy.' He loved that what we did to him was just so subtle that fans were going to endlessly sit there and stare at it just to figure out what was different. Annie's look was more severe, where I broadened her nose bridge and made the left side of her jaw look broken."

"But David was great, and he loved the process of wearing the makeup and going through it all. Once we had wrapped the shoot, I took the castings we did of their teeth and faces, as well as the extra vacuform pieces, and sent those to them as a 'thank you.' As it turned out, I ended up solving their inner artwork problem. So, on the album and on the CD, it's all the teeth and the face mask. He put all of those pieces to use. I thought that was really cool and very gratifying as an artist."

David Byrne poses after his makeup was completed by Gabe for a 2012 photo shoot. Photo courtesy of Gabe Bartalos.

Throughout his decades-spanning career, Gabe Bartalos has been fortunate to work alongside some of the greatest talents in the effects industry and collaborate with a vast array of filmmakers who helped shape the landscape of modern horror. Reflecting on the longevity of his career, he said, "I think that I'm really lucky to have gotten into it when I did. There was a foundation laid by those we still consider great, Rick Baker and Dick Smith being the biggest two, so there was a lot of excitement that fueled the industry to the point where it just exploded. That gave room for all of us."

"Now, once a big bang like that happens, every star is up to its own trajectory and [must] find its own orbit. I was lucky that all directors that I've worked with, and my fellow artists that have supported me, all came with a real love and a real honoring of creatures. We don't wink and nudge at the work we are doing. To all of us, this is really special stuff. Monsters and creatures are a wonderful byproduct of our fallacies and insecurities. They are fused to us and we wear it like a coat of arms. It's such a cool thing."

Gabe painting during pre-production on *Godzilla* (1998). Photo courtesy of Gabe Bartalos.

A bloodied Gabe looks rather cheerful on the set of *Saint Bernard* (2013), his second directorial effort. Photo courtesy of Gabe Bartalos.

"Then, when you take it further to the arts, when you push yourself to consistently make things better and you work with people who inspire you, it can allow you to find an amazing community of really good people. There are a lot of people in the film business for the wrong reasons, so if you are lucky enough to work with directors like Frank Henenlotter, Kevin Tenney, Tom McLoughlin, or Stuart Gordon, all these guys really love this stuff, and that helps you get through the dry spells and the more frustrating aspects of your job. I don't think I could have possibly gotten any luckier than I did in my early career."

17 Brian Wade

DURING HIS NEARLY FORTY YEARS in the effects industry, Brian Wade has contributed to over 120 film and television projects, collaborating alongside some of the greatest artists in modern makeup and working for numerous visionary filmmakers to boot. Growing up in Southern California meant that Wade didn't have to go far to pursue his love of monsters, which came along very early in his life.

Photo courtesy of Brian Wade.

"Part of my attraction to monsters came from when I was growing up," said Wade. "I watched a whole range of creatures and effects, whether it was the classics like *Frankenstein*, *Dracula*, and *King Kong*, or movies like *Them!* (with the giant ants), *Forbidden Planet*, or *The Day the Earth Stood Still*. Somewhere within all of that were elements of the films that had bits of what I consider to be magic, whether it was Robby the Robot, a spaceship, or Ray Harryhausen doing stop-motion. The thing that appealed to me was that you knew somebody was somehow making it happen, whether it was through stop-motion, a matte painting, a man in a suit, or someone with makeup."

"I'm not sure when the switch flipped for me, where I started to realize just what special effects were. Maybe it was me being a kid and having a child's curiosity, or maybe it was the odd bookshops you'd come across, where the owners of the shop would even think to carry something of that nature. But growing up in Southern California, there was this place called Hollywood Book & Poster Co., and that was a treasure trove to me because it had all kinds of film-related things there. I was always reading behind-the-scenes stuff, and that's where I found my first books on special effects."

"As a kid, I also liked magic, and I suppose in another way learning how to do special effects is like learning the secrets to a magic trick. I'm sure I'm not alone on this, but there was a little voice in my head that would somehow categorize the things I was seeing, whether I felt they were kind of goofy or done so well I was just captivated by them. Through all of the reading I did, I would come across the names of the different people involved in making these effects, but I usually couldn't talk to most of the other kids about my interests."

"My beginnings in makeup were all baby steps, really. Somewhere through my reading, I became aware of the different kinds of disciplines involved in all the things I thought were interesting. I loved reading about miniatures. I loved reading about props, stop-motion, and camera tricks—really, just about everything. It was all fascinating to me. Somewhere within that realm, I became introduced to the makeup aspect of filmmaking and the forefathers of all that we built upon, like Jack Pierce, John Chambers, and Dick Smith."

"I found Richard Corson's book on stage makeup, and it was really the only book with all of these behind-the-scenes things that actually taught

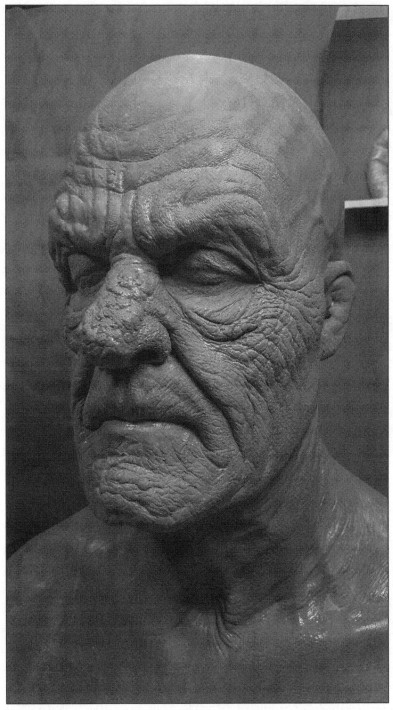

An old-age makeup designed by Brian. Photo courtesy of Brian Wade.

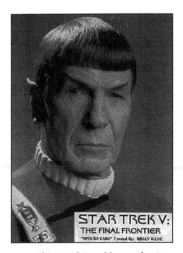

Brian designed Spock's ears for *Star Trek V: The Final Frontier* (1989). Photo courtesy of Brian Wade.

me something. I checked it out from the library and I just pored through it. So, that was my beginning, and a lot of the films that were coming out in my childhood, the ones I seemed to be watching, were Rick Baker effects films, so I was quickly becoming an aficionado of his work."

"In junior high, one of my friends' mothers worked for Don Post's mask company, and he told me he could get some materials through them, so that's how I got my first latex. I just started the processes of molding, doing a lifecast, sculpting a mask, pouring it up in latex, and making fake body parts. They were all these very basic, entry-level things, but it was exciting for me. I had always been creative and artistic, and I always drew, so there was even a part of my little brain that thought, *Maybe I'll be a comic book artist*, because I spent a lot of time drawing."

"I think I was in junior high school when one of the girls I knew had an older brother who was a big *Star Trek* nerd. She told me how they would go to these science fiction conventions, and she invited me to come along one time. The convention broadly covered both the science fiction and horror genres—really, it had everything. They had things like the original prop submarine from *Voyage to the Bottom of the Sea* and these stop-motion puppets from a low-budget film called *Laserblast*, which I had already seen. Once I saw those things in person, the craftsmanship kindled something in me."

"That convention was also the first time I met Rick Baker," Brian added. "I brought an issue of *Starlog* magazine with me, where they had profiled a film he'd recently done called *The Incredible Melting Man*. He took the time to speak with me, and I actually gave him my phone number and offered to help him out if he ever needed it, because it turned out I lived only two blocks away from him. I was just in junior high, but I was very enthusiastic. Meeting Rick somehow made me feel closer to special effects, like they were more of a tangible goal now. That was the moment when I said to myself, *This is what I want to do!*"

That pivotal meeting with his hero set Brian down a path he would continue to travel for the unforeseeable future.

"Like any other kid who went on to do this, I spent countless hours on my own trying to teach myself things, practicing and building make-ups on myself. There were failures, of course, but there were some successes, too."

"My lucky break came at the end of my junior year in high school, when one of my best friends at the time told me that he saw somebody making masks in their garage. I was very fortunate to grow up in Southern California, because there was a real big hub for that community in the San Fernando Valley. So, when my friend told me about what he saw, I grabbed a stack of my drawings and ran over there, and sure enough, there were a couple of guys working in their garage."

"I introduced myself to them, and they were Kenny Myers and Erik Jensen. Kenny Myers is one of the founders of Premiere Products, has his own line of makeups, and he's a really well-known makeup guy in the industry. Erik Jensen worked with Rob Bottin on many shows and with one of the ILM [Industrial Light & Magic] teams, too. This was back in the late '70s, and I'd come and hang out, help them whenever I could, and just learn about everything."

A lizard creature sculpture created by Brian. Photo courtesy of Brian Wade.

"One day, I got a call from Kenny, who told me that he might have a paying gig on a movie for me, which ended up being Roger Corman's *Galaxy of Terror*. That was my initiation into this world. From there, I worked on the *Piranha* sequel [*Piranha II: The Spawning* (1981)], too. After that, Erik told me that he wanted to put my name forward on a couple of projects—one might have been on [*Star Wars: Episode VI*] *Return of the Jedi*, but the other one was going to be working with Rob Bottin. I weighed out the pros and cons, but Rob was known as this awesome makeup effects guy who was doing some really mind-blowing things, and he had close connections with Rick Baker, too, so that just seemed like a more direct route to follow my own passion. So, Erik was kind enough to get me hired on John Carpenter's *The Thing*."

For an up-and-coming artist like Wade, being part of such an innovative and ambitious film like *The Thing* (1982) would prove to be beneficial to his burgeoning career, especially considering it would provide him with the opportunity to work under an artist who was known for pushing the envelope.

"Rob Bottin was truly the visionary behind why *The Thing* works as well as it does, and he was smart enough to surround himself with a talent pool that he trusted and that he could collaborate with. There was a fantastic concept artist named Michael Ploog, whom Rob worked very closely with. [Rob] would tell Mike what his ideas were, and Mike would sketch them out. Rob has an incredibly dynamic imagination and

Brian sculpting the full-size "Blair Monster" for *The Thing* (1982). Photo courtesy of Brian Wade.

a real gift for expressing what he's seeing in his mind's eye. He was just a 'more is better' kind of effects guy."

"*The Thing* became this rare occasion where there was this collision of talent between John Carpenter and Rob Bottin, and it was amazing. We also had an incredible amount of pre-production time to make this stuff happen, which provided Rob with a lot of opportunities to explore. I can remember on several occasions

Rob bouncing ideas off of me, and when you heard him tell a story, he would do it in such a manner that you were living the moment of the story right there with him. I would always find myself getting caught up in his stories."

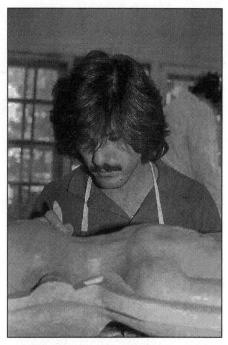

Brian working on an otherworldly creature for *Strange Invaders* (1983). Photo courtesy of Brian Wade.

"We were on that show for about fourteen months, and we had to put in some very long hours. Sometimes, we would just sleep in the shop for two or three days straight because we didn't even have the time to leave. But I think everyone who was on that crew would agree with me that there was nowhere else they would have rather been. It was a magical opportunity where I spent more than a year being schooled in all of the aspects of special effects, from design to sculpting to mold-making to casting and painting. *The Thing* was one of the strongest influences in the arc of my entire career."

Following *The Thing* (1982), Brian continued his journey into the professional world of special effects by honing his craft on films like *Psycho II* (1983), *Jaws 3-D* (1983), *Strange Invaders* (1983), and *The Last Starfighter* (1984). Eventually, Wade had the good fortune of working with another legend of modern effects, Stan Winston, when he was called to come on board James Cameron's *The Terminator* (1984).

"I'm not sure how it came about, but I believe somebody passed on my number to Stan, and he called me to come in for an interview," reflected Brian. "I guess there were two people—myself and one other—interviewing for one position, which I didn't really realize until I got there. I was fortunate and got hired to fill the position, though. When I started there, we were finishing up some work on the TV show *Manimal*, and I think we moved from there to a pilot [episode] called *Wishman*. Then, *The Terminator* came in."

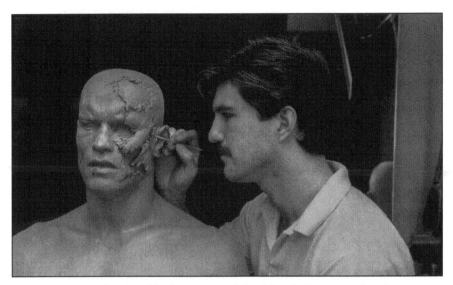

Brian sculpts Arnold Schwarzenegger's head for *The Terminator* (1984).
Photo courtesy of Brian Wade.

"I was there from the beginning, when the concept art was first coming in. I worked on the robot, some prosthetics, and a puppet head, too. Then, I actually had another job opportunity that came along, so I left *Terminator* in order to pursue that. But had I known what *Terminator* was going to become, I probably would have stayed. Even though I wasn't on *Terminator* through the filming, I did get to meet with Arnold [Schwarzenegger] and was there for the building of a lot of the effects."

"It was a great experience," Brian continued. "Stan was very supportive, and he let us do our own concept designs based off James Cameron's sketches. I look back at some of that work I did, and I'm like, *Oh my God, I'm just a baby.* But Stan was great, and he was very grateful for the work that we did. At the end of a show, he would invite us all over to his place and have these barbeques where he would be like, 'You see that, guys? That's the best steak money can buy, and you guys deserve that.' Stan was really just a fantastic human being all around."

Brian continued playing in the science fiction sandbox on *Starman* (1984) and *Enemy Mine* (1985), with the latter giving him the chance to once again work for another pioneer in modern effects, Chris Walas.

"I hadn't been in any direct communication with Chris Walas prior to *Enemy Mine*. He was from the Northern California camp of effects people. I was introduced to him through a colleague of mine, Stephan Dupuis, whom I had met on *Strange Invaders*. He told Chris to give me a call, and he asked if I would be willing to come for a few months and work up there. I thought it seemed like a new kind of adventure, so I said 'yes.' I had initially been hired to help out in the mold shop; because of the training I received, I had earned a good reputation in that department. Then, they moved me into sculpting, which I enjoyed even more."

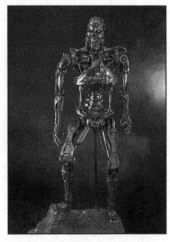

The robotic Terminator sculpture created by Brian. Photo courtesy of Brian Wade.

"*Enemy Mine* was an interesting show in that when I came on, it was still early in the development of the characters, so we went through one entire design and then moved on to another. Being a part of that was a really great experience because I got to see a full character come together, and there was a family environment there, which made it even more fun to be a part of. What's interesting is that *Enemy Mine*, much like *The Thing*, was a film that didn't seem to do that well when it was released in theaters, but has gone on to become revered by its fans, and that's pretty cool."

Wade continued to stay busy throughout the mid-1980s, working on a variety of projects, including Tom McLoughlin's *Jason Lives: Friday the 13th Part VI* (1986), which confidently resurrected Camp Crystal Lake's most notorious resident.

"Tom really did breathe some fresh air into that series," Brian said. "I know that *Friday [the 13th: Part] V [A New Beginning]* had gone on record as a huge disappointment, both financially and with the fanbase, too. I was contacted out of the blue by a gentleman named Chris Swift, who had been working for a company called Reel EFX. I went over there, and they were doing two projects simultaneously: one was called *The Lamp* [aka *The Outing*], and the other was *Jason Lives*."

"It was a whole different group of people I hadn't worked with before, and they brought me in to make some fake heads. There was already this decomposed dummy head of Jason that was going to be inside of a coffin, so that had some design cues on it already. We went to set, and the guy

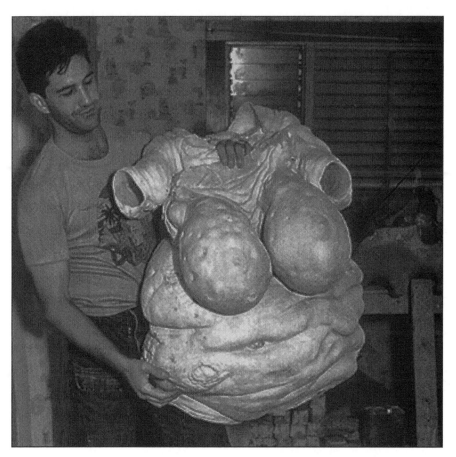

Brian with the witch suit he created for Steve Miner's *House* (1985).
Photo courtesy of Brian Wade.

they had cast as Jason, Dan Bradley, apparently looked a little too fleshy in the dailies, so the producers wanted to go ahead and recast Jason."

"They got a gentleman by the name of C.J. Graham, and in the whirlwind of everything, I was sent back from location to do C.J.'s lifecast. I believe I was there by myself, and I had to sculpt the Jason head and his hands over the course of a weekend, mold them, and then run them out with foam and bring all that back with me to Georgia to shoot the following week."

"*Jason Lives* was one of the best on-location crews that I have ever worked with. It was a small crew by modern standards, but everybody was very friendly and it was a great shoot. I know that Tom had some issues with trying to make things happen when they were being tight with the money. He had to find some very creative solutions for some issues he faced during the shoot, but he was a fantastic director to work with."

"I wasn't a huge *Friday the 13th* fan going into it, especially because I hadn't really seen the sequels at the time, but being a part of it was really special. It's one of those films that horror fans always ask me about to

The same year he worked on *Jason Lives* (1986), Brian also created the makeup for The Supreme Leader character (played by Anjelica Huston) for Disney's *Captain EO* attraction. Photo courtesy of Brian Wade.

this day, so I'm happy that people still enjoy it, even now. Plus, another reason *Friday VI* ended up being this big moment for my career was that I got a chance to play one of the ambulance workers, which was my first-ever on-screen appearance in any film. It was just a lot of fun."

While Wade had experienced an immense amount of good fortune at that stage of his career, one of the next films he was hired for allowed him the opportunity to work for his personal hero, Rick Baker, on the family-friendly comedy *Harry and the Hendersons* (1987).

"Throughout my career, as much as Rick was the single biggest inspiration behind me getting into the field, he was also the one who I was too nervous to ever interview with," Brian said. "Everybody else I was very straightforward with when I had to meet them, but I always thought, *My stuff will never be good enough to show Rick Baker*, so I always just psyched myself out when it came to him. One time, he had come by while I was doing some mold-making for Greg [Cannom], so perhaps he put it together that if I had been working alongside another great mold-maker, Gunnar Ferdinandsen, I had to be pretty good at what I was doing."

"At the time, I had been doing more sculpting, but when I did get the call to go work on *Harry and the Hendersons*, I thought, *I'm going to take the job anyway, because I'd love to be over there and see how things work, even if it's not in the department that I normally work in.* I knew it would be a great opportunity to see how things really are done at the highest of levels."

A look at the various versions of the "Regine bat" from *Fright Night Part 2* (1988), sculpted by Brian during pre-production. Photos courtesy of Brian Wade.

"*Harry* was, once again, one of those perfect situations where you had a great story, a great human cast, and then you had Rick Baker heading up the effects, and Kevin Peter Hall playing Harry. Kevin and I became friends on this one, too. My girlfriend and I used to hang out with him all the time. So there were a lot of great things that came out of working on *Harry*: seeing all the craftsmanship that went into creating Harry, making a lot of great friends, and it led to me being able to work with Rick again on a few projects, like *Gorillas in the Mist*, the *Beauty and the Beast* television series, and *Gremlins 2*. I know there's that saying, 'Never meet your idols,' but Rick was just fantastic. It was such a relief that someone I looked up to turned out to be an incredible human being, too."

Following *Harry and the Hendersons* (1987), Wade continued to hammer out an impressive path in special effects, contributing to several horror sequels, including *Critters 2* (1988), *Fright Night Part 2* (1988), *A Nightmare on Elm Street 4: The Dream Master* (1988), *Bride of Re-Animator* (1989), *A Nightmare on Elm Street 5: The Dream Child* (1989), William Peter Blatty's *The Exorcist III* (1990), and the aforementioned *Gremlins 2: The New Batch* (1990).

"I honestly don't remember too much of note from when I worked on *Dream Child*, but for *The Dream Master*, I worked on two different effects crews. I worked for Screaming Mad George on his crew, and we did the roach motel sequence where I sculpted the oversized cockroach and helped with Brooke [Theiss'] weird breaking arms effect. It was a weird job, especially because I had never sculpted a giant cockroach, not that it mattered one way or the other. George was the perfect guy to do something so bizarre with, and it's a fantastic little sequence in that movie, too."

"I also worked with Steve Johnson, who was in charge of a handful of little scenes. The biggest of them was a scene where all of these souls of Freddy's victims come out through his body and wreak havoc upon him. I had known Steve Johnson since the days when he worked at Rick Baker's [shop], and he was a very creative guy who always wanted to push the boundaries and ideas—not unlike Rob Bottin in that regard. So that was a really good occasion to be aboard Steve's crew, because he was doing some wild stuff, especially the Freddy torso, which ended up being something like fifteen feet tall. To create something like that was absolutely brilliant to me, and *Dream Master* ended up being one of the more fun *Nightmare on Elm Street* movies effects-wise."

"For *The Exorcist III*," Brian continued, "I was called in by Greg Cannom, who had been brought on to head up the makeup effects on the show. He was doing a couple of projects at the same time and wanted to give more of his personal attention to one of the other projects. For some reason that I'm still not aware of, there were some guys already working on *Exorcist III* that had gone to set, ended up being unhappy about something, and they walked from the show. So Greg needed to find someone to fill their shoes."

"Greg brought on myself and another incredibly talented makeup artist by the name of Mike Smithson. Unbeknownst to either of us, we were both somehow individually led to believe we were going to be heading up the on-set makeup on the show. Within the first couple of days shooting, we had this moment where we were both like, 'Hey, I thought I was heading this up.' What an awkward moment. I'd actually signed my deal memo with production as an on-set supervisor, and because Mike

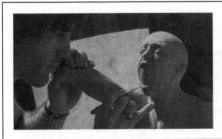

Prior to contributing to *The Exorcist III* (1990), Brian worked on Chuck Russell's 1988 remake of *The Blob* (1958). Photos courtesy of Brian Wade.

Seth Green poses on the set of *Idle Hands* (1999). Photo courtesy of Brian Wade.

was such a good friend of mine and I could see there were aspects of the work we were doing that were more important to him than to me, I had suggested that he should be in charge of certain parts of the show, and I'd be in charge of the rest. I even got him a well-deserved raise a few weeks into shooting, so everything worked out smoothly."

"The project had a lot of great makeup effects in it, and it turned out to be a great creative experience for both Mike and I, as well as Bill Forsche, a longtime talented colleague who joined us later on the project."

"Blatty struck me as being this intense personality," Wade added, "but as far as our interactions with him went, we had nothing but great experiences on that show. We were on top of doing what we were doing. Everything we were doing was looking good and getting done on time, and everyone was really pleased with our team. The most unique thing I remember about shooting *Exorcist III* was that William would keep the set fully refrigerated, and it was so cold in there that we could always see our breath. That was pretty wild."

As filmmaking technology became more advanced throughout the mid-to-late 1990s, Wade saw his opportunities to create lasting and unforgettable characters changing as well. He continued to keep busy doing traditional effects on a variety of projects, but eventually he got an opportunity to prove himself on a different landscape, lending his talents to bring the titular mouse to life in Rob Minkoff's *Stuart Little* (1999), as well as everyone's favorite mystery-solving pooch a few years later in Raja Gosnell's *Scooby-Doo* (2002).

"A big part of me being able to be a part of *Scooby-Doo* was because of my work on *Stuart Little*. That was one of the first movies that really raised the bar for those kinds of characters in live-action movies, so I thought for sure it would make for a great jumping-off point when I finally reached out to Jim Henson's Creature Shop. I had heard that they were doing *Scooby-Doo*, and I had an interest in working with them because I thought it would be another incredible and very different opportunity for me."

"I actually cold-called them and said to the girl answering the phone, 'Hey, my name is Brian Wade, and I'm the guy who designed Stuart Little. I understand you guys are doing *Scooby-Doo*, is there somebody I could talk to?' I had no idea if that would even work, but sure enough, she put

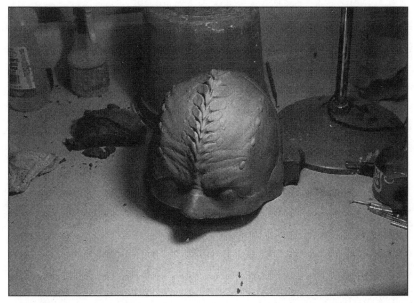

A Klingon brow piece sculpted by Brian for *Star Trek IV: The Voyage Home* (1986).
Photo courtesy of Brian Wade.

me right through and they had me come down and meet with them. They were working on a film based on Disney's *Country Bear Jamboree* ride at the time, and because they wanted to make sure that I would be locked in for *Scooby-Doo*, they had me work on that for a while."

"When we started on *Scooby-Doo*, we had to figure out just how we were going to approach this character and ultimately decided that we wanted him to look like the cartoon character, but more photorealistic. I wanted to make sure we nailed all of Scooby's trademark looks, the proportions of the character—including his oversized paws—and all of the characteristics to his face and snout. I ended up making a 1:1 scale sculpture of Scooby-Doo, which was later finished by a talented colleague of mine, Mario Torres. I'm told everyone was happy with it, because they made a full-sized stand-in puppet of the design for them to use on set. Later, as it turned out, the character was done entirely in CGI [computer-generated imagery]."

"Any time I've been involved with an iconic character that has an already established look, there's an equal measure of enthusiasm attached to it, and a pressure that comes from being given the direct responsibility of bringing that character to life. When those opportunities come up, they feel like they're once in a lifetime. I really get a kick out of it."

Throughout his career, Brian Wade has worked on nearly twenty different horror and sci-fi franchises, contributed to countless films from other genres, and has collaborated alongside some of the greatest talents in modern special effects. What's his secret? For Wade, it all comes down to just one word: passion.

"The biggest reason I'm still here is because of my passion for being creative, and that always comes through in my work. Usually, what keeps people working, in my opinion, is they do good work, they show up on time, and they are easy to work with. Those are the basics for anybody. I never got into this business because of a desire to be an award-winning makeup artist in this realm, because if you want to be an Academy Award winner, you also have to be the one on set applying these makeups all the time, and on occasion I get bored of all the waiting around on set. I primarily enjoy the making of this kind of stuff, starting from thin air and creating a character or creature, and bringing it completely to a finish. Either way, I've been fortunate that over the years I've found this happy balance of on-set work and studio work."

Brian works on a Thor sculpture for Shanghai, China's Disney Store.
Photo courtesy of Brian Wade.

"I do love applying makeups and going to set, but I just don't like all the waiting around. I would much rather spend that time keeping my hands busy on something else, and I love the creative process that happens in the studio, too. I've been a freelance artist almost the entire span

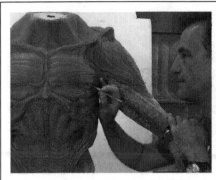 

Brian recently worked on the popular Netflix series *Stranger Things* (2016) and sculpted the Demogorgon creature on behalf of Spectral Motion. Photos courtesy of Brian Wade.

of my career, with some longer runs at certain effects studios, but I'm grateful for it, because being freelance means I've been flying without a net for years now. It can be quite a ride some days."

"Some people have been in the same company for twenty-five years, and that blows my mind. They love that rock-solid foundation, and I understand that, but to me, the variety keeps things interesting. Some days I reflect on it, and I feel like I'm a bit like a traveling salesman. I still don't know how I've managed it all, but I'm still here. I'm quite happy with how things are, and I have very few regrets about everything I've been a part of. I've been very fortunate from the very start, and I am grateful to everyone who has supported my work through the years."

18 Tony Gardner

FOR TONY GARDNER, longtime special effects artist and founder of Alterian Inc., it was his love of illusions that led him to pursue a profession centered on making audiences believe in the impossible.

"The start of my interest in filmmaking actually goes back to around age twelve, when I got my first Super 8 camera," explained Gardner. "I grew up in Ohio, so it wasn't like there were any resources at my disposal in regards to filmmaking. Whether it was film or makeup effects or spe-

Photo courtesy of Tony Gardner.

cial effects in general, none of that was even really looked upon as a career option where I lived. It was just an interesting thing that somebody else did far, far away, but it was more like a novelty or a hobby locally."

"I grew up doing magic tricks, and there was one moment I remember very specifically that started me on the path to film. When I was about eight years old, my grandmother bought me a magic kit that was quite involved. It had this whole setup with a little stage that folded out, and had all these cool tricks in it. I was opening it up and going through everything and the first thing that I pulled out was this black plastic card box. You put a card in it, closed the lid, and when you opened the box, the card would have magically disappeared. I didn't read the directions—I knew what it was—so I just put the card in the box, closed it, re-opened it, and suddenly the card was gone! It blew my mind."

"I was so excited, I ran into the next room to show my grandmother this cool trick. I was a little too excited, and as I went running out of the room, the box flew out of my hand. It hit the floor, the bottom of the box popped out, and then the card flew out from underneath that."

"My heart and my stomach completely sank. That's when I realized it was fake. Magic wasn't real. And for a while, I was completely depressed, but then I had this realization: *If I can create that same moment that I just felt for somebody else, how cool would that be?* So then I really got into magic seriously, and for me, 'magic' was all about that specific moment when a trick blows your mind, when you just can't believe what you saw was real. I would do magic at birthday parties as a little kid, and there's sort of a novelty in kids doing it, where you're allowed to be weird."

Once he realized the endless possibilities that film could offer, Gardner transitioned his love of creating illusions with live magic tricks to making movies when he was a pre-teen.

"My parents bought me a Super 8 camera for my birthday when I was twelve, and I started making little short films. I realized that if I wanted to film a magic presentation, I could stop the camera and then actually really fill an empty box or a hat up with stuff, and then start the camera back up, and suddenly something 'magical' really did take place . . . at least on film. It all looked so much more believable on film. Film seemed to give me so many more options than reality ever did."

"I started making little movies with my friends in the neighborhood and doing all sorts of crazy things: making our own versions of films we'd

A corpse created by Tony during his teenage years. Photo courtesy of Tony Gardner.

seen in theaters, or scenes that we liked from movies, even crazy stop-motion movies, including one with dozens of these furry things that, when
animated, looked like a swarm of creatures chasing us down the street.
That's when I began experimenting with makeup effects as well. I tried
out a really basic version of prosthetics at age twelve, where I would mix
up and tint flour paste and use that to animate the transformation of a
person's skin from normal into the dry, scaly skin of some sort of creature,
along the lines of stop-motion transformations on Lon Chaney Jr. in *The
Wolf Man* . . . just a more affordable version."

"As I got older, I was involved in a lot of different activities. I was all
over the place in regards to my interests. I was the epitome of what you'd
consider an ADD [attention deficit disorder] poster child back then. I
played drums in a band, I played string bass in an orchestra, was doing

magic, building creatures, making these short films, and was involved in the high school theater department. I was heavily involved in everything extracurricular above and beyond going to school and going to my classes—the normal academic stuff I was really supposed to be doing at that time. I also started getting involved in local community theater back then. I was doing really simple things for them, just making masks and things like that, or playing standing bass in their pit orchestra for the musicals. Nothing I was doing felt like it could ever be a career, though. They were all hobbies, in my opinion."

Despite the fact that he still saw prosthetics and mask-making as just a hobby, Gardner wasn't deterred from reaching out to several legends in the industry, fueling his desire to learn more and continue to hone his craft.

"I just started writing to people I could find any information on through books and articles," Gardner explained. "I started writing to Don Post, and I ended up getting a response from Don Post Jr., who then sent me a signed Don Post mask poster. Charlie Schram and Dick Smith were two more people who were so forthcoming with information. They would write back and send detailed explanations of processes and even slides or photos."

"Dick Smith sent me a signed photo of Hal Holbrook as Abe Lincoln, and I remember showing it to my friends in the neighborhood, and they were all like, 'First, who's Hal Holbrook? And who's Dick Smith and who's Charlie Schram?' There was really no one to share my interests with, so I felt like I was operating in a vacuum. What was nice, though, was that I was being recommended different books through those correspondences, which I could hunt down, and that helped me continue to learn and work with whatever resources that I could find out in Ohio."

"Three movies came out that changed my perceptions as someone who loved being creative," continued Gardner. "The first was *Planet of the Apes*, then *Star Wars* [*Episode IV – A New Hope*], and the final movie was *Alien*. I had seen a picture from *Alien* of the title creature somewhere, and just that one image really hooked me. I really wanted to go see the movie, but I wasn't old enough yet, so I eventually talked my mom into taking me to go see it. She hated me forever for having to sit through it, and I even made her take me back a couple more times to see it again. She'd learned her lesson, though, and would get me into the theater and then leave. I would sit in the theater and watch those three movies over and over, but *Alien* was the one that was truly inspiring; it was so original and unique."

"Around that same time, I was building a really large stop-motion spider armature to animate, about a foot and a half across. But then I saw *Alien* and thought, *Why not turn that spider into a Facehugger?* I was building it up on wooden dowels and wire—just really basic, simple stuff. I built up the forms and then the skin on the whole thing with cotton and latex tinted with food coloring. It had this long tail that was wrapped around the neck and it took forever to build. I think it turned out pretty good considering I was just learning as I went and going from whatever photos were available back then."

"But that's when I realized that there was really cool stuff happening in movies, and that there were resources available that made it possible to create your own versions of these inspiring creatures or characters if you put your mind to it, and then, it all clicked. There were no real directions as to how to build this stuff, just some great photos to reference. I was just figuring it all out as I went, and in hindsight, it's probably the best way to learn," Gardner added, "because you are constantly problem-solving and you quite often end up having to think outside of the box in order to pull some of this stuff off and make it work."

Once he graduated from high school, Gardner set his sights on attending college, where he was able to continue pursuing his passion for special effects through the school's theater department.

"When I went to college, *The Howling* and *An American Werewolf in London* were just coming out—two very big moments for those of us who love this stuff," recalled Gardner. "I went to Ohio University, this tiny little

The first Facehugger Tony ever created as a teenager. Photos courtesy of Tony Gardner.

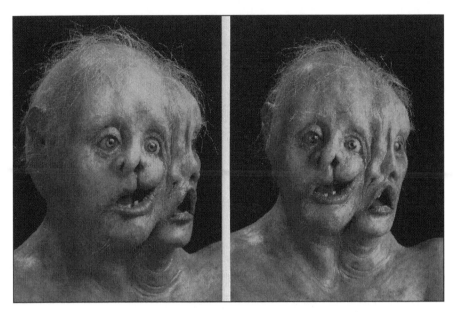

A two-faced monster Tony created at age eighteen. Photos courtesy of Tony Gardner.

college down near Ohio State [University], which had this really great theater department. There was no film department, so I signed up as a theater major and quickly discovered that the theater department was set up in this hierarchy, where the seniors got to do everything—they got to direct the plays, be in them, and just run the whole show. That meant as you went down the line, the juniors got to act or be part of the crew, sophomores were the grunts, and incoming freshmen were the grunts' grunts."

"But I could do stuff that other students couldn't do as far as makeup effects were concerned. I don't know how I did it, but somehow I ended up talking the college into giving me a room in the basement of the theater building, and buying these makeup materials that I couldn't afford to buy myself to use on theater productions there. They bought foam latex, dental stone, and all this stuff that I needed in order to do prosthetic makeup. The theater department was doing this play called *Dark of the Moon* that takes place in the South, and there was this weird, creepy mountain man, an old lady with a goiter, and all this other weird stuff in it that all had to be designed and created. The upperclassmen just trusted me to make it all happen, and all of the other freshmen were like, '*Who the hell is this guy?*' I didn't know what I was doing, either," Gardner added, "but I was doing it."

Just two of the makeups created by Tony during his college days.
Photos courtesy of Tony Gardner.

"That's when the theater department was starting to get kudos for putting on productions that were unique and different, instead of coasting on productions that would have been simpler and easier to do. I just soaked it all in and learned a lot from watching them reach out, try new things, and take chances. I really enjoyed the experience, but I realized that Ohio University didn't really have anything that even leaned towards filmmaking. I realized that if you wanted to be a newscaster, you were in the right place, but that was as big as it got there at that time."

Coming to the conclusion that his current educational choice wasn't doing him any favors when it came to achieving his dream of becoming a professional artist, Gardner knew it was time for a big change, one that would take him clear across the country to the West Coast.

"I decided to apply to USC [University of Southern California] for the simple reason that George Lucas and Dan O'Bannon had gone there. I was accepted by USC most likely due to the fact that I had a weird portfolio that was definitely different from all of the others with my Facehuggers, werewolves, and masks, but I didn't get into the film school. USC accepted me as a fine arts major and told me that the cinema school was a two-year program, and that I could re-apply to the film school the following year. I was excited."

"I also auditioned for the USC marching band and was accepted into the drumline. Their band camp started a week prior to school starting, so I decided to fly out a few days prior to band starting up, so I could have a look around this place called 'Los Angeles' beforehand. I brought all my makeup stuff with me, including this E.T. mask that I had made back at home, which sparked an idea in regards to how I could use my extra time there before band started. I had read that Steven Spielberg used to sneak onto the Universal lot prior to starting in the industry, so I thought I would try that, too, using E.T. as my way in the door. I was so straightforward with my approach to everything and went into it with a positive attitude; I had to try."

"So, I took a milk crate, stuffed a pillowcase, and turned it into a squat body and then attached my E.T. mask to it. Then, I wrapped the little guy in a blanket and put it in a milk crate to match the scene where E.T. rides on the front of Elliott's bike in the movie. I drove over to Universal Studios, parked down the street, and then walked in through the front gate carrying E.T. in a basket out in front of me, and just pretended I knew what I was doing. And sure enough, I walked right through. There I was on the Universal lot, and then it hit me: *So, now what do I do?* I didn't really think this plan through further than the challenge of just trying to get onto the lot."

A reanimated corpse created by Tony for *The Return of the Living Dead* (1985).
Photo courtesy of Tony Gardner.

"When I started my classes at USC, I realized almost immediately that I didn't really care for a single one of the art classes that I had," Tony admitted. "In a 3D Design & Composition class, we were doing these—in my opinion—really juvenile, simplistic, black-and-white paintings, and then gluing objects to them. I felt like I was back in junior high. I got so frustrated that I ended up going to all of my teachers and asked each one if I could turn my classes into some sort of independent study so that I could do something that I felt was more relevant to my interests, or I was going to go insane. Most of them agreed, but with the stipulation that I had to find somebody to be my teacher or mentor who was a professional artist within that arena, and it would be up to that person to grade my work."

"One of my film classes at the time was Drew Casper's Introduction to Cinema class, and I decided I would write my class paper on the use of mechanical effects as main characters in the film industry. I thought that I could use the paper as an excuse to interview people I also really wanted to meet. I chose Carlo Rambaldi because of his work on *E.T.* [*the Extra-Terrestrial*] and *Alien*, and Rick Baker, because he had just done *American Werewolf in London*. I also thought it would be interesting to interview Steven Spielberg, since he was directing films with these creatures in them as the main characters. This would give me three different perspectives that would make my paper interesting."

"So, I found Carlo Rambaldi's phone number in the phone book, which in those days meant going to a local phone booth in their area and going through the phone book for information. I found his name listed and called and asked if it would be possible for me to do an interview for a paper I was writing for a class at USC. It took a while to get it organized, but a date was eventually set. When I finally got to meet with him at his studio, his people left me in a room to wait for him. It turned out that it was his office. There were all these oversized chalk drawings up on the wall: a cat face, E.T.'s face, mechanical designs—all this stuff literally pinned up all over the walls. It was so cool. When he finally walked into the office, he seemed like someone so wise and established and comfortable in this world of film, and I suddenly felt so out of place."

"I was told that he didn't speak much English, and that I'd be talking to him through an interpreter—in the end I think it was actually Carlo's son. I would talk to him, he would turn and talk to Carlo in Italian, Carlo would respond, and then an answer would come back to me. So I felt even more awkward and kind of out of place. Somewhere through the course of our conversation, though, I shared that my grandfather had immigrated to the U.S. from Italy as a little kid. All of the sudden, Carlo laughs this big laugh and starts speaking in English with this thick accent. In my head, I'm like, *You fucker."*

"I think he was testing me or just messing with me, but it was a great icebreaker and the conversation ended up being really comfortable, and I learned a lot from him. He shared a bunch of sculptures and showed me around. It was a really cool experience."

Gardner's quest to secure his other interviews with Baker and Spielberg didn't go nearly as smoothly, but his pursuit of both ended up leading to some other amazing opportunities.

"I had gotten onto the Universal lot a few times by that point, so I knew where Amblin Entertainment was. I just went up and knocked on the door, and I talked to the people there and asked if I could interview Steven Spielberg for a paper. He wasn't there, though. I went back so many times after that, they eventually set up a real appointment."

"I remember the first time I went back, they said he was off filming, and there was a kid there playing video games who seemed about my age in a side room that was set up like a mini-arcade. He and I talked for a bit and then someone came in to get him, saying he had to go back to work. It turned out to be Zach Galligan from *Gremlins*, and that's what Steven was working on that day."

"I went back so many times, I literally became friends with the people in his office. Spielberg had a drum set, and I ended up re-tuning his drum set one day when I was waiting for him. I never did get him for any sort of sit-down interview for my paper, either, but I had great experiences trying. I think I got about three minutes with him when he blew in while working on scoring *Twilight Zone* [*The Movie*]. It was pouring rain and he was running behind. He ran into Amblin to grab some stuff and at least say "hello," and then we talked about Rob Bottin and cable-controlled creatures for a few minutes, and that was it."

"As far as trying to meet Rick Baker, I figured out where he lived as well, and just went up and knocked on his front door in North Hollywood. An older gentleman answered the door, and as I was talking to him and explaining that I was writing a paper, I kept looking past him at this giant painting on the wall behind him. It was a gorilla head, probably about four

Tony gives Gwyneth Paltrow's makeup a last look on the set of *Shallow Hal* (2001).
Photo courtesy of Tony Gardner.

or five feet tall—it was massive, super detailed, and looked like a blown-up photo. He eventually turned around once he realized that I kept looking past him, and he told me that it wasn't a photo, it was a painting, and that he had painted it. As it turned out, it was Rick Baker's dad, Ralph, and he proceeded to explain how he had painted all of the fine details on this gorilla."

"He told me that Rick was in England filming *Greystoke* [*The Legend of Tarzan, Lord of the Apes*], and he wasn't expected back for at least a month. But I stayed in touch with Ralph. I had turned one of my art classes into an opportunity to sculpt and create some masks. I needed to find an artist to critique my class work and grade it, so I eventually asked Ralph if he would be interested in being my advisor. He was actually doing the same thing for another student at the time and said 'yes.'"

"After all was said and done with my classes, Ralph said that he really admired my attitude and my enthusiasm to go after things. He asked me if I would leave a stack of slides of my work with him because he wanted to leave them for Rick to take a look at. He said, 'I'm not promoting you. I'm not pushing you on him in any way. I'm just leaving your slides with a note saying that your work is worth a look.' It was far more than I ever would have expected, and it was really nice of him to do."

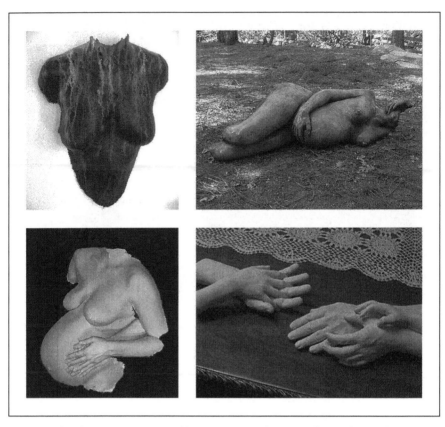

Several sculpting projects created by Tony prior to beginning his professional career in special effects. Photo courtesy of Tony Gardner.

Gardner soon realized Ralph's gesture would go on to make a big impact, though, after Baker returned from London.

"Rick eventually called me," Tony recalled, "and he mentioned the slides and the paper I was writing for school. I told him how that paper was already over, but I had another idea for a class next semester, so I still hoped to be able to meet him and do an interview. He agreed, and I ended up going to what was EFX Inc. [Baker's company] at the time."

"I went into the front office there and met Rick, and he was super nice and very personable, and also kind of quiet, like me. I asked him all the questions relevant to the paper and then we started talking about makeup and special effects in general. He asked me about myself, and I told him my interests, talked about some of the masks I had made, and all my experiences at school. He started quizzing me as to what resources I had access to work with and how I had done certain things—I felt like I was getting interviewed at the same time. He was actually writing stuff down on this little notepad, too, and I didn't really know what that implied, but the interview wrapped up, I thanked him, and I left. I was thrilled beyond belief—I had met everyone that I wanted to meet.

"I went back to Ohio for the two weeks of summer left before the new semester started," Gardner continued, "and I was feeling pretty good because I met all of the people on my list, I had a plan for cinema class next year that included another list of filmmakers to meet, so I was excited to get to kick back for a few weeks. I was home for literally two days and the phone rang. I almost didn't answer it since no one else was home at the time, but when I did, it was Rick Baker. We talked for a few minutes, just shooting the shit. I was thinking to myself, *My God, why is he calling me?* Then, he finally told me that he was starting a job on a music video and he was going to need some help in the shop, somebody to run around and pick up supplies, sweep the floors, and be a runner."

"He told me it was only about four weeks' worth of work, but at the end of the four weeks, he said he thought that at least I would know for

Tony at work on the "Moss Zombie" for Michael Jackson's *Thriller* (1983) music video.
Photo courtesy of Tony Gardner.

sure if this was the type of stuff I really wanted to be doing or not. He knew my interests were scattered all over the place, and thought that being around the shop watching what was going on would help me figure out what I wanted to do. I agreed to the job and told him I'd be back in about two weeks when classes started. That's when Rick said, 'The job actually started two days ago, and there's someone holding your spot right now.' He told me if I wanted the job, it was mine, and if not, this other guy would just stay there and be their runner. I told him I definitely wanted it and that I would be there as fast as I possibly could. I was pretty much shitting my pants at that point because I didn't think I would be working and doing anything professionally for a while, and here was Rick inviting me to be a part of the crew on a music video called *Thriller.*"

"Right after I hung up, my mom walked in the front door. I told her that I had to go back to California and I needed to get a flight out right away. She looked at me like I was crazy because I'd only been home a few days. I explained to her that I had a job opportunity that would last only four weeks and would be a great experience for me. I told her that school wouldn't be starting until I was already halfway through the job, and that I could handle the job and school at the same time. So she agreed to help me find my flight so I could get back out to California, and I started work the next day. I was so appreciative that my parents were so understanding and supportive at the same time."

While he may have initially thought he'd be able to balance his school and professional responsibilities at the same time, Tony quickly realized that his dream job was impeding on his ability—and desire—to continue his higher education.

"At first, things were okay because the job started out with a fairly straightforward schedule and pretty standard work hours, so I could manage everything there and still get my schoolwork done in the evenings. I even kept on as a drummer in the marching band. All of a sudden, though, everything sort of imploded. My hours on the video evolved into 9:00 a.m. to late into the evening [shifts], which meant there was no time for homework or even school itself, and at that point, I just wanted to drop out."

"Around that same time, Rick said that he liked how I was working out. He asked me to stay on and join the team, but with the stipulation that I had to find somebody else to take my place as a runner, which I did as fast as possible. All of a sudden, I was doing actual makeup effects work, and then I was asked to build a zombie on myself; everybody in the shop was going to be the close-up zombies in the video. What more motivation do you need to work until midnight than to build a zombie on yourself so you can be in a Michael Jackson video? That's when makeup took over as a top priority instead of classes, and I dropped out of USC."

"I was excited about everything that I was working on, and learning a lot of new stuff. I was put in charge of all of the background zombie masks construction, making bladders, learning how to make molds, and even painting. After the actual filming was over, John Landis invited me to the editorial [process] during post-production, because he had heard that I was really interested in filmmaking. He was kind of a smart-ass in the best way, and I gave it right back to him, and he loved that. We hit it off great from the get-go. So, besides working on the *Thriller* video and being in it, I got to watch the process of the video coming together from the very beginning, from the design sketches through fitting teeth on the dancers at rehearsals, all the way through to post-production. I was just soaking all of this stuff in and I knew then that I wanted to be a part of this creative process in **any** capacity," Gardner added.

"When *Thriller* wrapped up, Rick told me that he enjoyed having me be a part of his crew and that if something else came along again, he wanted to have me be a part of it. I was excited, but my parents weren't nearly as thrilled as I was. I remember talking to them about what Rick had said, and my parent's response was basically, 'Great. You've dropped out of college, and now you don't have a job. So what **are** you doing out there?' I didn't know. I spent the next three months basically doing noth-

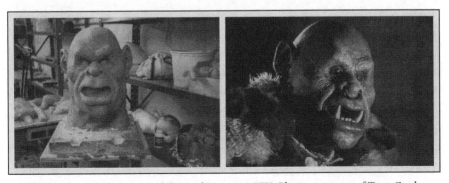

A Halloween mask Tony created during his time at EFX. Photos courtesy of Tony Gardner.

ing beyond my own little art projects and masks, which I think only left my parents even more unhappy about the choices I was making."

Tony persevered through that three-month rough patch, though, and the up-and-comer would reap the rewards for his patience with a steady flow of work that has kept him consistently busy for over thirty years.

"I remember after that time, Rick was offered *Starman*, and I ended up doing some prototype R&D [research and development] for an animatronic baby puppet, trying to make a flexible translucent skin, adding veins and a light source inside a test head, and all that stuff, just trying to figure out the materials and an approach. That's when I went from being that kid offered a one-time, four-week job, to having the situation turning around to the point where I spent the next four years working at EFX and getting the best on-the-job training you could ever ask for from the best person imaginable: Rick Baker."

"I ended up being there for about four years, through all sorts of different shows, meeting all sorts of different people through the different projects. It was a great time. Rick took on *Cocoon* after *Starman*, but as a

Tony poses with his creations for *The Return of the Living Dead* (1985).
Photo courtesy of Tony Gardner.

consultant, with Greg Cannom as the Makeup Effects Designer, and all of us already at Rick's went to work for Greg. Things were just sort of casual that way. Greg set up shop at Rick's as well, which made starting up really effortless. It was midway through this show that a friend from USC called and asked for a favor—something fairly basic, but something that ended up leading to me moonlighting on my first independent job for a few weeks."

"A fellow student at USC named Brian Peck had been cast in a film, and he asked me for a dental veneer top to make him look more like a punk rocker. The director liked the finished teeth enough to ask me to come out to meet with him and talk about his lead actress' teeth. So, all of a sudden, I was driving out to meet Dan O'Bannon at his house . . . the same Dan O'Bannon that had written *Alien*. It was a total film geek moment, but I think I held it together really well."

"To make a long story short, a few weeks later Dan ended up asking me to provide an animatronic puppet for the film that Brian was in, which was a low-budget horror film called *The Return of the Living Dead*. They were already shooting, and the company originally hired to do this half-corpse puppet had declared bankruptcy, but the puppet was due on set in two weeks. I was already working full-time on *Cocoon*, so of course I said, 'Yes!' (Who needs sleep, right?) Fortunately, Rick was cool with me working on the half-corpse at his shop at night."

"I pulled in Bill Sturgeon from Rick's to help me with the finger mechanics, and Scott Ressler helped with some of the fabrication. I had a great design to work from, too, from the amazing Bill Stout. I went on set with the puppet and ended up puppeteering the head, Brian Peck operated the jaw and read the lines on set, and I roped Bill Stout in to operate the spinal cord and the spinal fluid. I learned a lot in those few weeks, including the fact that I wasn't afraid to jump into pretty much anything."

"I was asked to do some 'split dogs' for a warehouse scene in the film as well," Gardner continued, "and also was asked to finish off a makeup that Bill Stout had started on Linnea Quigley, who played 'Trash.' I did all of that stuff in the kitchen of my apartment in Hollywood. It was fun to jump around and tackle such an interesting variety of things all for the same film."

"After *Cocoon*, we were all just kind of going with the flow over at Rick's, with nothing really lined up immediately. The makeup commu-

Tony (on the far left) helps block out a scene with director Dan O'Bannon (foreground) during production on *The Return of the Living Dead* (1985). Photo courtesy of Tony Gardner.

nity was a lot smaller at the time, so a bunch of us from different shops would go to a pizza place in Westwood on Friday nights just to hang out and catch up with each other. The guys from Stan Winston's shop [Stan Winston Studio] mentioned that they were going to be working on *Aliens*. Given that *Alien* was one of the films that got me interested in creature effects in the first place, I knew I had to be a part of it."

Looking to continue exploring the professional makeup world outside of Baker's domain, Gardner approached Winston about coming on board James Cameron's sequel, but he made sure to get his mentor's blessing first.

"The next Monday, I went into Rick's and explained to him that I'd love to work on *Aliens*, even if only for a week or two, just because *Alien* was a big part of my decision to do this kind of stuff. One of the first things I had built back in Ohio besides the Facehugger was a Chestburster. I probably would have built a full-sized costume if I had more resources at the time. Rick didn't have much going on, so he let me go work on my dream project over at Stan's."

"Stan brought me in at the very beginning stages of *Aliens*, where he and Jim Cameron were just starting to figure stuff out," Tony continued.

"They set me up in Stan's makeup room in the front of the shop, and my first job was sculpting the Chestburster. It was really weird, because I was sitting in the make-up room, and through the door beside me, Jim Cameron had set up shop in the break room. Stan was in his office another door down the hall. So there's Stan, Jim, and I up in the front of the shop, and every so often, the two of them would talk from room to room to each other. It was really fun, and it became really casual and fast-paced because it was just the three of us. The banter between them was really funny, and it was just a blast to see that kind of creative dynamic."

A behind-the-scenes look at Tony sculpting the Chestburster for *Aliens* (1986). Photo courtesy of Tony Gardner.

"So, I sculpted the Chestburster and then was also able to mold it, core the mold, run a skin, sculpt and mold the teeth—really follow this creature through the entire process. A few weeks in, the project started to take on more momentum and more space in the shop. The scope of it was incredible. We ended up building a full-sized Queen Alien out of garbage bags, cardboard, and foam core in the back parking lot just because it was the only space we had left."

"Jim [and Stan] had figured out this concept of strapping two stunt-men together on a rig inside the torso of the Queen, and he wanted to try it out and see how it would work. We all pieced this thing together and wrapped it up in black trash bags because Jim wanted the Aliens to all be black. I just thought it was so cool that they made the effort that they did to really figure it out right away, and that the director was there with us, doing it all alongside of us, too. It was so impressive to see that level of problem-solving happening right in front of you."

"From there, things got really busy. I bounced around on a couple different things, and so did everybody else. The Queen Alien was the pri-

Tony at work on the miniature version of the Alien Queen for *Aliens* (1986).
Photo courtesy of Tony Gardner.

ority at the time, and there was a miniature version that was going to be done animatronically to allow for faster and more controlled movements. Stan's shop was sculpting it, and then all those molds were going to go to a company called Doug Beswick Productions. Doug had done the stop-motion version of the Terminator, so he was going to do an animatronic version of this miniature Queen, as well as a small Power Loader with a miniature Sigourney Weaver strapped inside it."

"Then, I don't remember what it was a mold of, but I was cutting open a silicone mold with a razor blade. I was doing exactly what you're **not** supposed to do—cut towards yourself with a sharp blade—and as I was holding this mold with my right hand, I took my left hand and was pulling this X-Acto knife through the silicone, and somehow it caught, jumped out, and I ended up slicing my right hand open between my thumb and my first finger right down to the bone. It was this brief moment of, *What the hell?* Which was then followed by this vision of blood spraying, honest to God, for a good solid twenty feet—very Monty Python-esque."

"I went straight to the ER, got stitched up, and was unable to use my right hand after that. I had no movement in the fingers on that hand for almost a month. I basically had the ability to move my thumb and pinky finger on that hand and that was it. I'd cut through a bunch of nerves and they didn't know if I'd have full mobility with that hand again or not."

Although he was unable to do much with his right hand for quite some time, Gardner still found ways to contribute on *Aliens* (1986), even after Stan Winston's team left for the U.K. to set up shop to build the full-size Alien Queen.

"I felt pretty bad because I had suddenly rendered myself completely useless at work," Tony reflected. "As far as the timing went, though, Stan was getting ready to send his permanent crew over to England, and he asked me if I would go with his molds for the Queen Alien over to Doug Beswick's [studio] and follow through on the work needed there. Doug asked if I would like to come on board as the Cosmetic Supervisor for the Queen, Power Loader, and miniature Sigourney Weaver, which was great."

"I had no idea what to do as far as miniature clothes or anything like that, but I knew what sort of approaches I wanted to take towards the molds and materials for everything else. I ended up bringing in Shannon Shea and a couple other people to help me with the work and then, all of a sudden, I was kind of running a crew on my own. Doug was handling the mechanical shop and I was responsible for the cosmetic side."

"We had to ship our miniature stuff out to England in advance of the live-action shooting on *Aliens*, and since Stan would be working out the paint scheme for the Queen there, we just sent the Queen out flat black and left it to the team there to paint it once those decisions had been finalized. Nobody had made a decision on what the Queen Alien's teeth were going to be, though, prior to our ship date: were they going to be black or were they going to be white? No one had an answer for me, so I took it upon myself to cast up a couple heads with the teeth clear so that they had options on whichever way they wanted to go with the color. They wouldn't be stuck having to try to paint black over white or vice versa."

"And I guess when it showed up, Cameron really liked the clear look, and it stayed that way. It was one of those fortunate scenarios where something gets figured out almost by accident, which is always kind of fun, and to be a part of helping establish that look was really cool. I really felt like at that point, my short little career had come full circle from copying *Alien* to working on *Aliens*," added Gardner.

"From there, Doug Beswick was brought onto *Evil Dead II* to handle two specific effects sequences. One was an animated sequence with Linda coming back to life and dancing, basically like a Ray Harryhausen scene, and the other was a giant demon head and tree branch that come into the house at the end and attack Bruce Campbell. It was a great experience. There were so many techniques being used on that film that I had never seen before. It was amazing."

"Doug had me sculpt a couple of different concept maquettes of this creature's head coming through a doorway. The idea was to scale up our creature head as large as possible so that you could use the real actors' faces inside this giant creature costume and have all their faces pushing through it, as if their souls were trapped within this creature's body. It went

Tony poses with the giant demon head on the set of *Evil Dead II* (1987).
Photo courtesy of Tony Gardner.

A behind-the-scenes look at how the giant demon head was shot by Sam Raimi on *Evil Dead II* (1987). Photos courtesy of Tony Gardner.

through several different approaches in regards to execution and became something massive, almost the size of a Volkswagen bus in the end, given that the face had to be on a rolling platform that was counter-weighted."

"One of the things that Sam realized with this thing being so big was that if the creature can't get in the door, what pushes Bruce towards the creature's mouth? The vacuum that was pulling everything in the room towards the door was suddenly blocked by the creature's giant head. Sam's solution was that a tree branch from one of the possessed trees outside the cabin would break in and help "feed" Bruce to the head. So, Doug built this giant rig with a welded aluminum frame, and then Theresa Burkett and Mark Wilson came in and created soft, flexible bark over the whole thing out of sheet foam and oatmeal mixed into latex."

"My time on *Evil Dead II* felt like I was part of this really cool, creative, weird art studio type of environment, where all of these creations were being built that were completely different from one another, but they were all for the same film. Some of the techniques were really old school and some were pretty complicated. Every once in a while I couldn't help but take a step back and go, *Wow, this is really inventive."*

"The more I'm talking about it now, the more I'm realizing that shows like that don't happen all that often anymore, in regards to having to problem-solve on the spot and be quick on your feet. Now it seems more like everyone sits in a dark room in front of monitors, designing and building the stuff you'll see on screen. A lot of the creative, hands-on type of problem solving you just had to do back then, you were forced into it because you had a problem to address and a situation you needed to come up with a solution for right away. You had no choice. Quite often now, that 'thinking on your feet' experience doesn't really exist, and I feel like we've lost a little bit of that excitement."

Shortly after filming wrapped on *Evil Dead II* (1987), Tony spent some time just doing his own art projects, but it wasn't long before Greg Cannom pulled him in on a project he was busy with at the time, Joel Schumacher's *The Lost Boys* (1987).

"I remember being told that Greg was going to be using Rick's shop for *Lost Boys*," Gardner recalled, "and I was renting space in there already, working on my own art projects in a back corner. Greg was okay with the arrangement, though, which was really nice of him. At one point, the

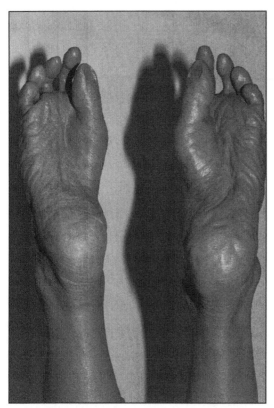

workload on *Lost Boys* got really big all of the sudden, and Greg ended up asking me to help out on some stuff. I agreed, and the first thing I did was sculpt the prosthetic makeup for Kiefer Sutherland's stunt double. I had to make him look like Kiefer in his prosthetic vampire makeup, so that was a cool process."

"Then, they decided that they wanted to have this little kid [Chance Michael Corbitt, who played Laddie] be seen as a vampire, so I sculpted that one, too, which was interesting, given his face was so small and so round, and the design was so angular. There's a scene where the vampires

The feet sculptures (without the claws) from *The Lost Boys* (1987). Photo courtesy of Tony Gardner.

Kiefer Sutherland lining up his hand for the sunlight shot on *The Lost Boys* (1987).
Photo courtesy of Tony Gardner.

are hanging upside down and you see their weird, clawed feet. Greg's idea was that the big toe would be opposable like a thumb, and those feet would mutate to the point where anatomically they could hold the weight of these guys hanging upside down. I thought it was a really cool idea, and I got to build these insert feet. I also worked on a vampire [Brooke McCarter's character, Paul] melting in a bathtub and a few other odds and ends. I was really enjoying the opportunity to learn new things on such a cool show."

"They were filming the scene where the boys are crawling out of the cave and Kiefer reaches to grab them, gets hit by sunlight, and his arm bursts into flames. Joel didn't want shiny burn gel on a stunt guy's arm. He wanted the flames to be right on the surface of the skin and to really be able to see the flames dig into the skin. Plus, they wanted the hand to articulate, so they decided at the last minute to do an animatronic hand."

"I had the hand closest in size to Kiefer's, so we cast my hand and then it was up to me to take it from sculpture through to completion,

The prosthetic hand created for the bathtub scene in *The Lost Boys* (1987).
Photo courtesy of Tony Gardner.

including running the foam. When we took it to set, somebody else puppeteered it, but it was fun to actually go on the set and watch, since it was the only time I had an opportunity to go on set for the whole show. One of the other things shooting that day was a giant burning dummy of Ed Herrmann for the finale scene, which was really cool. They decided that they wanted to see him as a vampire before he was incinerated to have a more dramatic death, so Greg had built this really cool full-body puppet of the actor that would be set on fire. Unfortunately, you never see it in the final edit of the film."

"There was so much to learn from on that film," Gardner continued. "Joel Schumacher is a very visual guy with a lot of really great ideas, and he would shoot a lot of footage. I learned on that one, though, that once a film got into editorial, things could change because of pacing or clarity, and effects sequences could be cut way down or get cut out altogether. It was interesting to see the effects work trimmed down to be a part of the story and not a distraction from it, but it was also sad to see some of the stuff go."

After getting to mix it up with vampires on *The Lost Boys* (1987), Gardner had the opportunity to contribute to two projects that were similar in nature: *Harry and the Hendersons* (1987) and *Gorillas in the Mist* (1988). Gardner credited those years in the late 1980s as being some of the most imaginative and inspiring times he ever experienced as an artist. On *Harry and the Hendersons* (1987) in particular, Gardner saw the creative boundaries of special effects being pushed in very different ways.

"Rick [Baker] had asked me to come back and help finish up some stuff on *Harry and the Hendersons*," Tony said. "When I came onto *Harry*, they were already towards the tail end of their build. I had to fabricate a Harry head for the stunt dummy in the scene when he gets driven around and then launched off the car. I ended up casting up and assembling the dummy out of the molds of Harry's muscle suit."

"Rick had this cool idea for an animatronic insert piece that could fit into Harry's under-skull, making it so you could take the animatronic mask off of [actor] Kevin Peter Hall and put it on this animatronic version of his head so that Harry could do things that Kevin couldn't do. Harry was supposed to lick a TV set, and Rick wanted him to have a long tongue like a dog's, so instead of trying to do something that could fit inside the limited space within the head when Kevin was wearing it, Rick's logic was that if we took Kevin out of the equation, there would be all of this available space to have this three-foot-long tongue that could come out and lick the TV set and pull back into the head, all in one shot. It worked perfectly," Gardner added, "and Rick had figured out a cool way around what had initially been a very daunting problem."

"The only part of Kevin that was visible when he was wearing the Harry mask were his eyes, so we had to recreate that part of his face as part of the animatronic 'insert head.' I sculpted the eye orbits and eyelids to fit over animatronic eyes, which was something completely new for me. I had wanted to do mechanical eyelids on the half-corpse for *The Return of the Living Dead*, so it was interesting to work with animatronic eyes and figure out clearances, closure, and tear ducts so that it all looked real in close-ups and still worked mechanically. To be able to do it on mechanics that were this precise was an eye-opener . . . pun intended."

"When you're creating a makeup or animatronic character on an actor, more than half of the success of that character is the actor inside the character that's bringing it to life and making it appear realistic or believable. Kevin Peter Hall literally brought Harry to life. Harry was Kevin and Kevin was Harry, and there was so little difference between the two—it was amazing. The original design included contact lenses that were more primate-looking, but they ditched the lens idea because Kevin was so expressive and was able to do so much with just his eyes. While the lenses looked more correct for the species, Kevin's eyes added so much personality and humanity to Harry. It was fascinating to watch the character come alive."

"It's unreal where your mind goes when you're watching something that is crafted as beautifully as Harry was. The suit was almost secondary to Kevin's performance, but only because everything just felt so real. It was so well-done that you didn't think of it as a suit."

For the final project he worked on with Baker, Gardner married his own love for animals with the world of special effects in some rather extraordinary ways while gearing up for Michael Apted's *Gorillas in the Mist* (1988).

"That was my last show with Rick," Tony said. "At the beginning, it was very much that same sort of relaxed family dynamic we'd had when we started on other shows, because there were just a few of us on board at that point and we had a nice amount of lead time to prototype and figure things

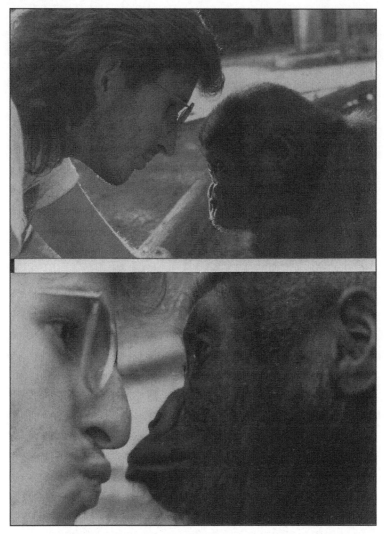

Tony with Marcus the gorilla. Photos courtesy of Tony Gardner.

out. I had done an exhibit for the L.A. Zoo on my own prior [to *Gorillas in the Mist*], and had established a relationship with the zoo that allowed us access to the primate area in the mornings, prior to the zoo opening.

"We could sit down with one of the baby gorillas named Marcus in the mornings, which was awesome. We would sit outside of the enclosure, which had glass walls, and the animals would sit on the floor on the other side of the glass and play right in front of us. We brought the smaller sculptures with us and sculpted right in front of the animals. Marcus would put his hand up on the glass, and I could measure his palm, or even hold my sculpture up right next to his hand. At one point, I was able to sit with Marcus in his pen with him in my lap. I'm a big animal lover, so I was in heaven."

"We ended up building a life-sized animatronic baby gorilla puppet based on Marcus. Even when it didn't have fur yet, and the body was just a ball of foam, you could still see this thing literally coming to life. It was amazing to watch the guys puppeteer it. I can still remember it so vividly because it felt like we were building this complete little character that was so endearing. We weren't just building an animatronic robot. There was a personality to this little guy, and it felt that way from the very beginning, which was nice."

"Rick put me in charge of a prototype gorilla suit for proof of concept, where we'd be using animatronic eyes instead of the actor's eyes inside the head. It would mean that the entire face would be animatronic. We had 'gorilla parts' in the shop that fit Rick already, so our approach was, 'Let's build it out of stuff that already exists, make a new animatronic head, adjust a few things, and see what we get.' We took it up to Griffith Park and we had Rick in the suit and were filming some footage of him jumping out of the brush at the camera and just walking by, doing a couple of different moves to see proportionally how the head looked to the body and what angle the wearer needed to be in order to pull the concept off. We learned a lot of great stuff that day, but more than anything it was fun to take Rick out there and see him running all over the place as a gorilla."

"Being in charge of the prototype suit for *Gorillas in the Mist* was the first time that I was responsible for somebody inside a suit," Gardner continued. "There was a whole new set of responsibilities that came into play that I wasn't expecting. An almost parental and protective feeling kicks in when your job responsibilities suddenly include making sure that an actor is okay and safe. There was this whole serious layer added on to an experience that had previously been just 'fun.' The responsibility for the person inside the suit in regards to their health and well-being suddenly became more important than anything else, because their well-being became my responsibility, too, in addition to just getting my 'creature job' done. It was another one of those moments where you go, *I really respect the people that can do this on a daily basis.* It's like a prizefighter and his support team. I took my work on that one very personally and very seriously."

In the late 1980s, Gardner officially branched out on his own to form his now hugely successful company, Alterian Inc., which has contributed to hundreds of film and television projects, music videos, and commercials over the last few decades.

When asked whether or not it can be heartbreaking to watch something you've worked on for months be sent off and become the responsibility of someone else, Gardner discussed how it's definitely harder for him to do so now, especially since running his own company can often leave him tied to his studio.

"When you're working for Rick and watching the stuff go off to location with him, you know it's in the best hands possible, so it's not really hard to watch it go in those instances, other than just wanting to be there. It's harder now, actually, because I'm trying to run a business, which means I can't leave the shop as easily because I'm the guy in charge. Over time, you get used to watching your 'baby' go off and become part of a movie, but passing that off to somebody else can definitely be difficult."

"It was funny, because after *Gorillas in the Mist*, I interviewed for the [1988] remake of *The Blob*. They had someone lined up to do the major makeup effects for the film, but they needed to bring in someone else to do some smaller stuff. I went in and interviewed for those smaller pieces, one of which was the projectionist character caught up in the Blob on the

Tony gets wet on the set of *The Blob* (1988). Photo courtesy of Tony Gardner.

ceiling. The bulk of the effects were going to be handled by Greg Cannom, which I thought would be great because we had an excellent rapport, so that would be a blast. Then Greg had a conflict and had to pull out, so production asked me if I wanted to take over Greg's workload and they would find somebody else to do the effects that I was originally going to do."

"I wasn't sure I was ready to run a shop of the size that would be needed to do Greg's workload," Gardner admitted, "and I didn't have a space that size available to me, either. The producers had decided to rent out a big warehouse in Hollywood for Lyle Conway's crew. They were bringing Lyle in from London to do the Blob creature itself. Production thought that they could divide that warehouse space in half, and have the creature crew on one side and the makeup effects crew on the other. With both of us in the same building, the look of everything would remain consistent. I was nervous because I had run smaller shows at other people's shops before, but I had never done anything at that level."

"The schedule was really tight. I hired a bunch of friends, and we just dove in and started sculpting maquettes for each of the death scenes. About two weeks into it, I thought to myself, *Oh my God, this is a blast!* I totally loved everything about running a shop, especially the process of incorporating everybody's ideas and collaborating together. It was a lot of fun for me, and that moment was the point where I knew that I could do this, and that I **wanted** to do it again and again."

"My wife (fiancée at the time), Cindy, was the Makeup Effects Coordinator for our side of the shop. She had come from a background in production coordinating for film, so this wasn't so different. Working together was great, especially considering the long hours, and we realized we were a good team. The two of us worked really well [together], and our skill sets complimented each other. I'm the art half and she's the smart half. We knew that if we didn't kill each other by the end of *The Blob*, we could do this. And right when *The Blob*'s extra photography was over, we got married and went off on our honeymoon.

Tony preps a victim on the set of *The Blob* (1988). Photo courtesy of Tony Gardner.

Even though Gardner knew he would be able to work alongside his wife, he soon found out that wasn't going to be the case when it came to another business partner he ended up buying out of the company after its first year in operation.

"When I was ready to start my own place, there was a co-worker I had worked with previously who wanted to team up with me," Tony explained. "We partnered for a couple projects, *Darkman* and *Dark Angel* [1990], and I quickly realized that I didn't want to be in a partnership with somebody else. I worked great with my wife and I'm into this because I love it, and this person seemed to have a completely different agenda. It didn't seem right on so many levels, so I wrapped up within a year's time, and then I bought him out and that was the end of it."

"After *Darkman* was over, I was back on my own again. That's when we actually started Alterian proper, and boy was it a slow start-up. We decided that we would make some Halloween masks given we had some time to kill. We ended up launching a whole line of Halloween masks. We were frustrated buying masks that were thin and didn't keep their shape, and we wanted to make a few masks the way we remembered them as kids: slightly oversized and cast in really thick latex. Our little mask project grew into the Alterian Ghost Factory, which ended up becoming its own entity in its own building with its own crew. Chet [Zar] and Loren [Gitthens] went over there from the main shop and ran that for almost a whole year."

"We were starting up the *Swamp Thing* [1990] TV series around the same time we were starting the Ghost Factory. We had to do masks for some *Swamp Thing* background characters, so I approached Universal and asked if they were interested in letting us do masks of Swamp Thing himself for the general public, and suddenly we had the licensing for *Darkman* and then for *Swamp Thing*, and we got into *Army of Darkness* masks after that. Warner Bros. heard about what we were doing and had us do characters for the Warner Bros. stores for a while, too, including a bunch of the *Looney Tunes* characters. We started a series of 'Ghost Maker' mask kits as well, one of which became the design for the *Scream* mask. Things were taking off, but we realized that doing these masks was full-time work, so we had to pick one or the other because we could only handle so much. We had to prioritize."

For the aforementioned *Darkman* (1990), Gardner reunited with Sam Raimi on his very first comic book-style cinematic endeavor.

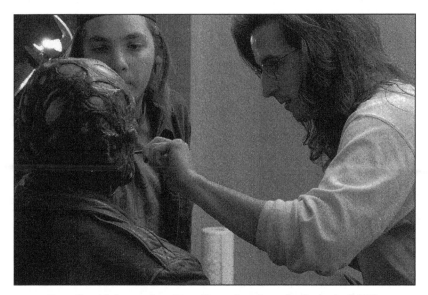

Tony (far right) at work on Liam Neeson's makeup for *Darkman* (1990).
Photo courtesy of Tony Gardner.

"Sam had tried to set up *The Shadow* as a movie, but he couldn't get the rights," Tony recalled, "so he basically said, 'Screw it, I'm going to go do my own thing.' He took *Phantom of the Opera*, *The Shadow*, and a couple of other things and came up with something totally new."

"In the beginning, he came to us with some designs for the main character that had already been done elsewhere, but he wasn't happy with them. He thought they were 'too gooey,' as I remember him saying. He wanted to see if we could come up with another look for the character, something a bit more 'dried out,' so we started out just doing character designs for him. It turned out that what he really wanted to do for *Darkman* was to have a character that was a living version of the poster art from *Evil Dead II*—which was basically a skull with regular human eyes in it. I thought it was the coolest idea ever."

"We were doing the designs of Darkman in the pre-Photoshop era, so we were creating these colored pencil designs of the character with different looks, but just couldn't quite nail the image the way Sam had described it. Colored pencils tend to soften things a bit. One night at home, I just felt really inspired and I sculpted out this bust of the character and put some glass eyes in it. It was mostly a skull, with bits of burned skin and muscle here and there. I put shoulders on it and sculpted a trench coat with a high collar at the last minute, with just a rough form for the coat. I don't remember if I sent over a picture or if I showed the sculpture to him, but Sam saw that and he immediately asked me to do the movie. He went to bat for me with Universal."

"I got sat down by Universal before we started and they asked me if I had ever done a makeup of this kind of complexity before. I told them I had, but I hadn't really," Tony admitted. "I just knew that I knew what I was doing, and I really wanted the opportunity. That's really the story of how all of these jobs went back then—you were solving a problem and doing

A conceptual bust created for the titular character in *Darkman* (1990). Photo courtesy of Tony Gardner.

something that nobody had ever done or seen before, sometimes with no precedent. And Universal just let me go at it."

Once he began working on *Darkman* (1990) full-time, Tony soon realized that some of the assumptions he had made about who would be playing the titular hero (which helped inform his initial design of the character), wouldn't play out the way he expected. However, those idiosyncrasies ended up paying off in dividends in other ways.

"Honestly, I had assumed Bruce Campbell was going to be Darkman. I remember thinking that Bruce's angular face would totally match up with the aesthetics of the sculpture that I had done, and we could adapt that makeup design to his face with no problem at all. But while they were in the process of casting the film, Sam came to me and told me that the studio had someone else in mind, and he said I would love him. That's when I found out it was Liam Neeson, and I remember at the time, when I was doing my research and looking him up, thinking, *Oh my God, this guy has way more of a square head and jawline, and a broken nose. What are we going to do, because he's totally the opposite of the design?* I thought we were going to have to do a complete do-over of the design from the beginning."

Tony also performed as the character Lizard Man in *Darkman* (1990). Photo courtesy of Tony Gardner.

"In the end, of course, what I thought were 'issues' were the character traits that make him recognizable for who he is, so I realized that everything that I thought might be a handicap actually turned out to be a major asset to the look of Darkman. It was obviously a learning experience from that perspective, but it was really challenging, too. Prosthetic makeup is obviously an additive process, so I had to figure out how to keep that makeup as thin as possible and really dig into the skin and make it look like there was depth to the burned areas. That's when I decided that I was going to build up his entire head proportionately so that the good side looked balanced with the burned side. He ended up wearing a good half-inch of foam on the good side of his head," Gardner added.

"That allowed us to carve into the face enough to give a sense of depth, and then use dark colors and even black around the areas where you wanted it to look deeper in the corners of the mouth and stuff like that. It was all about figuring out proportions all the time so that he looked balanced out, and not like a giant Q-tip head wearing shoulder pads."

"Liam also has really big hands, and I wanted to make gloves for him so he could take the hands off and on, and we could change the stages of the dirt and bandages just by changing his gloves. Liam was really conscious of not keeping his hands up by his face a lot because his hands were disproportionate. We also built animatronic hands and forearms, so that when Darkman fought Smiley in the warehouse, and Dan [Bell] got punched by Darkman, it looked proportionate and didn't look like he was getting punched by somebody wearing a boxing glove. Liam actually puppeteered quite often, too, so that anything with the animatronic hands would also have a sense of his performance in it."

"The whole experience all the way through the end was truly great. Liam had to wear that full makeup twenty-something times and he never complained once. We always made sure we had smoothies or something with protein in it for him to drink so he could look after his health. During breaks, you would see him take a

Some of the cast and crew of *Darkman* (1990) pose for a shot (Tony is sitting in the front right, giving the thumbs up). Photo courtesy of Tony Gardner.

muffin from craft services and pound it flat with his fist to feed it in through his teeth, because he could only open his mouth so far. He always told us, 'It's not a problem. It's a challenge.' I took that positive mindset with me for the rest of my career. I thought he was pretty brilliant in that way."

Around the same time he was working on *Darkman* (1990), Gardner was brought on to contribute to another modern cult classic, Clive Barker's *Nightbreed* (1990), becoming involved with the reshoots the producers were doing to add more gore-flavored effects to the film.

"*Nightbreed* was a really weird one for me because we were only involved with the reshoots," Gardner explained. "The producers wanted to add a bunch of scenes, and some of them involved makeups and characters that were in the film, but we had to give them a different look. For example, there was this priest character [Ashberry, played by Malcolm Smith] that had gone to the dark side. They sent over the prosthetics from London and said that they needed me to create this character again and copy what he looked like in the film, but we needed him to look like he'd been burned for this new end scene. We had to work with David Cronenberg's character [Dr. Philip K. Decker] as well, but that was literally just—for lack of a better term—'mask wrangling,' because that character just wore a zip-up mask."

"There was a scene added where the killer comes into the hotel check-in area, and then the lady who checks people in finds the manager's decapitated head resting on the desk's sign-in ledger. They needed a

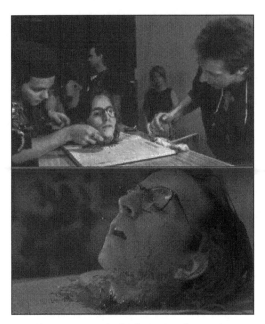

Tony prepping for his big scene during the *Nightbreed* (1990) reshoots. Photo courtesy of Tony Gardner.

fake head, so *Nightbreed* was the beginning of my career as a severed head in the movies. It ended up being me wearing a severed neck prosthetic, with my head up through a fake desk, with the ledger cut really well so that I could get my head up through it. We also did the scene where John Agar is being tortured and he's tied up in Christmas lights and sliced up. My experience on the show was literally only a few days on set. They were all with Clive and a really tiny crew, so it was really fun to step in and be part of the post-production process. Everybody was super nice, and I really enjoyed working with Clive."

Tony's involvement on the reshoots for *Nightbreed* (1990) would lead to more incredible collaborative opportunities with Barker in the future, but prior to that, Gardner once again reteamed with Sam Raimi for a third project, *Army of Darkness* (1992), to handle Ash and Sheila, the main characters of the *Evil Dead* 2 (1987) sequel.

"Sam already had KNB [EFX Group] working on the skeleton army," Gardner recalled, "and he asked if I would like to do all of the makeup effects involving Bruce Campbell and Embeth [Davidtz], because he really loved what we'd done on *Darkman* and he really wanted me to take the same full-head prosthetic makeup approach towards Bruce's character on the film. Sam wanted us to mess up Bruce's whole body—he wanted to see Ash's limbs and head get cut off and then come back together. My thinking was that if Ash were to get reassembled and then reanimated, it would be interesting if the pieces reassembled inaccurately and were a little misaligned. Along those same lines, what if his jaw was barely hanging on, and he used a rope to tie his jaw into place, along the lines of Jacob Marley in *A Christmas Carol*? I was pitching ideas like that to Sam, along

The "Evil Ash" character being sculpted during pre-production on *Army of Darkness* (1992).
Photo courtesy of Tony Gardner.

the lines of 'Frankenstein meets Jacob Marley,' and he thought it was an interesting idea."

"To be honest, I was kind of going down the punk rock Frankenstein road with Evil Ash and Evil Sheila, whose character became my homage to the Bride of Frankenstein, which only seemed appropriate. When we got the script and I saw dialogue like, 'Gimme some sugar, baby,' and all of the other classic Ash lines, I knew there was going to be a chance to have some fun with this one, so I wanted to push this punk rock look a little bit."

"Bruce was also giving us feedback on our work, and he was just as articulate as Sam in his vision for the characters in *Army of Darkness*. That made it really easy to just dive into everything with some confidence. Certain scenes were talked about being homages to particular old films or scenes from old films, so there was always a point of reference for us, too. There were days when it was technically super challenging, but it was one of those things where every one of those challenges was something fun. We felt like we were doing something that hadn't been done before, and so much of the weird stuff that we did succeeded because Bruce really

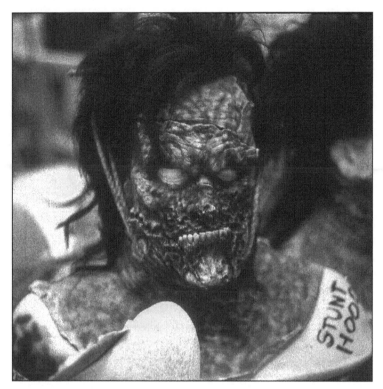

A stunt hood created for the "Evil Ash" character from *Army of Darkness* (1992).
Photo courtesy of Tony Gardner.

sells it in the film. The stretching faces, the different lengths of the arms, the mini-Ashes, and things like that—Bruce just being Bruce really made *Army of Darkness* what it is."

In the early 1990s, Tony was asked to provide a zombie and a talking cat for a Disney movie that also involved cutting the zombie's head and fingers off and driving a bus over the cat. The movie didn't sound very Disney-esque, and its name was *Hocus Pocus* (1993).

"As soon as I read the script, I knew who had to play the zombie . . . I just didn't know his name," Gardner said. "There were these McDonald's commercials on TV at the time with this skinny character with an animatronic moon head named Mac Tonight. He was super animated, had a lot of character, and never spoke a word. I remember thinking that if that actor could make it look easy and fun wearing a heavy animatronic head, then watching this same guy playing a gangly zombie [Billy Butcherson] with his mouth stitched shut would be amazing."

"I tracked down Steve Neill, who had done the Mac Tonight head, and he happened to have a bust of the actor who had worn the head sitting out behind his garage, an actor named Doug Jones. Steve let me borrow the lifecast, and I made sure that we sculpted every character design for Billy Butcherson on that lifecast. If the studio wanted that design, they were going to need to hire that actor—it was that tight to his face. I had never worked with Doug, I just had a feeling he would be a perfect fit."

"Margaret Prentice and I applied Doug's makeup every day, and every day the three of us would marvel at the sets and Bette Midler—literally everything about the film. Being on that soundstage on the Disney lot was one of the most amazing experiences. I met a really cool producer on that set, too, who was also the originator of the story of the movie: David Kirschner. It turned out that the plot of the film came from a story that David had made up to tell his daughters when they were little, and as a kid he had a cat named Binx."

In the mid-1990s, Clive Barker called upon Tony Gardner and Alterian once again to lend their talents to *Lord of Illusions* (1995), Barker's

Tony touches up Doug Jones' makeup between takes on the set of *Hocus Pocus* (1993).
Photo courtesy of Tony Gardner.

feature film adaptation of his horror noir short story, "The Last Illusion." Looking back, Gardner reflected on his memorable involvement with the project.

"*Nightbreed* led to Alterian doing all of the character designs for *Lord of Illusions*. But at the start, the production company was talking to Steve Johnson and myself about doing the effects for the film. We had to bow out after the initial design phase, as we had a conflict with a pre-existing commitment to another project that suddenly had a green light."

"As production on our other project wound down, Clive's group contacted us about a nightmare sequence that they wanted to shoot some practical effects for, with people's heads melting and these weird slug-headed creatures revealed underneath. So, we were asked to come in and design and build these really cool, weird, translucent, hot-melt vinyl heads that had these stylized mechanical rigs inside them. You could see through the skin through layers of veins, and while this animatronic head pushed forward, the skin sloughed off, the eyes pushed out on stalks, and there were four weird orifices in the face that literally expanded with this black/brown slime oozing out of them. It was this really organic, disgusting, cool thing. So our experience on *Lord* was a very odd one for sure, but it was nice to have closure at the end of it, and to be able to go on set with Clive and shoot a bunch of stuff with just him and a small crew again. That was great."

"One thing I don't talk about too often is the fact that Clive and I were actually going to open a haunted house on Hollywood Boulevard at one point," Gardner revealed. "It was going to be in the Vogue Theatre across the street from the Egyptian Theatre. We designed it as a walkthrough experience, with a tour guide in this weird world we had created for the first part, and then you were on your own for the remainder of the experience. The rooms and set pieces were designed, and the look of all of the characters, too. We were to the point where we had storyboards for the whole backstory of the place, and had designed a line of toys based on some of the characters, and we had even sculpted one as a multiple piece model kit."

"But then we got the seismologist's final report back on the building's infrastructure and were told that essentially everything needed to be retrofitted. It would have basically been smarter to tear the whole building down and start over. There were also tenants in storefronts on the front of the building that would need to get bought out. We didn't have the additional funds for any of that, so once that seismology report came back, it all just imploded. We hit all of these problems trying to find a new location in the area and eventually just bailed on it. We figured we would still do it someday, but then a couple of years later, Universal Studios started doing Halloween Horror Nights and that's when we realized there wasn't a need for our project anymore."

Around the turn of the century, Tony had to do in-depth research for his bullet-centric work on *Three Kings* (1999), resulting in some inquiries from law enforcement.

"In the late '90s, I was hired to provide makeup effects for a film called *Three Kings* and managed to get David O. Russell, Warner Bros., and myself in trouble before the film was over. I had been asked to create a few effects where the camera actually 'went inside' an actor's body to show the damage that a bullet could do, as well as the aftereffects of that damage. This was pre-CGI, so it all had to be created practically. By the time the film was finished, I had been investigated by the FBI, Arizona State Police, and the Missing Persons Division, and had to write a press release for Warner Bros. to hand out at the gate. Turns out people thought that we had taken a homeless person off the streets of Phoenix and shot them up with a high-speed camera recording it all. We took it as a compliment and a testament to the realism of our work."

"One of the actors that I was applying prosthetics on for *Three Kings* was actually a director named Spike Jonze. Spike introduced me to two musicians afterwards who went by the name of Daft Punk, who wanted to create some sort of disguise mask or helmet. We did lifecasts of the two musicians—Thomas Bangalter and Guy-Manuel de Homem-Christo— and worked out some designs in clay over their lifecasts based on some sketches that they brought out to us. The entire experience involved new materials and new processes, including LED technology, metal plating, and minor programming—all things we had never done before. Spike told them that I was the guy who could figure it out, and we just learned as we went. Best to dive in and figure things out, instead of passively standing back—you never know where that mindset might lead you," Tony added.

"Beyond the three different iterations of the robotic helmets, there were multiple music videos, as well as an experimental feature film called *Daft Punk's Electroma*. All of the various projects with the people at Daft Arts were super collaborative experiences, and *Electroma* was one of the

Tony pictured with the helmets he created for *Daft Punk's Electroma* (2006).
Photo courtesy of Tony Gardner.

first film projects where I ended up involved on the production side as well as the makeup and costuming effects. I learned a lot."

In 2003, Tony picked up the mantle for one of the genre's most beloved icons when he tackled the special effects and animatronics for Don

Tony makes some adjustments to Chucky on the set of *Seed of Chucky* (2004).
Photo courtesy of Tony Gardner.

Mancini's *Seed of Chucky* (2004). The ambitious sequel required Alterian to provide three fully animatronic characters: the film's titular antagonist (voiced by Brad Dourif), Chucky's main squeeze, Tiffany (voiced by Jennifer Tilly), and their offspring, Glen/Glenda (brought to life with a vocal performance from Billy Boyd).

"I was brought in on *Seed* at literally the last minute," recalled Gardner. "My involvement started with a couple of really vague phone calls at first, where I was being asked if I could make a talking baby about toddler-size that could walk around. I think they were trying to suss us out. By the time I got the call explaining that they were making the next *Child's Play* movie, I was also told that it would be shooting in Romania in about three months, and they needed to have three animatronic characters built for this one. So we just hit the ground running, and without much reference material to work from other than some photos. There really wasn't time to think."

Seed of Chucky (2004) may not have been nearly the box office and critical success its immediate predecessor was, but the fifth installment of the *Child's Play* (1988) series was noteworthy for several reasons, including the fact that Gardner got to die on screen as himself.

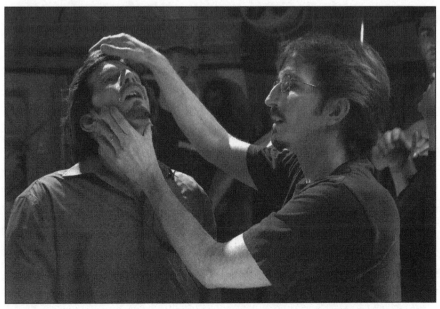

Tony preps "himself" on the set of *Seed of Chucky* (2004). Photo courtesy of Tony Gardner.

"Don sprung the idea for my cinematic death on me right at the beginning. He told me that Chucky and Tiffany kill the special effects guy in the 'movie within the movie,' and he asked if I would be up for auditioning for it. I told him I didn't know if I'd be any good, but I was willing to do the audition. I went in and had to do the character's death scene as my audition, which was a completely different scene in that first draft of the script, with Chucky and Tiffany tying this guy down on a table and playing the game *Operation* on him while he was alive, cutting out different organs. So Don filmed me on his kitchen table acting this whole scene out on video, and that tape went to Universal. I guess I did okay, because I got hired. That audition tape is still out there somewhere. I dread the day someone finds it."

"It was both good and bad playing a character in the film. 'Good' because I obviously had easy access to myself for lifecasting and matching up the dummy during pre-production, but 'bad' once we went to film the death scene. Everything felt so fractured for me on that shoot day; we had all three puppets working in that scene. That meant that we had twenty-some puppeteers working. I was supervising them and also puppeteering

Jennifer Tilly poses with Tony (and his severed head) after his demise on the set of *Seed of Chucky* (2004). Photo courtesy of Tony Gardner.

on each character, and I had to rig my body so we could dismember it, then clean up, put on my wardrobe, and go shoot out another scene in character. After that, I would segue back to puppeteering. When it was over, I thought it was hilarious that we actually got through the day. That was definitely film insanity at its finest."

While he may have been under the proverbial gun that day on set, it's Tony's utmost desire to continue to live up to fans' expectations for the Chucky films, especially since he knows they're so passionate about their beloved characters.

"There was some pressure, for sure, when I first came onto *Seed*," Tony said, "because the fanbase is huge and they're very savvy. We had to make sure we got things right with both Chucky and Tiffany, but it was trial by fire, honestly, especially on set. Every aspect of it was brand new to us, but we survived it, and we must have done okay, because they asked us back for the next two. *Curse [of Chucky]* was an experiment with Chucky wearing a 'Good Guys' skin over his own, which I think we took too literally at the time. So on *Cult [of Chucky]*, I became very obsessed with making sure Chucky's look feels genuinely authentic, especially for the fans."

"I had a laser scan done from an original Chucky doll, and we scanned the original clothing, too. I know that the sweater varies from film to film, but beyond that sort of gray area, I was obsessed with making sure we got his anatomy and proportions perfect for *Cult*. The studio was very supportive of that, too, and Don was of the same mindset. There were a few tweaks made for mechanical reasons, but they were minor. It was nice being able to recreate the character true to David Kirschner and Kevin Yagher's designs from the original film."

"*Cult of Chucky* and *The Bad Batch* were two films where I was involved from the earliest stages of the script all the way through post-production, and where I was also credited as a Producer or Co-Producer on the films. Being responsible for the big picture as well as a specific department—not to mention being on set and doing makeup or performing a killer doll at the same time—hasn't seemed as nerve-wracking as I was expecting, to be honest. Your responsibility is much larger, but it seems like a natural extension of the creative process, and being a part of the production team involved with overall problem-solving is just one more aspect of helping put together a product that you can be proud to put your name on."

"Team Edna" poses with John Travolta behind the scenes on *Hairspray* (2007).
Photo courtesy of Tony Gardner.

With over two hundred film, television, and music video credits (one of which he directed himself for Daft Punk) on his résumé, there's no denying that Tony Gardner has firmly established himself as one of the most influential and innovative makeup effects artists to come up during the last forty years in the industry. He blew genre fans' minds with his half-corpse zombie in *The Return of the Living Dead* (1985), he's contributed to countless horror and sci-fi films, and worked alongside some of the biggest directors ever. He helped define the trademark look for one of the most popular electronic music acts of all time, and has even suffered cinematic deaths in his career, most famously by the hand of Chucky. Additionally, Gardner's efforts have been recognized with multiple prestigious awards and nominations, including an Oscar nomination for Alterian's work on the comedy *Bad Grandpa* (2013).

While he can't really pinpoint one attribute as the key to his longtime success in a sometimes unforgiving field, Gardner says it's the problem-solving aspect of his profession that keeps him going.

Tony goes over the script with an otherworldly cast member in *Cast a Deadly Spell* (1991). Photo courtesy of Tony Gardner.

"Any job that pushes you creatively is definitely the most rewarding job I could ask to be involved with. If somebody tells me that something can't be done, I'm the first one in line for that job. I want to do it, I want to figure it out, I want to problem-solve. The stuff that is creatively challenging is definitely more rewarding throughout the entire process. Once you solve the process, then you have to pull it off. All of that stuff energizes me as an artist, and it was so cool that I was able to ride in on this wave of innovation in regards to practical effects in this business, where the work was literally hands-on, and the constant mantra was, 'We've got to figure this out one way or another.' So few jobs require that kind of thought process."

Tony touches up actor John Lehr on the set of one of GEICO's wildly popular caveman commercials. Photo courtesy of Tony Gardner.

"Every experience I've had doing makeup professionally, save the one year with the business partner, has been really positive. I've found that things that I've done twenty years ago are still relevant now. Something that we did with the mask business way back when came into play

(Left to right) Don Mancini, John Waters, and Tony Gardner pose together on the set of *Seed of Chucky* (2004). Photo courtesy of Tony Gardner.

as we were recently making prosthetic molds for *The Mist* TV series. That tornado of our youth, trying out all of this stuff now that we're all a little older and a little wiser, we're able to put it to good use."

"I just feel like I've always been a creative and collaborative artist," Tony added, "and even now I'm just as much of a collaborative, creative guy as I was back when I first started out. I feel fortunate that I'm able to continue doing the stuff that I'd still be doing even if no one paid me to, honestly, because I love doing it so much. Not everyone gets to be that lucky."

19 Steve Wang

WHILE HE MAY HAVE GROWN UP almost seven thousand miles from Los Angeles, special effects virtuoso Steve Wang's early obsession with masks eventually led him to Hollywood, where he would spend most of the 1980s and 1990s establishing himself as a respected artist in the industry.

Photo courtesy of Steve Wang.

Yoda, as created by Steve, age fourteen.
Photo courtesy of Steve Wang.

"I moved here from Taiwan when I was almost ten years old," recalled Wang. "I had this fascination with masks, but in Taiwan our notion of masks is a cardboard face with eyeholes poked out and rubber bands around the ears to hook it to your face. When I saw these vacuform *Ultraman* masks that were being given away as part of a local theater's coloring contest, I became obsessed with them. I did the coloring contest and I didn't win, but somehow I knew that masks really drew me in."

"Within a month of being here, I went to a toy store called King Norman's in San Jose, and there were just hundreds of masks. They had the Ben Cooper masks with the box plastic costumes, they had Don Post masks and the Be Something Studio masks, too—just every mask you could think of, and seeing these full rubber heads with hair punched in or glued onto them just blew my mind. I was in heaven. That day, I was with my grandmother and I begged her to buy me the most horrible ape mask, but to me, it was gold."

"After that, I was so obsessed that I started saving money to buy masks whenever I could. I did this for about four years and I accumulated about thirty masks. That's when I decided that wasn't enough for me anymore—I wanted to know how to make all these things."

Unsure of exactly how to get started, Wang turned to a popular resource for horror fans from his generation, *Famous Monsters of Filmland*, which helped put some of the pieces in place and started him on the path to becoming a makeup artist.

"As a kid, I was always very artistic. I did a lot of drawing, but I had never done any sculpting, and that felt like it was the next logical step towards making masks. I didn't really know what sculpting was, but once I discovered *Famous Monsters*, I found these pictures of Rick Baker, Dick Smith, and Stan Winston, and they were standing there with a clay sculpture of a head or a body part. That's when it all clicked."

"I went out and bought some clay and started using spoons and forks to sculpt masks. There was this issue of *Cinemagic* magazine that came out with Kirk Brady, where he had made these amazing full-head masks that came down to the shoulders and neck—I actually bought one years ago that somebody stole from me,

Masks created by Steve at ages fifteen and sixteen.
Photo courtesy of Steve Wang.

unfortunately—but he did a whole tutorial on how to make masks from sculpture to molding to casting, and that was what taught me how to do it. I started making plaster molds, I started casting my own masks, and that was the beginning of my makeup effects career," Steve reflected.

Steve spent the next several years honing his craft day in and day out, much to the chagrin of his mother, whose plan to get him out of the house eventually backfired on her.

"I fell in love with making masks and that's all I did for five years, all on my own. Some of my masks I would work on for eighteen hours a day. I was insane. It would take me thirty days to sculpt one mask, and my mom thought I was nuts. She got scared that I was becoming a recluse, so she asked my older brother's friend, Johnnie, 'Hey, can you meet my son Steve and get him out of the house, take him to the discos or parties, and have him meet some girls or something? I'm worried about him.' So Johnny came into my room one day and the first thing he asked me about were my masks, because he was so amazed by them."

"Then, Johnnie asked me if I had ever heard of fan conventions, where you can do costume contests and all that stuff. And the next thing you know, my mom saw us in the garage building my first full-body monster suit. She about had a fit! Long story short, Johnnie started hanging out less and less with my brother and became more my friend. We started hitting all of the conventions and doing all of the costumes we could make. I ended up getting him into the industry in the '80s, too."

Before Steve made the transition down to Southern California, he found a longtime friend and peer in another rising talent in the realm of

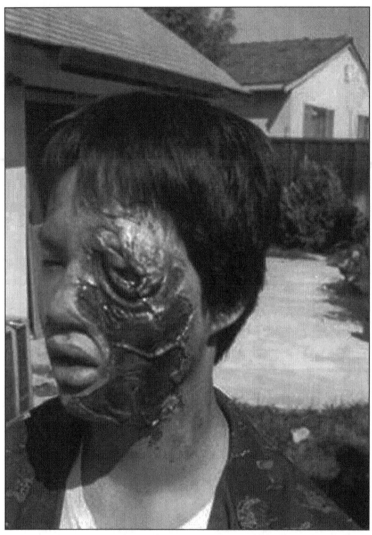

A "ripped face" makeup created by Steve, age fifteen. Photo courtesy of Steve Wang.

special makeup effects, someone who became instrumental in preparing him for the professional world that awaited them in Hollywood.

"When I was seventeen, I met this fellow artist named Matt Rose, from Santa Clara. He became one of Rick Baker's main guys for decades. We became friends instantaneously and I knew he was into making masks, too, so he invited me to come by and look at them. I went to his house and that's when our friendship really began. He just made these beautiful masks, and Matt was way ahead of the curve on everything he was doing.

We put together a mask business the year I graduated high school, and basically for a whole year we were in this little shack in his backyard, creating a whole line of masks and 3D T-shirts that we sold to all of the local costume companies. We even did mail orders, too."

"We balanced each other out," Steve added. "Matt is not so business-minded. He gets very emotional, and my family has owned different businesses, so I'm probably a little more relaxed about all that stuff. I remember we were going to this costume shop one time that I used to buy masks from. So, we go there and lay our masks out and Matt tells me, 'I hate this guy because he always bullies me into selling my masks for cheap.' Now, I know that these masks sell out every year and the owner always doubles the price, so because of what Matt said, I knew exactly how to play the situation. I ended up raising the prices on the guy without him even knowing it, so we made even more money that year."

"After a year or so of doing our mask business, we met Bob Burns at a local convention, and we knew that he had mentored Rick Baker when he

was a kid. We instantly hit it off with Bob and he invited us to come to L.A. so he could take us around to L.A. Effects [Group] and a few other places. We took a weekend trip down to L.A. and Bob took us around. We met Bob and Denny Skotak, who worked on the Academy Award-winning [effects] for *Aliens*, and a whole bunch of really cool people."

"A few months later, we talked about moving down to L.A. pretty seriously to pursue a career. As far as feeling like we were ready, we never felt like we were ready because we were both nineteen years old, just young kids out

"Bugman" mask created by Steve for Don Post Studios. Photo courtesy of Steve Wang.

of high school, but we wanted to get into the business really badly. So Bob and Denny called up Matt and one of our other friends, Mark Williams, to come down and work on the *Alien* derelict ship because they were doing *Aliens* at the time. They had the original spaceship from the first movie, but it was all falling apart because it was a big plaster structure with actual clay, sculpted and painted directly over. So Matt and Mark moved down to restore that ship."

"During that time, I was working at a computer hard drive place, reworking hard drives and stuff like that. At night I would go to Matt's house because I had gotten a job with a Japanese museum to create a full-body creature suit, so I would work on that project over there. As soon as that was finished, I packed up and moved to L.A., and Matt Rose, Mark Williams, and I all shared an apartment together."

"I thought that I would take a couple weeks off to see L.A. and then try to get some work, but the very first week I got a call from Matt. He said to me, 'Hey, we need more people at Stan Winston's. We're doing *Invaders from Mars*, do you want to come in?' I went in and met with Alec Gillis and was hired on the spot just to help out, doing lab work stuff, cleaning molds, and casting foam. Eventually, that all led to painting a lot of stuff and then going on set. I met Stan while I was on set, and that was an amazing learning experience for me because I learned how he works. Still, to this day, I work that very same way whenever I'm on set, too."

Oni demon created by Steve, age nineteen. Photo courtesy of Steve Wang.

"I also learned some really important lessons about how the industry works on *Invaders*," Steve continued. "When I first got into the business, maybe I had a different point of view about it, but for me, it wasn't important to just be the sculptor or to just be the painter. I always felt it was important to learn everything. I just wanted to learn, and I thought if you wanted to be a good artist and be technically proficient, you have to know all of this stuff that no one cares about. So I was just really happy to be given those tasks."

"What I learned was that ultimately, if you have the ability and you have the chops, you'll get more and better opportunities if you

Steve painting one of the Drones on the set of *Invaders from Mars* (1986). Photo courtesy of the Stan Winston School of Character Arts.

just keep working hard, because the bosses that you work for are not stupid. They see if you can do something well and they'll want you to continue doing more of the artistic stuff. That's exactly what happened with me at Stan's. The first year I was there, I was only on *Invaders from Mars* and was one of the lowest-paid guys just doing lab work, even though I got to paint some cool stuff and I had a lot of fun."

Shortly after getting his feet wet while working on *Invaders from Mars* (1986), Wang was given another chance to prove himself as an artist when he interviewed for effects legend Rick Baker, who was gearing up for the family comedy *Harry and the Hendersons* (1987).

"Right towards the end of *Invaders*, Alec Gillis told all of us that Rick Baker was going to be hiring for *Harry and the Hendersons* soon, so everybody called in and made an appointment to meet with Rick. All of us that were on *Invaders* were literally going to interviews thirty minutes apart. When I met Rick, it was amazing because he was my idol. Matt interviewed, too, and it was funny because we came back from our meetings and we were like, 'Wow, isn't Rick's shop awesome? Did you see this or that?' And, as it turned out, Matt and I were the only ones who got the full tour at Rick's, and we were hired on the spot as sculptors starting in two weeks. We went from being the two lowest guys on *Invaders* to sculptors on *Harry*, and the rest of the guys who had been bullying us that got hired for *Harry* were all going to be working in the mold shop."

Right around that time, Wang also came on board John McTiernan's *Predator* (1987), and while the final design of the interstellar warrior has

Steve sculpting the muscular details on the titular alien hunter from *Predator* (1987). Photo courtesy of the Stan Winston School of Character Arts.

now become synonymous with Steve's illustrious career, he was involved with the project much earlier than many fans may think.

"The funny thing is that a lot of people don't realize I actually worked at Boss Film [Studios] when they were on *Predator*. After I finished at Rick's, I got a job with Kevin Yagher and then shortly after that, I interviewed with Steve Johnson at Boss Film. He hired me on the spot as a sculptor and even got me into the sculpting union."

"I met Screaming Mad George there, who became a really good, dear friend, and we both got into the union at the same time. I can't confirm, but I think we were the first Asian guys to get into the sculptors' union, too. But, while at Boss, I was just a sculptor; I had no idea they were having all of these problems [on *Predator*] until after I was already gone. They all came back and said that the film had been put on hold. I know that Steve Johnson wasn't very happy with the design because he had pushed for another design he had done, but Fox came back and said, 'No, this is our design, this is what we want to do.' Steve was quite against that whole thing, but it was his job to build it, so they built it knowing that it wasn't going to work, and it just didn't work, of course."

"Right around this time, I went in for an interview for *The Monster Squad*, which was the next project Stan was going to do. I showed Stan these aliens I had painted for *The Collector*, which was a Chevy commercial directed by Doug Trumbull, the legendary visual effects artist behind *Blade Runner* (1982). Doug shot it in Showscan, which was a new technology at the time, and Stan was pretty blown away. He asked me how I painted everything and I told him that it was done entirely using airbrush techniques. So I left and Matt said to me later on, 'I don't know what you said to Stan, but now he's telling us everything has to be airbrushed from now on.' So that was pretty cool to hear."

Steve and Matt were tasked with creating the Gillman for *The Monster Squad* (1987). While their version of the creature eventually became a landmark creation in the world of special effects, the design process was somewhat bumpy in the beginning.

"Stan had already done these original designs of each character they wanted in *Monster Squad*, and it was up to the assigned artists for each monster to take that idea to the next level. I had done a paint design for the Gillman, but the presentation was horrible. It was done with colored pencils and it was all muddy and dirty. It wasn't quite what I wanted to convey. I was trying to tell Stan that I was going to do a camouflage paint

Original creature costume that Steve created for Screaming Mad George's annual Halloween contest. It won first place. Photo courtesy of Steve Wang.

job that was a color scheme based on nature, because no one had really done that to that degree. I wanted to introduce it for this character, but when I showed Stan the paint design, he said 'no,' because the rendering looked horrible. I had no idea how I was going to convince him."

"During that time, there was Screaming Mad George's Halloween contest for industry professionals. This was a contest he created to give young makeup artists the opportunity to meet Dick Smith, Rick Baker, Stan Winston, and Tom Burman, and to put their work in front of those legends. It was George's version of *Face Off* at that time. I made this creature with a hermit crab shell, and it had a crab arm on one side and a human-type crab arm on the other. It was pretty garish, and I couldn't even see out of it. It was so uncomfortable."

"The story I heard is that when I came out, there was a big 'whoa' from the audience because no one had seen that kind of paint job before, and I won first place in the monster suit category. So when we were done, Stan came up to me and said, 'Is this how you want to paint the Gillman?' And I said, 'Yeah, something like this.' All Stan said was 'good,' so I was able to convince him on my vision through the contest."

Steve Wang and Matt Rose's work on the Gillman creature during the sculpting phase for *The Monster Squad* (1987). Photos courtesy of Steve Wang.

The final Gillman design by Steve Wang and Matt Rose for *The Monster Squad* (1987).
Photo courtesy of Steve Wang.

"In fact, Stan was so excited to see the paint job, that on a Sunday, he brought his wife to the shop just to see the progress. Stan would never come in on the weekend, so I could tell he was excited about it. Plus, the technology to create a seamless suit like that hadn't happened yet, so that was one of the contributions that Matt and I made to the business on *Monster Squad*. That approach has now became the industry standard."

Over the next few years, Steve continued to stay perpetually busy on a variety of films, including *Hell Comes to Frogtown* (1988), *DeepStar Six* (1989), *Food of the Gods II* (1989), *A Nightmare on Elm Street 5: The Dream Child* (1989), and *Spaced Invaders* (1990). In 1989, Wang returned to Rick Baker's Cinovation Studios to join another landmark effects film, *Gremlins 2: The New Batch* (1990), which ambitiously introduced audiences to many new versions of the titular creatures.

"When we first got *Gremlins 2*, Rick actually gave us three months for an R&D [research and development] period, which is rare," Steve explained. "I have never been on another project where we had that amount of time. In those three months, we did a full-size Gremlin suit for an actress to wear. We also did a full animatronic Gremlin test, made different

A completed Mohawk Gremlin for *Gremlins 2: The New Batch* (1990).
Photo courtesy of Steve Wang.

types of puppets and marionettes, and Rick just shot the shit out of all these things, just to test everything out ahead of time. What it ultimately came down to was that everything that was done before was still going to work, but because we understood the materials better at that point, all we could do was just figure out the best way to do it all."

"The first thing we had to figure out was how to mass-produce these things. Because we had different artists working on different parts of these creatures, how do we do that and keep everything going smoothly? Matt and I were tasked with creating a production line. The first thing we would do was a generic core of the different creatures—Mogwais and Gremlins—and we made mass molds of those so people could just grab them and sculpt out their designs on top of the generic versions. Everything would just be modular and fit together."

"After that, we were all tasked with our own Gremlins, and from that point on we had pure freedom. I had expected Rick to be all over us, but he would give you almost no input ever. I asked Rick, 'So, how do you see Mohawk?' And all he would tell me was that he thought Mohawk should be a black-colored Gremlin. That was about it. So, every two days I would do a maquette, and after doing something like fifteen of those in a month, I asked Rick to tell me which one he thought was going in the right direction. I finally got him to pick one design he liked, so I started sculpting it, but he never came by again. Just as I was about to finish the sculpt, he told me to just go ahead and mold it, so I did. I even did the paint job on it with no feedback, but when Rick showed it to Joe Dante, Joe loved it and it was approved."

"As a kid still developing, part of me was seeking the approval of somebody that I really respected," Steve explained. "I didn't know if I was

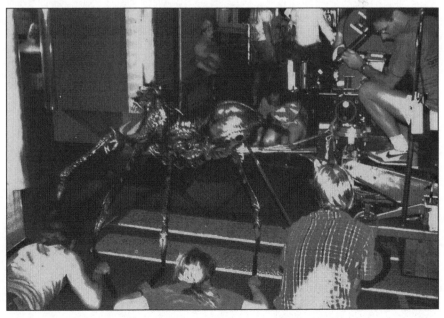

A behind-the-scenes look at the Spider Gremlin puppetry on *Gremlins 2: The New Batch* (1990). Photo courtesy of Steve Wang.

ever going to get that, but luckily, it did happen eventually from Rick, and looking back at Rick's hands-off approach, I thought it was amazing that he had this team of young kids and just let them go and do all this stuff on their own. It was incredibly trusting of him, but I think he knew he put the right team together. Matt did Gizmo and he looked amazing, and he also did Lenny, the big, goofy Mogwai. I designed the paint jobs on Lenny and George as well, and I also got to design and be in charge of building the Spider Gremlin."

"Almost a whole year had gone by from when we started working on *Gremlins 2* to the point where we were working on set. I remember the first shot we did was when Mohawk busts out of the console. After the dailies came back, Rick came in with a big smile on his face, saying, 'He looks great! Everybody loves Mohawk,' and I finally got the first confirmation that I was doing something right—one year later," added Steve.

Shortly after *Gremlins 2: The New Batch* (1990), Steve was at a crossroads in his career. Feeling burned out by the effects industry, he searched for a new creative path to follow.

The Guyver and star David Hayter pose on the set of *Guyver: Dark Hero* (1994), which Steve directed. Photo courtesy of Steve Wang.

"I decided to change careers near the end of *Gremlins 2*. I got right into the business very young, but I was working so fast and so hard that within four years, I was literally burnt out. There was just so much negativity in the business. Plus, as an artist, if you get stuck in one place too long, you become stagnant. I want to consistently be around guys that are my caliber or higher, so I can look at their stuff and realize that I've got to do better and get inspired by their work. I jumped around for a while, but then I got bit by the film bug really hard."

"I had made a Super 8 film and it was a pain in the ass, just absolute torture. But at the end of it, I knew I had to make more. So, after *Gremlins 2*, I kind of gave up on makeup effects for about eight years. I did a couple more projects here and there just to pay the bills, but I was more invested in my filmmaking world, where I was writing a lot and trying to get films made. That was an interesting journey because I did a lot of growing up during those years."

"Filmmaking is painful. It's transformational. You go in thinking you're a certain person, but by the end, you're someone else completely. You know the old saying, 'Adversity introduces a man to himself?' When you're on a skewer, resting on top of a fire, that's when you start to learn who you really are. Sometimes you're surprised in a good way and sometimes you're surprised in a bad way. There are so many pluses and so many minuses. A big part of it comes down to politics. There have always been politics in filmmaking, and there always will be."

"For example, I was an Executive Producer on my own TV show called *Kamen Rider: Dragon Knight*, and I spent three years on it creating forty episodes. Everything went smoothly. We shot 120 days straight with two crews, and we just kept working towards finishing those forty episodes. Even within a system that worked as well as that one did, there was always some asshole that ruined it for everyone at some point, so I would have to go put fires out all the time. You can't control it."

A background ape sculpture created by Steve for *Planet of the Apes* (2001). Photo courtesy of Steve Wang.

Although he faced his fair share of personal and professional challenges while pursuing creative endeavors outside the world of makeup effects, all of those experiences made a world of difference once Steve returned to his roots.

"The single best thing about leaving to go make movies and then coming back again was that when I came back, I was like a little kid in a candy store. I was completely reinvigorated. I had a newfound energy, a newfound interest in sculpting, painting, and making monsters, and now, it's been twenty years since I've been back, even though I had to leave for a few years to do *Kamen Rider*. But I'm just as excited now as I was when I was a little kid."

Wang brought that enthusiasm onto the set of *Hellboy* (2004), where he collaborated with Guillermo del Toro, a highly passionate filmmaker who also has a background in special effects. For the ambitious comic book adaptation, Steve was tasked with bringing Abe Sapien [played by Doug Jones] to life, which was no easy feat considering the demands that the character's appearance required.

"I was brought into Spectral [Motion] by my good friend Mike Elizalde to work on Abe," Steve recalled, "and I believe it was Jose Fernandez who had already done the maquette. Guillermo was really happy with that already, and so he wanted me to do the paint job, which Guillermo loved in the end. It was my job to figure out how to do this makeup, because I knew we couldn't do it as a suit—it would look too bulky. I wanted to do something that was very graceful and slick."

"One day, Guillermo came up to me and showed me a picture of the actor he hired, and the guy was like 5' 5", very muscular and short. I looked at the maquette of Abe again and told Guillermo that the guy in the picture was not the guy he needed—he needed Doug Jones. Doug Jones had worked with Guillermo on *Mimic*, and the very next day Doug came in the office, met with Guillermo, and got the job."

"Abe's makeup was very challenging on a technical level. We had about five months to do it, and it wasn't enough time. There were so many things that needed working out because it had to be a seamless makeup. There were all of these translucent, stretchy parts that had to look sexy when they were retracting. It couldn't be floppy, so it had to be made smaller to stretch. Also, because of the materials we were using, nothing would glue to this stuff, so we had to sew in hooks and all this crazy stuff

The Marcus makeup created by Steve for *Underworld: Evolution* (2006).
Photo courtesy of Steve Wang.

to apply it to Doug. The first time I applied Abe, it took about eight hours, and Doug was great throughout the whole process."

"Normally, when you're applying a makeup, you have to go around [the actor] and glue and position yourself. With Doug, as you're gluing, he's twisting his arm for you by himself so you don't have to move, you don't have to ask him to do that, he just does it. Doug always knows what's going on with his makeups and he always helps out. He's so great."

Over the last several decades, Wang has continued to keep himself on the cusp of cutting-edge effects, contributing to films like Tim Burton's *Planet of the Apes* remake (2001), *Underworld* (2003), *Blade: Trinity* (2004), *X-Men: The Last Stand* (2006), and *Aliens vs Predator: Requiem*

(2007). Then, in early 2013, he teamed up with Eddie Yang to open Alliance Studio, where they have found other avenues to keep their passion for creating special effects alive.

The *StarCraft II* Kerrigan statue created by Alliance Studio on behalf of Blizzard Entertainment. Photo courtesy of Steve Wang.

Steve posing with creations he made for an instructional video for the Yoyogi school in Japan. Photo courtesy of Steve Wang.

"If you want to survive, you have to adapt—it's as simple as that," Steve emphasized. "You have to not be afraid of change and you have to just go with it and adapt. That's part of the reason I was able to innovate a lot of new technologies in the makeup effects business, because I'm always looking to do something different. I love that. It's exciting, and I embrace new technology. My business partner, Eddie Yang, and I both come from the traditional effects world, but now he's mostly digital. With him doing digital and me doing practical, we're the perfect match at Alliance because we utilize all of the technologies to do our job."

"These days, we're getting huge jobs from Blizzard Entertainment, Riot Games, and other video game companies to create these immense character statues, and that's been pretty cool. Somehow, following my passion and turning down other big jobs in the past means I now get to do something that I'm really passionate about, and over the years it has really paid off. Now, all these different companies hit me up to make these statues, and that is one of the biggest things that we do at our studio—we do a lot more of that than film work, actually. Beyond just being able to create amazing art, the best thing about this kind of work is that we get to see fans' eyes light up when they see what we do. You don't get those kinds of reactions from studio executives anymore, so that interaction is such a refreshing thing to experience at this point in my career."

20 Todd Masters

GROWING UP IN THE PACIFIC NORTHWEST, special effects artist Todd Masters knew early on that he was destined to follow a creative path.

"I was a very weird child," Masters reflected, "and I guess I was far more ambitious than most of the kids I grew up around in Seattle. My dad had an 8mm camera, which I had some interest in, but I immediately broke it, playing around with it. I was one of those kids that was just like,

Photo courtesy of Todd Masters.

413

Oh, how's this work? I think I'll take it apart, check it out, and look at all the little mechanics, but then I could never figure out how to put it all back together."

"Later on, I earned my own camera and I started making little experimental films, and for whatever reason, I thought it would be really smart to make my book reports as little movies. I remember thinking, *Oh, that'll be easier than writing it,* and even though they were just kind of silly, my teacher did think it was creative and let me get away with it because at least I was doing the work."

"My parents were really great about letting me follow this unusual path, not knowing if it would ever come to much," Masters added. "With just one wrong turn, I could easily have been a homeless person without their support and encouragement. They were always really good about saying, 'Hey, kid, do you need a workspace? Here, have a workspace.' Or my mom would say, 'Oh, do you need to use the oven to cook your monster stuff?' She didn't care if our pot roast tasted like foam latex. That really allowed me some confidence, and I didn't have to worry about screwing up much. I could just dream up what I wanted to do, and they gave me an ability to follow that dream."

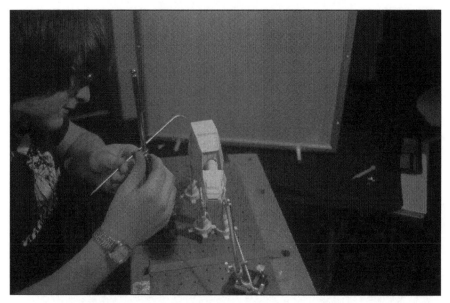

Todd animating a miniature AT-AT from the *Star Wars* (1977) universe.
Photo courtesy of Todd Masters.

Shortly after learning how to properly use a camera, Masters ran into a few problems with his friends, who weren't always reliable participants in his film projects. Undaunted, Masters devised a plan to create his own stars, and began studying the art of stop-motion animation.

"I started having problems with my cast showing up whenever I wanted to shoot something," explained Masters. "They were my neighborhood friends, and while we would have fun, they often didn't show up for their call times, and it was kind of frustrating for me. So then I had this brilliant idea, that instead of filming human actors, I was just going to make my actors and animate them myself."

"I loved *Rudolph the Red-Nosed Reindeer* and all the Rankin/Bass animated movies of that era, but I didn't really know much about the process. I figured out with my camera that I could do everything one frame at a time, so I started putting my juvenile art skills to use to make these little clay creatures. I had heard about this guy named Will Vinton, who was in Portland—not too far away—so I looked him up in the phone book, called him up, and asked him for some advice."

"Will was doing early claymations at that point—this was long before his studio became big time (eventually becoming the award-winning LAIKA studio of today)—and he was very helpful and led me to some techniques and other people that were doing this kind of work. I continued going back to various phone books (which I mined out of the Seattle Public Library). I would look up any FX [special effects] artist that I had heard of for more answers. I called model animators Jim Danforth and Ray Harryhausen (even though Mr. Harryhausen was in England) and makeup FX artist Craig Reardon, to name a few. I would just cold-call these people out of the blue and ask them all sorts of questions."

"That's how my hobby turned into my life's passion. I got into mold-making all by myself, and I was able to find a couple of books to help me out further. There wasn't much information on materials available at that time. Right around then, I called up Dick Smith—also out of the blue—and I think he yelled at me, which is something I'll never forget."

Masters wasn't satisfied to only work in stop-motion animation, though. "I've always had this need to keep learning about anything and everything I could. I would do a lot of research over those years, and I kept teaching myself more and more techniques by making a lot of mistakes along the way. Eventually, around the age of twelve, I got a job. I found an animation company that was in South Seattle—a really crappy part of town—and I'd take the bus down there. I would work with them on whatever animation projects they had going on."

"I remember that one of the films I worked on was an educational birth control film, so as I was working, I was learning about animation and the birds and the bees at the same time. I remember coming home after a long day and my parents asked me, 'Oh, what'd you do today?' And I responded, 'Oh, I just painted, like, eight hundred sperm.' That's an interesting conversation to have with your parents at age twelve."

"There wasn't much of a movie business happening in Seattle until a bit later," Masters continued. "I started interning at a film processing lab in Seattle that happened to be working on *Star Wars: Episode V, The Empire Strikes Back* at the time. So here I was, this kid who was not even in high school yet, and I'm on the optical printer for the sequel to *Star Wars*. I remember seeing the snowspeeders come in on blue screen, sideways, on VistaVision film. That was really cool."

"At that young age, I had already enjoyed a bunch of varied experiences where I was dipping my fingers in a lot of different stuff, just working wherever I could get more knowledge; I wanted to learn as much as I could. I did graphics, photography, radio, journalism, and studied all types of art as well."

Once he graduated high school, Masters found himself at a personal crossroads. The next logical step would be to attend college or a trade school, but after some disappointing replies from colleges, he knew exactly what he needed to do to continue growing as an artist.

Todd at work on the set of [*Star Trek:*] *First Contact* (1996). Photo courtesy of Todd Masters.

"By the time I was eighteen, I had applied to a bunch of big art schools, and they all turned me down. I guess they wanted candidates that had already been through a junior college. That was a bummer, so I decided to go to a local art school in Seattle, but ended up staying there for only a day. It wasn't for me. What the art college was promising I'd be able to do with them by the third year was really at a novice level, at least for me, with what I had already accomplished by that time. I had already worked professionally, made movies, done animations, and had all of this optical printing knowledge. No art school could really touch that, as far as I could see, even the big ones that turned me down."

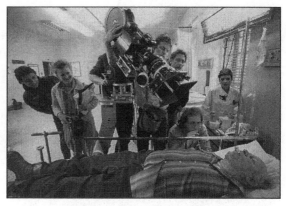

A behind-the-scenes look at the cult classic *Blue Monkey* (1987). Photo courtesy of Todd Masters.

"So, I decided I needed to do something very different than art school. I packed up my Volkswagen bus, moved away from my parents, and drove down to Los Angeles to see if I could get a job—any job—with all the contacts I'd made from my phone book calls along the way."

Somehow, Masters managed to pull off the impossible: he landed a job with a top effects house almost immediately.

"Day one that I was in Los Angeles, I got picked up by Boss Film Studios and started working on *Big Trouble in Little China*. That got me in the door during the heat of '80s genre films. I also was working on *Night of the Creeps* around the same time with Jim Danforth and Ted Rae. I wanted to work for everybody that I could and learn as much as I could. And I did as many projects as I possibly could."

"While I wasn't great at a lot of things early on, I had a lot of experience that many others that were starting out didn't have," Todd continued. "Plus, I had learned to do practically everything, even if I wasn't good at it all yet. Because I had been doing stop-motion and knew camera and visual effects back when not many FX people knew that stuff, I would often get hired as a stop-motion assistant, or a visual effects assistant, and developed a reputation as a person that was able to work out a variety of problems."

"Something I picked up early on was how to manage various personalities and people. I would study how my supervisors dealt with unhappy clients and learned basic people skills and how to handle stress, etc. From my earlier days as a graphics artist, I already had some basic business

Actor Doug Jones as Cochise from the
Falling Skies (2011) television series.
Photo courtesy of Todd Masters.

experiences and how-to-deal-with-clients experience, and I soon became the go-to, on-set rep and a get 'er done guy."

As he continued to cut his teeth at Boss Film Studios and elsewhere in the mid-1980s, Masters absorbed as much knowledge about the business side of the special effects industry as he could while working alongside several influential artists and FX technicians, including a maverick MUFX artist of that era, Steve Johnson.

"Steve was one of the guys I found in the phone book, too, and he offered me the job at Boss Film—he was my supervisor there. When it was time to break away from Boss, he and I started our own studio and worked independently while sharing a studio space together. He soon grew out of that space and started his business, XFX, at another location. I had this choice of either going to work for him or going off on my own. So, I finished up my last project with him and decided to go off on my own. I officially started my own company, MASTERSFX, in 1987, and it seems like it's just been one very long day ever since," Todd added.

Although he was still relatively young and new to the Hollywood effects industry, Masters wasn't fazed by stepping out on his own, even when he was still establishing himself.

"When I was growing up, I would look at these magazines and see people like Rick Baker and Rob Bottin, who were both very young when they first got started. In fact, I think Rob Bottin was something like fifteen years old and he was already running his own freaking Hollywood show. Those guys inspired me. And I'm still that same kid I was back then, even today—I just don't have my mullet anymore."

From the get-go, MASTERSFX found a great amount of success on a plethora of projects, including *Howling IV: The Original Nightmare* (1988),

A creepy character Todd created for the *Tales from the Crypt* (1989) episode "Only Skin Deep" (which initially aired in 1994). Photo courtesy of Todd Masters.

The Return of Swamp Thing (1989), *A Nightmare on Elm Street 5: The Dream Child* (1989), and *Look Who's Talking* (1989). In addition to his big-screen successes, one of Masters' largest career breaks came in the world of television when he began working on HBO's *Tales from the Crypt* (1989) series.

Masters' involvement with *Tales from the Crypt* (1989) also led to handling the ambitious effects on Ernest Dickerson's cult classic *Demon Knight* (1995), which featured an incredible amount of practical effects. According to Masters, he and Dickerson used *Tales from the Crypt: Demon Knight* (1995) as their own platform to not only make a great horror film, but to pay homage to some of their favorite movies as well.

"The scene where Billy Zane punches through John Schuck's head was an homage that we wanted to do in honor of Peter Jackson's wicked *Dead Alive* [a.k.a. *Braindead*], which many of us saw at a midnight screening while working on *Demon Knight*. Then, the demon-birthing scene was our tip of the hat to Ray Harryhausen's skeletons in *Jason and the Argonauts*. Both Ernest and I were big fans of Harryhausen's, and we were influenced by his work to modify an elaborate setup for a scene that was originally written a different

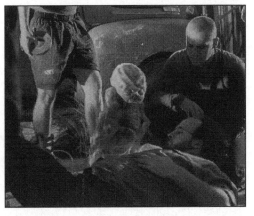

Actor Billy Zane and Todd Masters prepare for the "demon birthing" scene in *Tales from the Crypt: Demon Knight* (1995). Photo courtesy of Todd Masters.

Todd (kneeling, second from right) poses with his team, the demons, and actor
William Sadler on the set of *Tales from the Crypt: Demon Knight* (1995).
Photo courtesy of Todd Masters.

way. We had to rely on a few tricks to pull all of that off with the budget,
so in some cases, simpler was better."

Even though he wasn't afraid to go old school, that doesn't mean that
Masters didn't look towards the future, either, as he continued to set both
himself and his studio apart by fully embracing the oncoming wave of
technology that was changing the world of practical effects throughout
the 1990s.

"When digital became accessible, we pulled it into our company's
pipeline way before everybody else was even thinking about it," Todd explained. "It was all basically the same stuff I had learned way back while
doing graphics and opticals, in terms of setting up shots and lining up
elements. Back in the Seattle optical FX house, I learned to break it down
into practical digital associations that we'd sometimes call 'handshakes.'
So we were always looking at ways we could bring technology into the
mix while still using our practical FX developments, too."

Throughout the 1990s, Masters continued to adapt and change with
the emerging digital technology, long before it became the norm in Hollywood. Known for utilizing mixed methodologies—blending practical FX

with digital VFX [visual effects]—Masters and his team have evolved certain cinematic illusions over the years.

"In *Star Trek: First Contact,* there's that gag with the Queen Borg's head and shoulders," Masters said, "and if you go back and look at that gag that Tom Savini did with Kevin Bacon's neck [in *Friday the 13th* (1980)], where the arrow pierces through, that's a very similar slant board rig, where Kevin's real head was there on the pillow, but the rest of his body was hidden in the bed. Savini fabricated a neck and shoulder piece to come off at an angle to create the illusion of Kev's body on the bed. That's essentially what we did for the scene with the Queen Borg in *Star Trek: First Con-*

Actor Jonathan Frakes poses with Alice Krige (as the Borg Queen) between shots on the set of *Star Trek: First Contact* (1996). Photo courtesy of Todd Masters.

tact, when she comes out of the rafters with only her head and shoulders and then she plugs into her body. It's essentially the same trick, just spun a little differently. Instead of hiding things with a pillow and a bed sheet, we were matting her body out using a blue screen."

"That became a big moment for *First Contact.* We did it at a time when people weren't seeing how practical and visual effects could really benefit each other. Because I had experience with both effects and how they can work in that 'handshake,' our studio was able to step in and offer up some unique options."

The elaborate mechanical rig used to bring the Borg Queen to life on *Star Trek: First Contact* (1996). Photo courtesy of Todd Masters.

When it comes to finding inventive ways to solve problems, Masters has never been one to shy away from a challenge—even if that challenge includes creating hundreds of killer slugs and some of the biggest practical effects ever conceived for the big screen. That's only a hint of what Masters and his crew tackled for James Gunn's ambitious horror comedy *Slither* (2006), which was produced by Gold Circle Films.

"Gold Circle wanted something to show off at AFM [American Film Market] long before we started shooting *Slither*," Masters recalled, "and they asked me if I had any makeup tests or anything that I could

A close-up look at actor Michael Rooker in his monstrous state for *Slither* (2006). Photo courtesy of Todd Masters.

give them to help sell James' vision. And while we did have some stuff, I thought about what my personal hero John Lasseter might do in these instances. He's a smart guy, and he used to insist that Pixar Company's (at that time only a software company) early tests would always include a little story within it. Not just another technical 'shader' test, but instead, a little toy's story, or a ball or a light. And they developed into what they are today from these tests. So I said, 'Well, I don't really want to shoot 'just a test.' Let's shoot something with more of a story to it that we can present to give people a real idea of what to expect from this film.' And that's when James and I sat down and created our own 'rip-o-matic' for *Slither*."

"A rip-o-matic is basically ripping off another movie's tone and establishing shots. We then shot our own scenes and added them to make a mini-teaser. James wrote voiceovers, and then we shot the rest in our L.A. shop. We tested the Grant character (played by our foam-runner at the time, Ken Culver) in an early third-stage makeup, we got some friends and actresses to shoot other creepy scenes, and then we put this trailer-looking thing together. It turned out very cool, and I did pretty much all the visual effects myself over several flights, back and forth between L.A.

Dan Rebert touches up the Grant puppet between takes on the set of *Slither* (2006). Photo courtesy of Todd Masters.

and Vancouver, as I recall. When people saw it, they loved it, and that helped sell the movie."

While Masters was used to utilizing both practical and digital effects on his films, there was one aspect of *Slither* (2006) that came as a real shock.

"I worked heavily on *Slither* with Dan Rebert, who was our supervisor in our L.A. shop. He had a lot of weird material knowledge that we had developed for a couple of other shows previously. We were really starting to get into the translucent membranes, weird bladders, and intrinsic colors. What was interesting about Dan's involvement was that he brought a lot of his materials knowledge in from sex toy businesses that he used to work at."

"As it turned out, the material he used for sex toys was what we needed to create these slugs, so we bought up every single possible sex toy we could to repurpose them for *Slither*. In fact, because we were making this during one of the Iraq wars, and because it was a petroleum-based product and there was a shortage in petroleum because of the war, that meant these toys weren't being manufactured at all. We tried calling up one distributor who was out, and we asked them, 'Well, if you don't have

A behind-the-scenes look at the enormity of the Grant puppet used during *Slither* (2006). Photo courtesy of Todd Masters.

any more, do you know where we can get them?' And they said, 'No, no, no, you don't understand, none of us have any more—period. The planet is out!' And that was all because we used this material on *Slither*."

"One day I was giving a new client a tour of the shop right after we had just bought a whole bucket-load of sex toys. There was this table in the back of the shop that had a mountain of vaginas and penises piled on it that were being cut up so they could be melted down. And so, here I am, just casually walking our client through all of that and still trying to convince them that we were a professional studio," Masters reflected, blushing at the memory.

Something else Todd was not prepared to handle on *Slither* (2006) was a reluctant co-star who had no idea just what was in store for her character later on in the script.

"One day, they sent us Brenda [James], who also happens to play a character named Brenda, to be molded for her giant fat suit that was set to explode in *Slither*'s third act. When she showed up, she said to us, 'Well, what am I doing here? Why am I being cast?' And we were like, 'I'm guessing you didn't read the script?' She had only read the first few scenes and had no idea she was going to be this huge flesh-ball in the movie. When she found out, you can imagine that Brenda was a bit horrified."

"That suit has got to be in the record books for the world's biggest prosthetic," added Masters. "I don't know of many prosthetics where you have to crawl in through the ass of it. All in all, it was a twelve-foot-diameter ball of silicone fat. It was pretty amazing."

Just a few years later, Masters worked with another horror maestro who has since gone on to bigger projects, Scott Derrickson, who was at the helm of 20th Century Fox's 2008 remake of *The Day the Earth Stood Still* (1951). Even though he enjoyed collaborating with Derrickson, Masters wasn't particularly fond of contending with the politics of a big-budget studio project.

"As the saying goes, when you do the bigger shows, that means more meetings, more memos, more opinions, and a lot less creativity. When you do smaller movies like *Slither*, you have a certain kind of freedom where you can be a lot more hands-on. When you work on big movies, you are always dealing with a committee."

"So, when I came onto *The Day the Earth Stood Still*, they were already somewhat into pre-production, and many FX decisions had al-

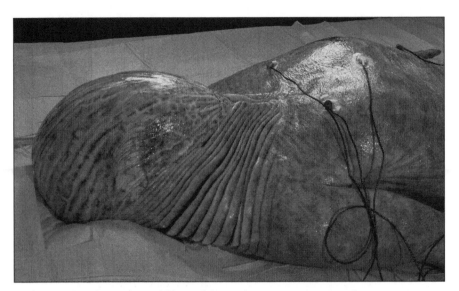

Throughout his career, Todd has collaborated on numerous science fiction projects, including *The Day the Earth Stood Still* (2008). Photo courtesy of Todd Masters.

ready been made. They had already begun working with some visual effects companies on creating the look of [the alien] Klaatu, and initially I was worried about how I was going to design him, but the visual effects company said to me, 'Hey, don't worry about it. We've already designed Klaatu.' I thought we were set."

"They gave me a web address so I could check out the designs and get a sense of what I needed to do in order to make this into something tangible," Masters continued. "And when I got into the folder, I saw that there were something like five hundred different Klaatu pictures in there, and they were all just a little bit different. So I asked them, 'Well, which one is Klaatu, because they're all slightly different?' And they proceeded to tell me that it hadn't really been decided yet. So, we took it from there and turned their designs into a classic monster maquette (a scaled-down study model of their character)."

"We had a meeting and I came in with this Klaatu maquette, and Scott immediately went, 'That's it!' Sometimes directors have a hard time really seeing things with all of this digital shit, so when you can realize it with something that's tangible, it allows them to see their 'real' angles and how the forms will play in light. To see how it looks and to experience it within a true space can be hugely beneficial."

An unfortunate victim is prepped on the set of *American Mary* (2012).
Photo courtesy of Todd Masters.

Masters' ability to adapt served him well on *The Day the Earth Stood Still* (2008) and on countless other projects in the 2000s and into the following decade, including *Snakes on a Plane* (2006), *The Haunting in Connecticut* (2009), *30 Days of Night: Dark Days* (2010), a reunion with James Gunn on *Super* (2010), *Red State* (2011), *American Mary* (2012), and *Elysium* (2013).

"My career might hit on that classic idiom, where the hardest part is just showing up. And not only did I show up, but I always made sure that I took my responsibilities seriously. I made sure that I connected with people in a positive way. It's the greatest job in the world, to make rubber monsters, and I'm proud to be doing just that."

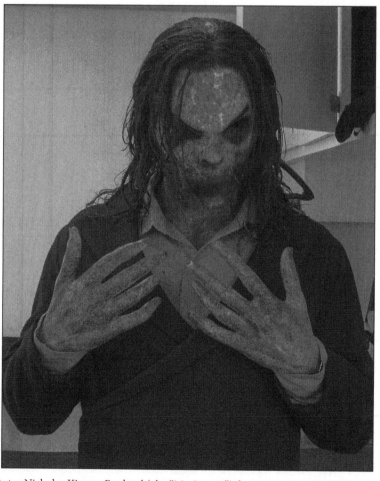

Actor Nicholas King as Bughuul (aka "Mr. Boogie") from Scott Derrickson's horror film *Sinister* (2012). Photo courtesy of Todd Masters.

"Many of us that have been in this crazy monster business are still in good communication with one another," Masters added. "There are only a few of us that have been able to keep it all going since the '80s. We all know everybody like family. We've seen each other grow up and age. We all go to each other's parties . . . we go to each other's funerals. I'm friends with pretty much every owner of every shop, so it has been nice to have all these positive relationships with everybody over the decades. Back in the day, we used to have these crazy Halloween parties in our studios, which I guess we've now grown out of. Now others are carrying on the tradition on rare October nights when all of us FX folks costume up and destroy someone's backyard or shop."

"Now, all of our monster shops are having to face the future, looking at how digital FX has eaten its way into our businesses, like Ms. Pac-Man. We're all wondering, 'What's next?' So it's good to have great relationships with these people, because we're all facing a similar future, and we're not all having to deal with it on our own."

For over thirty years now, Masters has consistently found ways to persevere through the changes that have hit the special effects industry, and it all comes down to a little planning.

"I've always sat down and made these goals that are basically in this linear line that I just chop into years. Essentially, that's my way of projecting what my five-year plan is. Sometimes I'll go longer and sometimes I'll go shorter, but this has always given me the ability to look at the business from various vantage points, where it could even be for today or tomorrow. That's something I've always done, and I got that from my dad."

"But for as much as I love planning, I also love the surprises that come with this work. A lot of us special effects artists are people that drive to work in a slightly different way every day. We want to have some challenge, some unique problem to deal with, and in the '80s and '90s, when we had to consistently reinvent things all the time, that was the fun of it. It still is the fun of it."

"How do you make the impossible possible? How do you make a fantasy creature look like a real, living, breathing entity? How do you make this gore gag work realistically? How do you make this stuff work repeatedly on a set with sixty people watching you, where you cannot fuck it up? It's almost like being a magician, and for me, that's both the sweat of it and the fun of it."

Todd (kneeling, far left) and his crew pose with a special friend.
Photo courtesy of Todd Masters.

"I'm never going to be the type of person that just wastes time, where I'm sitting around just watching TV all day on a Saturday, or taking a trip to the beach. I'm not built that way. I want to produce movies. I want to make monsters. I want to keep creating, because to me, it's not really work. It's art. Like the Muse song says, 'Don't waste your time or time will waste you.'"

Made in the USA
San Bernardino, CA
11 August 2020